The Best Available Evidence

Decision Making for Educational Improvement

W0013632

Edited by

Paul Newton and David Burgess
University of Saskatchewan, Canada

SENSE PUBLISHERS
ROTTERDAM/BOSTON/TAIPEI

A C.I.P. record for this book is available from the Library of Congress.

ISBN: 978-94-6300-436-7 (paperback)
ISBN: 978-94-6300-437-4 (hardback)
ISBN: 978-94-6300-438-1 (e-book)

Published by: Sense Publishers,
P.O. Box 21858,
3001 AW Rotterdam,
The Netherlands
https://www.sensepublishers.com/

Chapter 3 was originally published as Newton, P. M., & Burgess, D. (2008). Exploring types of educational action research: Implications for research validity. *International Journal of Qualitative Methods, 7*(4), 19–30. Reprinted with permission.

Printed on acid-free paper

TABLE OF CONTENTS

TABLE OF CONTENTS

PREFACE

This volume is born from a landscape where educational improvement efforts are being directed by calls for *evidence*—evidence that is commonly presented as non-problematic and representative of a unitary corpus of "what we know." Throughout this book, we characterize three broadly conceived classes of knowledge and evidentiary claims within contemporary educational improvement discourse: (a) *explanatory*—primarily quantitative approaches; (b) *interpretive/constructivist*—primarily qualitative approaches; and (c) *practitioner-driven*—primarily participatory approaches (Guba & Lincoln, 2005). Practitioners and policy-makers are confronted with multiple forms of educational research to consider. We hope that this edited volume will add to the conversation with respect to the use of research and evidence in educational improvement in pre K-12 and post secondary contexts. The authors in this volume explore the potential, intricacies, and limitations of a number of research approaches and the implications for the application of research evidence in education.

In Chapter 1, José da Costa begins by establishing that evidence from quantitative research requires a sophisticated understanding on the part of consumers of research about concepts of significance, importance, and the validity of research findings. He argues that educational policy makers and practitioners require a significant ability to understand "threats to validity" in quantitative research, and he suggests potential methods to ensure more mature and informed approaches to research-based policy making in education.

In Chapter 2, Bonnie Stelmach examines the challenge of transferability or generalizability of qualitative academic research to address the needs of large-scale reform and improvement agendas. She begins her chapter with a discussion of the confusion between constructionist and interpretivist qualitative research paradigms. While acknowledging the limitations of qualitative methodologies, she rejects attempts to measure the veracity of knowledge claims by holding such methods to the standards of quantitative approaches—paying particular attention to the evidence-based education movement and such initiatives at the *What Works Clearinghouse*.

Chapter 3 includes a discussion of practitioner research and action research with respect to issues of validity. Paul Newton and David Burgess reconceptualize validity as a contingent concept dependent on the purposes of the research. In this chapter, they present three action research modes that call for different approaches to validity and the justification of knowledge claims.

Derek Stovin, in Chapter 4, discusses the potential for narrative forms of research to inform educational improvement. He begins by providing a description of narrative approaches within qualitative research followed by the presentation of examples of the use of narrative approaches in educational research. Finally, Stovin explores the potential for narrative research to inform decision making and policy making in education.

In Chapter 5, Cherkowski and Walker propose alternate ways of measuring schools for the purpose of improvement. They draw on literature from "positive psychology" to assert that happiness and well-being are central aims for educational improvement efforts. They suggest that traditional school improvement efforts are based in deficit models, and they explore the potential for appreciative approaches. They conclude with a framework for understanding schools as sites of human flourishing and explore the implications for educational leaders.

In Chapter 6, Scott Tunison outlines some of the potential risks inherent in data-driven accountability systems and suggests a robust set of ethical practices for data use and deployment. He argues that foundational to ethical data practices are the notions of relationships, mutual trust, and respect.

Chapter 7 is a venue for Pamela Timanson and José da Costa's look at the literature concerning organizational learning, learning organizations, and learning communities in organizational studies and educational administration. They identify the potential for restructuring school as learning organizations and explore the tensions and contradictions of using such structural lenses to improve schools. In particular, they challenge the notion of using the learning organization concept to leverage system-level goals and priorities advocated in the interests of educational improvement and reform, and second that educational reform and localized educational improvement efforts are historically linked with current emphases on accountability, new public management, and standardized testing in the English-speaking world.

In Chapter 8, Vicki Squires explores the role of data, accountability, and institutional assessment in post-secondary institutions. She discusses the emerging practices of assessment (particularly in the student services areas) and its role in institutional planning and decision making. She uses several examples of assessment projects to illustrate the principles of effective data use in post-secondary institutional improvement efforts.

In a similar vein, Robin Mueller explores change and improvement in post-secondary education in Chapter 9. In this chapter, she reviews the history of universities and examines current trends in the evolution of post-secondary institutions. Finally, Muller suggests frameworks for thinking about change efforts in the post-secondary sector.

In Chapter 10, Erika Smith and Richard Hayman review issues facing post-secondary institutions with respect to emerging technologies. They explore the problem of the rapidity of change in the area of emerging technologies and the challenges this presents in acquiring timely and relevant evidence for change efforts. In this chapter, they suggest potential practices for addressing the evidence gap for decision makers in post-secondary contexts.

We would like to echo the comments of our contributors in suggesting that practitioners, graduate students, educational leaders, and policy makers would benefit from a level of sophistication as "readers" of the best available evidence. This evidence-informed decision making is dependent upon (a) an ability to determine the relevance and utility of evidence, (b) an ability to determine the strengths and limitations of the various forms of evidence, and (c) an understanding of the ethical and moral implications of evidence and data.

ACKNOWLEDGEMENTS

We would like to offer our sincere thanks to our colleagues, family, and students for their support as we worked through this edited book. Our colleagues in the Department of Educational Administration at the University of Saskatchewan (past and present) have been central in our development as scholars and have offered encouragement throughout this and our other scholarly endeavors. To our current and former graduate students, your work provides the impetus to contemplate the ways in which research and evidence contribute to the improvement of educational institutions. Also, regularly overlooked when we seek to offer gratitude, our colleagues who work tirelessly as practitioners and leaders in educational institutions. We owe a debt of gratitude to you for your diligent work in the field, and we owe a debt of responsibility to reflect more often on the ways in which research and evidence might be produced that can make a real difference in the lives of instructors, leaders, and students. Mostly, we would like to express our most sincere gratitude to our contributors, whose work represents a novel contribution to thinking about evidence and educational decision making. We also thank you for sticking with us on the longer than expected journey. Finally, to Michel Lokhorst at Sense, thank you for your advice, guidance, and patience.

Teresa, Connor, and Sean; and Liam and Lauren, thank you for your patience, stability, support, and love throughout.

JOSÉ DA COSTA

1. EVIDENCE-DRIVEN POLICY AND PRACTICE IN EDUCATION

Issues of Veracity in Quantitatively Based Research

For several decades, calls have been made by a variety of researchers and practitioners for basing decisions in educational policy and practice in evidence rather than on more traditional and common approaches grounded in personal political ideology or personal preference and preconceived notions drawing on unsystematic analysis of anecdotal data. Even unsystematic interpretation of data gathered through large-scale initiatives, which are conducted very systematically (e.g., provincial or state administered achievement tests, Program for International Student Achievement – PISA, Trends in International Mathematics and Science Study – TIMSS), often result in invalid conclusions and invalid courses of action based primarily in preconceived ideologies. Interestingly, despite the numerous calls for grounding decision making in data, policy development often still seems to be based on selective application of research supporting decision-maker predispositions.

Basic types of rationalistic research fall into three main categories: descriptive, correlational, and experimental. As the name implies, descriptive research provides descriptions, typically drawing on descriptive statistics (e.g., mean, median, mode, standard deviation, range, etc.) to give readers a sense of the context being studied. Correlational research focuses on how two or more variables change together, either in direct or inverse relationships. The most basic measures of correlation rely on Spearman (non-parametric test of association between two variables), Kendall (non-parametric test of dependence between two variables), and Pearson (parametric test of association between two variables) correlation coefficients or derivatives of these. Experimental research and, the closely related, but methodologically more problematic, quasi-experimental research, allows researchers to explore how variables are related to each other, either directly or inversely, just as with correlational research, and it allows researchers to make claims about cause/effect relationships. Educational policy makers and practitioners often read any of these types of research and begin, erroneously, imagining how to enact change that will lead to desired outcomes, whatever they might be. Even educational policy makers and practitioners who recognize the fallacies of drawing on descriptive or correlational research to make changes to their context, may make inappropriate decisions with regard to practices and policies when outcomes from carefully controlled settings are applied in field settings which do not match the experimental setting contexts. Decisions

P. Newton & D. Burgess (Eds.), The Best Available Evidence, 1–18.

of this type are often based on imagining a desired outcome described in research, then ignoring many contextual factors while implementing the method described in the research gathered (e.g., the current trend to try to mimic the outcomes of Finnish schools, as described by people such as Salhberg, 2011 without heeding his warnings of the political and social complexity of the system).

This non-systematic and biased approach may be exacerbated by additional issues of validity and reliability of research conducted in field settings (i.e., classroom or school settings using *ex post facto* and quasi-experimental designs). As anyone who has conducted field-based research knows, classrooms and schools are not ideal laboratory settings where extraneous variables can be carefully controlled, or indeed, even monitored and noted. Such field-based research is messy and requires much replication before confidence in findings can be firmly established. Furthermore, measurement of abstract social phenomena is fraught with difficulty. Measurement in the field of education, and in the social sciences generally, attempts to link highly abstract constructs (e.g., efficacy, achievement, satisfaction, etc.) with empirical indicators. Empirical indicators form the evidence seen to be a central tenet of empirical sciences which draws on data, collected through any number of ways or instruments, either to lend credence for or refute researcher hypotheses (Popper, 1972). Confounding factors, however, can contaminate evidence and often lead to seemingly contradictory results across, what may appear to be, very similar studies. Many of these contradictory results can be traced back to issues of validity of the method and the subsequent veracity of the findings.

The fundamental purpose of this chapter is to focus on issues that should be taken into account when considering research and its applicability to research consumers' contexts by assisting the practitioner or policy maker who desires to move beyond basing decisions on pre-dispositions or "gut instinct." This chapter is divided into five sections, Section one deals with threats to validity of research conducted using quasi-experimental and ex post facto research designs. The second section focuses on issues created when violations of assumptions underlying statistical analyses are not reported and on issues to consider when reading research utilizing parametric statistical analyses. Section three addresses the issues inherent in traditional null-hypothesis significance testing and the need to shift to estimation and effect size measures. The fourth section explores ways of establishing and understanding the importance (as opposed to the statistical significance) of statistical findings. Having dealt with the aspects necessary to assess the quality of evidence and the data underlying the evidence, the fifth section explores the policy-making and decision-making literature specifically identifying the problem of not drawing systematically on research to inform policy and practice.

Threats to Validity

The need to understand what constitutes valid data and the ability to draw appropriate inference from those data to inform decisions must be understood not only by researchers, but also by consumers of research. Validity in research is not new and many seminal works have been written on the topic from quantitative and qualitative perspectives. Some of the more well known include: Campbell and Stanley (1963, 1966), Cook and Campbell (1979), Guba (1981), and Lincoln and Guba (1985). Foundational to notions of what constitutes credible research for grounding decisions are four overarching (i.e., applicable to empirical qualitative and quantitative forms of research) conceptions of validity originally described by Guba (1981): (a) truth value, (b) applicability, (c) consistency, and (d) neutrality. While Guba's 1981 paper focuses on validity in qualitative research, he provides useful conceptions proposing parallels between quantitative and qualitative research that are particularly helpful for thinking about validity broadly. More specific, but still in keeping with the broader conceptualizations of validity, to research conducted from a rationalistic paradigm was the validity framework proposed earlier by Campbell and Stanley (1963, 1966), refined later by Cook and Campbell (1979). Their framework for considering validity for research conducted in education, and the social sciences generally, is based on the need to identify potential sources of invalidity in research when intact groups of participants, or those who self-selected for participation become the source or sources from which data are gathered. Much rationalistic field-based research, just as laboratory-based research, seeks to explore and understand cause/effect relationships. The four areas of potential invalidity named are, in essence, areas that must be considered in establishing cause/effect relationships. In order to do so, researchers must be able to:

1. Establish that changes to a presumed cause (i.e., the independent variable) are related to changes in what is thought to be an effect (i.e., the dependent variable); in other words, there is co-variation between the cause and effect.
2. Ascertain temporality of the cause and effect (i.e., establish that the presumed cause did occur prior to the presumed effect).
3. Rule out plausible alternative explanations, or at least establish that the presumed cause is, truly, the most reasonable explanation for the observed outcome. In fact, when alternative explanations exist for the observed outcome, one cannot have any confidence in the presumed cause/effect relationship.

In meeting these three criteria in rationalist field-based research, specifically, researchers and research consumers must be very concerned with: (a) internal validity, (b) construct validity, (c) statistical conclusion validity, (d) external validity, (e) reliability, and (f) objectivity. While brief descriptions of these forms of validity are provided below, the reader is encouraged to read the very detailed discussions of validity offered by Stanley and Campbell (1963, 1966), Cook and Campbell (1979), and the many others whose ideas have evolved from these seminal works.

Internal validity. Internal validity refers to researcher control over research variables in the study setting. This includes control over variables of which the researcher may not even be aware. These variables may cause outcomes that may

3

be incorrectly attributed to variables of interest. Lack of researcher control over variables not central to the research at hand can lead to confounding of factors believed to cause effects observed in dependent variables. The central question researchers and research consumers must ask themselves about research findings is: what besides the independent variables of interest may have led to the results being observed?

In laboratory settings, researchers most typically rely on random assignment of subjects to treatment and control groups in order to randomly and evenly distribute all characteristics participants bring (e.g., random assignment of any characteristics which may be possessed by research participants, examples may include height, weight, intellectual capacity, etc.) between the comparison groups making them equivalent prior to administration of any treatment or implementation of any program. Field-based researchers typically do not have the benefit of being able to randomly assign participants to either treatment or control groups, these researchers most often have to work with intact groups. In schools these intact groups may consist of classes, schools, jurisdictions, or other units over which the researcher has no control with respect to who is in the group. In order to establish, at least, some degree of certainty that effects observed in a dependent variable are due to the independent variable of interest, researchers are well advised to systematically consider and rule out the threats to validity as described by Cook and Campbell (1979). These include:

1. History – something, besides the treatment, which occurs between a pre-test and a post-test that causes post-test results increase or decrease.
2. Maturation – skills develop or deteriorate due to age progression.
3. Testing – familiarity with test or questionnaire format leads to improved performance.
4. Instrumentation – observers gathering data change in systematic ways.
5. Statistical regression (i.e., regression to the mean).
6. Selection bias – participants self-select on the basis of some criterion or multiple criteria of interest of which the researcher is typically unaware.
7. Mortality of study participants (particularly problematic if certain sectors of participants drop out of the study causing groups to become biased in particular ways).
8. Interaction of history, maturation, testing, or instrumentation with selection bias.
9. Ambiguity about direction of cause/effect relationship.
10. Diffusion or imitation of treatment (i.e., without researcher knowledge, control or comparison group members interact with the members of the experimental group and learn about and are effected by the treatment meant only for the experimental group).
11. Compensatory equalization of treatments (i.e., the control group receives treatment conditions without the knowledge of the researcher, for example

when teachers share materials with each other because they perceive them to be beneficial).

12. Compensatory rivalry (i.e., John Henry effect).
13. Resentful demoralization of respondents receiving less desirable treatments, or no treatment, with these people purposely sabotaging study results (Cook & Campbell, 1979).

Construct validity. Researchers have a responsibility to carefully define the research constructs central to their research focus. These constructs and the relationships found amongst them are, usually, the focus of rationalistic research. Problems in defining the constructs or researchers' inabilities to describe the relationships between and among the constructs can allow for rival explanations of the mechanisms underlying what is observed. If one considers such constructs as intelligence, love, efficacy, self-esteem, achievement, learning, to name a few, the complexities underlying these are great. Even with carefully crafted definitions it is still possible for others to misunderstand what the "label" means. For example, many lay people would consider learning and achievement to simply be synonyms for the same construct, however, a careful examination of these quickly reveals them as different. A variety of considerations must be attended to by researchers to ensure strong construct validity. These are:

1. Adequately defining constructs such that clear operational definitions are understood by the researcher and the consumers of the research, an operational definition is one that is worded such that it can be measured.
2. Mono-operational bias refers to a very narrow or limited operationalization of what is being measured, this is best attended to by using multiple indicators of a particular construct (e.g., operationalizing student achievement could be done through standardized tests, examples of student work, and teacher opinion).
3. Avoiding mono-method bias involves collecting indicators of a construct using a variety of methodological approaches (e.g., paper-and-pencil questionnaires, interviews, observation, etc.).
4. Hypothesis guessing in which the research participants try to guess what the researcher is looking for, then they provide the answers, usually, that the researcher is predisposed to hearing or seeing.
5. Evaluation apprehension connects to people's general desire to be positively evaluated, often responses to questions, written or oral, will be tempered such that, as an individual, the respondent's reputation or expertise is not called into question (e.g., teachers rate their school highly because it is a reflection on them).
6. Expectancies – researchers, regardless of the research tradition they gravitate toward, observers, supervisors, research participants, etc., all have beliefs about an almost infinite number of topics and issues, these predispositions often result, if not carefully accounted for, in findings that reflect the predispositions rather

than the actual research outcomes (e.g., researchers find what they are looking for, teachers gathering data on behalf of researchers see effects they believe they should see).

7. Confounding of constructs occurs when something, other than what is thought to be the independent variable, causes the observed effects in the dependent variable (e.g., in single group grade one classroom study, is the development of reading ability a function of a particular reading program or approach to teaching, or is it a function of an excellent teacher who knows how to provide students with appropriate scaffolding, or both?).

8. Level of constructs refers to the "amount" of the independent variable needed to cause an observable effect on the dependent variable, this is partly related to the power (i.e., the ability of the research to correctly reject the statistical null hypothesis) of the research as well as to the sensitivity, including the validity and reliability, of the measuring instruments.

9. Interaction of testing and treatment can threaten construct validity when measures influence the observed outcome of the treatment (e.g., a pre-test may provide students with clues about the "correct" answers).

10. Interactions of different treatments, which may be inadvertently introduced by the researcher or teachers in classroom field settings, may have a synergistic effect that cannot be teased apart by the researcher even if she or he becomes aware of the interaction.

11. Restricted generalizability across constructs is often problematic in field settings in education as researchers use different operational definitions of the same construct (e.g., student achievement is often measured by standardized achievement tests, but what is found to be related to this operationalization of achievement is limited since teachers are responsible for many other aspects of students' education including socialization) (Cook & Campbell, 1979).

Statistical conclusion validity. At its most fundamental level, statistical conclusion validity deals with the question, "is this study sensitive enough to detect a difference or a relationship if one exists?" Seven threats exist to this form of validity, namely:

1. Low statistical power (e.g., the sample size and the effect size of the quality under investigation, either singly or in combination are simply too small to be measured).

2. Violated assumptions of the statistical tests (addressed in more detail in the next section of this chapter).

3. Fishing and error rate (e.g., statistical results that occur mainly by chance).

4. Reliability and validity of data collection instruments (e.g., the measuring instruments provide data that are repeatable and reflect the construct under study; as an example, IQ tests are often accused of measuring reading ability to a large extent).

5. Reliability of the treatment implementation or data collection implementation (e.g., treatments are administered to all groups as intended by the researcher, or data collection instruments are administered under the same conditions for all participants).
6. Random irrelevancies in the research setting (e.g., in field settings research conditions are often changed, knowingly or unknowingly, by teachers, parents, administrators, etc.; even a fire alarm ringing during one group's experience will create a random irrelevancy for the group).
7. Random heterogeneity of the respondents (e.g., the refers to the possibility that a treatment or set of questions may affect a particular type of person differently from others, this could manifest in many ways, but gender, age, etc. are some possibilities) (Cook & Campbell, 1979).

External validity. The concept of generalizability is at the heart of external validity. At issue is the ability to apply what has been learned from the participants in the specific research context to other contexts. Generalizability falls into three basic categories related to persons, settings, and times:

1. Participant selection (e.g., systematic differences between the participants in the research sample or samples and the population to which the results will be generalized).
2. Setting (e.g., differences in context between where the research is conducted and the settings to which the research will be generalized).
3. History (e.g., differences in temporal context between when the research is conducted and the time periods to which the research will be generalized) (Cook & Campbell, 1979).

As the context in which the research was conducted and the context to which the researcher is interested in generalize diverge, the less certainty there can be that the research findings will, indeed, apply to the larger context.

Violations of Statistical Assumptions and Appropriateness of Analysis Method

All statistical analyses, those that compare groups and those that explore relationships between or among variables, are founded on particular assumptions regarding the characteristics of the sample or the population from which the sample is drawn. At the most fundamental level, non-parametric analysis methods are distribution-free (i.e., they do not come from populations in which the particular characteristic is normally distributed, for example "income") and can be used for analysis of nominal, ordinal, equal interval, and ratio data (Gall, Gall, & Borg, 2007; Gay, Mills, & Airasian, 2012). The main assumptions underlying the most fundamental non-parametric statistical analyses are that the data are collected from a random sample and that the data come from individuals that are independent of each other. However, non-parametric statistical analyses tend to be less powerful than parametric statistical analysis techniques (i.e., they are less likely to detect a *true difference* if one actually exists—less likelihood of a Type II error).

Parametric statistics, on the other hand, have more underlying assumptions but are appropriate for equal interval data and ratio data, in addition to randomness and independence, the most fundamental analyses must also be based on data that are normally distributed and exhibit homogeneity of variance. More advanced non-parametric and parametric analyses will have additional assumptions that must be met in order to use them appropriately. Violations of the statistical assumptions, knowingly or unknowingly, often lead to analyses that support incorrect conclusions about the substantive question at hand.

Tests for assessing the extent to which assumptions are violated are available and should be reported by researchers. Interestingly, many research reports do not provide the reader with any assurance that assumptions underlying the statistical tests of significance have been met. Educational policy makers and practitioners are cautioned to look for assurance in research reports that statistical test assumptions have been met.

Earlier it was pointed out that parametric analyses are appropriate for equal interval and ratio data. Interestingly, many educational surveys and data collection instruments collect categorical or, at best, ordinal data (e.g., Likert-type scale gathering satisfaction data, where: 1 = "strongly disagree," 2 = "disagree," 3= "neutral," 4 = "agree," 5 = "strongly agree"). While categorical data are often reported as frequencies and analysed using non-parametric statistics, it is not unusual to observe ordinal data being treated as though they were on an equal interval or ratio scale with means and standard deviations being reported. This is highly problematic since the research consumer can have no confidence that the differences in means and standard deviations between two groups or between two observation points from the same group are meaningful. This, of course, leads to problems of validity of the claims made in the research report.

Educational policy makers and practitioners are cautioned to look for evidence that statistical analyses are appropriate to the kinds of data gathered (i.e., categorical, ordinal, equal interval, ratio) and that the report writer has provided assurance that the underlying assumptions for the statistical tests have been met. This is not to suggest that consumers of research must be able to conduct these analyses, but they should look for the assurances before simply accepting conclusions and recommendations made by the researcher. This is also not to suggest that research reporting that an assumption underlying a statistical test has been violated should be entirely dismissed, however, it should be taken cautiously.

A Different Way of Thinking about Significance

Traditionally, students learning about null-hypothesis significance testing (NHST) using inferential statistics were taught to select the "risk," the alpha (α) level,[1] they were willing to take in rejecting a false null-hypothesis (i.e., type I error) and to clearly set out the statistical null hypothesis and the statistical alternate hypothesis in advance of whatever analysis they were going to conduct (e.g., Gall et al., 2007; Glass & Hopkins, 1996; Hopkins, Glass, & Hopkins, 1995). Social science research conventions typically set the alpha level at the 0.05 level (i.e., the researcher is willing to make a type I error 5 times out of every 100 times that a random sample could be drawn from a population for the research). In educational research that may have higher potential for harm, researchers may adopt a more conservative alpha level of 0.01 (i.e., theoretically the researcher is willing to make a type I error only 1 time per 100 times that a random sample could be drawn from a population for the study). For exploratory research, researchers may make a case for relaxing the alpha level to 0.10 (i.e., the researcher is willing to make a type I error 1 time in 10 times that a random sample could be drawn from a population for the research). After *a priori* setting the appropriate alpha level for determining when to reject or not reject the null hypothesis being tested through the inferential statistical analysis, researchers could then gather their data and conduct their analyses, ultimately finding evidence for rejecting or not rejecting the null hypothesis of difference or null hypothesis of association. Unfortunately, this sets up a dichotomy that simply paints the world as black or white: significant or not significant. This view of research is grounded in the probability logic in selecting samples from a population, significance simply leads the researcher to *not reject the statistical null hypothesis* or it leads the researcher to *reject the statistical null hypothesis*. It is simply a binary (Neyman & Pearson, 1933). While this may be a very reasonable approach in areas of research in which true random samples can be drawn from infinitely large populations, it is fundamentally flawed in research drawing on participants who volunteer and who are available to actually participate in research.

It is fairly common knowledge that in research publication, results that are non-significant (i.e., the null hypothesis is not rejected) typically do not get published. Cumming (2013) summarizes: "a 'statistically significant' effect in the results section becomes 'significant' in the discussion or abstract, and 'significant' shouts 'important'" (p. 3). This in combination with other factors, for example, statistical analysis software packages that are much more user friendly and accessible to researchers whose understanding of statistical analysis theory and methodology may be somewhat lacking, has led many researchers to engage in what Cumming (2013), and others, refer to as "cherry picking"—conducting analyses in which data from some participants are left out, some variables are left out, some variables that had not been considered originally are included, in the interest of capitalizing on what are actually random differences, or chance, in datasets. These researchers really have no idea whether or not they happened to have randomly drawn (or the sample may not be random at all as highlighted by Cook and Campbell in their threats to validity) a sample that is truly representative of the population from which it was drawn, and to which they wish to generalize.

A second caution is offered here in relation to statistical tests of significance. While many statistical analysis approaches exist to ensure that researchers retain control of the alpha level when examining relationships among multiple variables or multiple groups, there are instances in the research literature in which multiple univariate analyses have been conducted, as though the data for each analysis was gathered independently from a different randomly selected sample. This leads to issues in which pre-existing relationships between multiple variables or constructs are overlooked, a factor stemming from inter-dependence of individuals from one test to the next (e.g., Hopkins et al., 1995; Glass & Hopkins, 1996; Sprinthall, 2011). Furthermore, research reports using this approach increase the chances of making a type I error (i.e., reject the null-hypothesis when it is actually true). In fact, every univariate statistical analysis adds to the probability that a type I error will be made, however, neither the researcher nor the research consumer will know in which analysis in the series of analyses this occurred.

Educational policy makers and practitioners are urged to look for clear evidence that research reports are not simply capitalizing on chance to report findings that emerged. This is true of research that reports p-values without consideration for their hypothesis-testing purpose as well as research that ignores the increased probability of finding a "false positive" result. Having identified two very important drawbacks of NHST, the question of what alternatives are possible to address these problems remains. Literature emerging over the past decade may offer a way out by focusing on transparent reporting of research, analyses that emphasize *importance* of findings over significance, and replication of research to enable multiple approaches for establishing the robustness of research findings

Research Transparency, Importance, Cumulative Evidence

As highlighted above, dissatisfaction with NHST approaches have been surfacing in various research communities. Fidler (2010) points, in particular, to the dissatisfaction with Null Hypothesis Significance Testing amongst psychologists. In fact the 1994 edition of the American Psychological Association (APA) Publication Manual calls for reporting statistical power along with effect size statistics of statistical analyses. This guidance as well as an alternate recommendation to provide confidence intervals related to reported statistical analyses is provided in the most recent edition of the APA Publication Manual (2010). In addition to the approximately five-dozen APA published journals, many other journals, not associated with APA, also make use of the APA Style Manual for article submissions. Psychological Science, the journal of the Association for Psychological Science (APS), "the highest ranked empirical journal in psychology" (Sage Publications, n.d., n.p.), which has authors adhere to the APA Style Manual (2010), as of January 1, 2014, emphasizes in its submission guidelines to authors: "to include effect sizes accompanied by 95% confidence intervals rather than standard deviations or standard errors" (APS, n.d.).

The APS goes further by describing the need for published research to be transparent in terms of reporting sufficient detail for research replication. Furthermore, data analysis emphasis needs to shift from NHST to reporting confidence intervals (CI) and effect size (ES) in an effort to demonstrate the practical importance of findings. Finally, suggestions are emerging in this community for (a) the establishment of dissemination venues for replication studies and (b) commitments from researchers to their various research ethics boards that they will report all research analyses, not just those that result in "significant difference" (APS, n.d.).

Research transparency. Very typically, research journals impose word limits on the length of articles they will publish. This forces authors of these articles to make decisions about where to "prune" words in order to stay within the word limits. Several journals, with Psychological Science leading the way, have moved to not including word counts from the methods or results sections:

> Effective January 2014, the Method and Results sections of either Research Articles or Research Reports do not count toward the total word limit. The aim here is to allow authors to provide clear, complete, self-contained descriptions of their studies, which cannot be done with restrictions on those sections. (APS, 2015, n.d.)

This shift is not to encourage authors to simply become more verbose in their descriptions, the emphasis is on providing fulsome, but cogent, descriptions of the methods and results. Anyone reading a research article written in this journal should be able to replicate, identically, the research being reported. Educational policy makers and practitioners should look for complete descriptions of research methods and results in any research they read. The method section of any research report should provide the *step-by-step recipe* for how the study was conducted and how the data were analysed. When descriptions are lacking, the conclusions and recommendations should be treated with caution since it is impossible, as a consumer of that research, to know what was omitted and how that might affect the results being reported.

Confidence intervals and effect size. The discussion of the practical importance of findings is one that should be of interest to educational policy makers and practitioners, alike. It is not unusual to find studies using NHST approaches reporting "significant" findings that are practically unimportant. Since significance in NHST analyses is a function of, both, effect size and sample size, a study having a large sample size, even when the observed effects are small, is very likely to lead to the conclusion that a significant finding has been identified. Two main approaches for addressing this issue have been identified in the literature: CI and ES.

Reporting of CIs provides consumers of research with a sense of the precision of any estimated result. For example, pollsters regularly survey people on a variety of topics, these are sometimes shared via news or other media. While descriptions of the methods used are very terse, usually the pollsters will report how many people were surveyed (the "n"), the percentage who responded in each particular way (the "point estimate"), and the amount of potential error present in the point estimate (the estimate of the possible range the point estimate actually represents): the confidence interval. Using the example of the pollster who might report on the proportion of the population who supports a particular political party in an upcoming election, a point estimate and confidence interval might be reported as 35%, with a margin of error of plus or minus 5%, of people surveyed support Party X. Given the size of the sample the consumer knows that as little as 30% of the actual population might support Party X or as much as 40% of the population might hold this opinion. This is not a new concept and extensive descriptions of confidence intervals for parametric and non-parametric measures of association and difference are available (e.g., Glass & Hopkins, 1996; Hopkins et al., 1995; Pedhazur, 1997; Sprinthall, 2011).

The second approach, reporting ES, addresses the issue of practical importance also from the point of view of the problem created by studies making use of large sample sizes. In such studies, minor differences between groups or weak correlations between variables can result in significant findings given NHST approaches. These trivial group differences or weak correlations are of very little value in educational settings. Imagine for a moment that a study finds that PISA scores can be raised by 0.1% across an entire province or country by implementing a particular instructional strategy; furthermore, this strategy will only require an increase to the provincial or national education budget of 5%. Most people would agree that the cost would not justify the gain: the finding, while statistically significant, is not important. A budget increase of this magnitude should be expected to result in a greater substantive gain. ES addresses this issue by taking into account the gain without the effect sample size plays on NHST. Put another way, ES provides the reader with a sense of the magnitude of the relationship between variables or the differences between groups.

Just as with determining CIs, methods for determining ES for parametric and non-parametric measures of association and difference have existed for many decades (e.g., Glass & Hopkins, 1996; Hopkins et al., 1995; Pedhazur, 1997; Sprinthall, 2011). Examples of ES measures of association include correlation (r), explained variance (r^2), coefficient of contingency (C), Cliff's d, Cohen's d (probably the most common ES indicator used in parametric tests of difference in social sciences research), Hedges's g, eta-squared, omega-squared, and many others. While the purpose of this chapter is not to provide in depth understanding of these measures, it may be useful to understand how to interpret ES coefficients.

It is noteworthy that there is not universal agreement as to the exact break-points for small, medium, and large effect sizes. Approximate values of small, medium, and large effects for three sample ES measures are shown in Table 1 (Sprinthall, 2011).

Using ES to gauge the magnitude of differences between groups or the magnitude of the association between variables provides consumers of research with a metric

Table 1. Approximate values for interpretation of three samples ES coefficients

Effect size	C	r^2	Cohen's d
Small	0.10 to 0.25	0.10 to 0.25	0.2 to 0.5
Medium	>0.25 to 0.40	>0.25 to 0.50	>0.5 to 0.8
Large	>0.40	>0.50	>0.8

that does not change conceptually from study to study and does not suffer from the pitfalls of NHST approaches.

In addition to looking for and using practical approaches to establish the utility and magnitude of effects, using measures of association or of difference, educational policy makers and practitioners are also urged, as suggested by the APS (n.d.) and Cumming (2013) to look for cumulative evidence. Synthesizing the findings across research studies in a form of meta-analysis (Glass, McGraw, & Smith, 1981) is beyond the ability, and often, interest of educational policy makers and practitioners. Consumers of research are encouraged to seek out meta-analytic research that systematically brings together the works of different researchers studying the same or very similar research questions. A variety of frameworks for this type of synthesis have been proposed, a few include: (a) Meta-Analysis Reporting Standards as proposed by the APA (2010), (b) Cooper (2010) provides a meta-analytic framework consisting of seven inter-related steps, and (c) Cummings (2013) provides a brief description of techniques for combining CI results from different studies.

While research consumers who lack the expertise to conduct these statistically based meta-analyses may feel overwhelmed by the suggestions above regarding meta-analysis of research findings, this is not to say that a statistical approaches are the only way to synthesize research findings. Less formal approaches drawing on qualitative analysis techniques can also be employed which thematically cluster studies' contributions on particular topics. This is particularly true if careful attention is paid to understanding the meanings of CI and ES when reported.

RESEARCH AND THE CONTEXT OF POLICY AND DECISION MAKING

Some of the early writing around policy, specifically the adoption of innovations from an adult education perspective, would lead the reader to believe that policy development and implementation is a relatively linear process in which credible evidence simply needs to be obtained (i.e., through research) and disseminated (e.g., Rogers' diffusion of innovation theory—Rogers, 1962, 2003) to the appropriate people for implementation. Building on the work of Bryce Ryan and Neal Gross (1943), who drew on the work of Gabriel Tarde (1903), the French sociologist responsible for describing the "S" shaped diffusion and adoption of innovation curve with Iowa farmers and their adoption times for new hybrid corn (i.e., innovators, early adopters, early majority, late majority, and laggards), Rogers (1962) differentiated between diffusion and adoption in that diffusion was a process that occurred among groups of people as they learned about new approaches. Adoption, he argued, was an individual process in which a person made a commitment to implementation. To reach implementation commitment, Rogers identified five stages individuals move through: (a) first developing knowledge of the innovation, (b) developing an attitude toward the innovation, (c) making a decision to adopt or reject the innovation, (d) decide how to implement the innovation if it is seen as worthwhile, and (e) confirm that the decision was a good one. Rogers also identified four pre-conditions impacting whether a decision is made to implement an innovation or not, these include: (a) the decision maker's previous practices, (b) whether the individual felt the innovation potentially addressed a need or problem, (c) the innovativeness of the decision maker, and (d) norms of the social context within which the individual operated. Finally, of critical relevance to the central discussion in the present paper was the role of mass media; Rogers argued that an individual's awareness and understanding of an innovative idea is most effectively influenced through the use of mass media and its ability to inform, in lay terms, innovators of leading research and innovations.

Looking for policy development literature reveals a perceived gap between research and practice exists, surprisingly, in the field of medicine. In the first of a series of eight papers focused on the gap between research and practice in medicine, Haines and Donald (1998) argued that

> ...how best to promote the uptake of research findings has been fuelled by a number of factors including the well documented disparities between clinical practice and research evidence of effective interventions. Examples include interventions in the management of cardiac failure, secondary prevention of heart disease, atrial fibrillation, menorrhagia, and pregnancy and childbirth. (p. 72)

Haines and Donald (1998) went on to argue that "there is also growing awareness that conventional continuing education activities, such as conferences and courses, which focus largely on the passive acquisition of knowledge have little impact on the behaviour of health professionals" (p. 73). Drawing on Rogers' (1983) diffusion of innovation work, Haines and Donald crafted their argument about how to close the research practice gap by focusing on the care provider and the patient. Keeping in mind that Haines and Donald's target audience was health care professionals, they identify two general categories of barriers preventing the implementation of research in their practice: environmental and personal. Within these two categories they identified specific areas of barriers; those which influence or are influenced by the government level policy makers in the health care area include:

1. Lack of financial resources,
2. Health policies which promote ineffective or unproved activities,
3. Influence of the media on patients in creating demands or beliefs,

4. Impact of disadvantage on patients' access to care,
5. Obsolete knowledge,
6. Influence of opinion leaders, beliefs and attitudes (e.g., a previous adverse experience of innovation),
7. [Patient] demands for care, and
8. [Patient] perceptions or cultural beliefs about appropriate care

The parallels to education are strikingly similar!

In another British study focusing on an historical view of what has driven higher education policy in the U.K., Shattock (2006) argued that from the 1930s to present, policy decisions have not been driven by research conducted by scholars within the higher education community. Shattock examined the tension between the internal Higher Education political forces (the "inside") which exist within the Higher Education institutions themselves and those political forces from various levels of government who often control purse-strings (the "outside"). He notes that prior to the mid-1970s, in the U.K., higher education policy was driven primarily from the inside, but since that time, policy has been driven from the outside. Shattock cited the 2003 White Paper, *The Future of Higher Education* (DfES), in which six themes driving U.K. higher education into the future were affirmed; these he demonstrates are derived "from a Treasury belief, fostered by OECD and the European Union..." (p. 136).

An examination of the American post-secondary education system suggests that higher education in that country is driven from the "inside" by the market forces that directly affect the institutions (Trow, 2003). Interestingly, Trow's assessment of the American higher education policy shaping forces paralleled Shattock's assessment of the U.K. situation with respect to the lack of influence by research conducted by scholars focused on higher education—research appears to be irrelevant.

There are a number of lessons this brief sampling of policy development from three fields suggests for broad scale policy development and decision making in basic education. First, if we are to believe the innovation diffusion theory perspective, the key is to identify innovators (i.e., risk takers and able to cope with uncertainty) and early adopters (i.e., people who have a high degree of "opinion leadership" and who serve as role models in their communities) to promote ideas (popular media is one important means) to stakeholder groups (i.e., educators, parents and business community members—the voters, various levels of government). Indeed these innovators and early adopters are likely members of the stakeholder groups just mentioned. Haines and Donald's (1998) contribution to medical policy making helps educators to identify similar barriers that must be overcome in order to implement new educational approaches; these are:

1. Lack of financial resources;
2. Educational policies promoting ineffective or unproved activities;
3. Influence of the media on parents and students in creating demands or beliefs;

4. Impact of disadvantage on students' access to education;
5. Obsolete knowledge;
6. Influence of opinion leaders, beliefs and attitudes (e.g., a previous adverse experience of innovation);
7. Parent and student demands for education; and
8. Parent and student perceptions or cultural beliefs about appropriate education.

The insight that is potentially most troubling in this exploration comes from the higher education field. Clearly, policy making in basic education shares much with post-secondary education. The higher education experience in the U.K. and the U.S. would suggest that research from within the academy is not particularly relevant; not because such research does not exist, nor because it does not have something relevant to say about higher education, but because politicians and other decision makers, whether they are from the "inside" (i.e., university presidents) or the "outside" (i.e., government ministers) typically choose not to pay attention to it. They are more focused on pre-existing ideology and beliefs than they are on what scholarship from the field has to offer.

Innovation in k-12 policy making and decision making generally follows the same patterns described by Rogers (1962). In particular, educator decision making is very much dependent on Rogers' pre-conditions for adoption of innovative thinking or practice. Typically, evidence contradicting existing beliefs requires suspension of those beliefs rather than simply ignoring the contradictory evidence because it does not fit with decision-maker pre-dispositions. This requires explicit effort to accomplish as, often, contradictory evidence is simply discounted without a thorough analysis of its veracity.

BRINGING THE THREADS TOGETHER

This chapter calls for changes in how research is viewed, critiqued, and used by educational policy makers and practitioners. Returning to the ideas underpinning this chapter, that is, the need for educational policy makers and practitioners to draw on research findings for enacting changes in policy and practice, a variety of observations are offered.

First, field research is extremely messy because researchers are unable to control for all of the unexpected possible threats to validity. Having said that, field research also has great potential for contributing to our understandings of educational processes since teaching and learning takes place in field settings. It does not take place in carefully controlled laboratories.

Consequently—the second point that needs to be highlighted—consumers of research must develop fundamental understandings of research design and be acutely aware of the potential threats to the different types of validity so they can assess the robustness of the research method. In other words, consumers of research need to be able, with confidence, to identify threats to the validity of different types of research, which can cause rival explanations for results to become tenable. This requires understanding research method to identify where threats to validity may exist as well as understanding educational context to be able to imagine the competing rival explanations for research findings. In field-based research there is no perfect research method, anything a researcher does to mitigate one validity related issue invariably creates or has the potential to create a methodological problem: minimizing the threats to validity while maximizing the trustworthiness of research becomes the quest.

Third, consumers of research need to develop, minimally, a level of understanding of statistical data analysis techniques that enable them to comprehend the ideas underlying those techniques. Knowing some fundamental approaches and their theoretical underpinnings allow for research consumers to understand the basic elements of research focused on exploring hypotheses of difference and research focused on exploring hypotheses of association. This also means understanding the importance of not violating the assumptions underlying the statistical approaches, or, alternately, recognizing when statistical assumptions have been violated and what that means in terms of the research findings being reported.

Fourth, consumers of research are encouraged to seek research that de-emphasizes NHST approaches, instead looking for research that reports the results of quantitative analyses in very practical terms of CI and ES. The educational policy maker and practitioner is reminded to be very skeptical of research that focuses on and emphasizes NHST approaches discussing findings on the basis of low p-values only.

The final point that will be highlighted is the importance of drawing on the insights gained from multiple studies. This is not an exercise in finding only those studies that resonate with the educational policy maker or practitioner. Without a question, it is possible to find research that supports virtually any point of view; however, if our purpose is to advance practice on the basis of research, it is critical that the literature considered on any topic be balanced and evaluated through a critical lens.

Addressing these issues will enable educational policy makers and practitioners to make changes supporting educational improvement. To do so, though, requires that decisions be made based on credible evidence gathered from multiple studies that are selected to provide balanced views of the state of the art. Both educational policy makers and practitioners need to be aware of their biases and beliefs, hold them in suspension as advocated by Dewey (1933), to avoid drawing only on research aligned with their pre-dispositions for informing their decisions and actions.

NOTE

[1] One-tailed and two-tailed tests of significance and the effect of these on alpha levels will not be dealt with here, for in depth explanations of this, please refer to any introductory statistics text.

17

REFERENCES

Association for Psychological Science. (2015). *Submission guidelines*. Retrieved from http://www.psychologicalscience.org/index.php/publications/journals/psychological_science/ ps-submissions

Association for Psychological Science. (n.d.). *Manuscript structure, style, and content guidelines*. Retrieved from http://www.psychologicalscience.org/index.php/publications/journals/ms-structure-guidelines

Campbell, D. T., & Stanley, J. C. (1963). *Experimental and quasi-experimental designs for research*. New York, NY: Rand McNally & Co.

Campbell, D. T., & Stanley, J. C. (1966). *Experimental and quasi-experimental designs for research* (2nd ed.). New York, NY: Rand McNally & Co.

Cooper, H. M. (2010). *Research synthesis and meta-analysis: A step-by-step approach* (4th ed.). Thousand Oaks, CA: Sage Publications.

Dewey, J. (1933). *How we think: A restatement of the relation of reflective thinking to the educative process*. Boston, MA: D.C. Heath and Co.

Fidler, F. (2010). The American psychological association publication manual sixth edition: Implications for statistics education. In C. Reading (Ed.), *Data and context in statistics education: Towards an evidence-based society* (Proceedings of the Eighth International Conference on Teaching Statistics. Ljubljana, Slovenia). Voorburg, The Netherlands: International Statistical Institute. Retrieved from www.stat.auckland.ac.nz/~iase/publications.php

Gall, M. D., Gall, J. P., & Borg, W. R. (2007). *Educational research: An introduction* (8th ed.). Toronto: Pearson.

Gay, L. R., Mills, G. E., & Airasian, P. W. (2012). *Educational research: Competencies for analysis and applications* (10th ed.). Toronto: Pearson.

Glass, G. V., & Hopkins, K. D. (1996). *Statistical methods in education and psychology* (3rd ed.). Toronto: Allyn & Bacon.

Glass, G. V., McGaw, B., & Smith, M. L. (1981). *Meta-analysis in social research*. Beverly Hills, CA: Sage Publications.

Guba, E. (1981). Criteria for assessing the trustworthiness of naturalistic inquiries. *Educational Communication and Technology Journal, 29*(2), 75–91.

Haines, A., & Donald, A. (1998). Looking forward: Making better use of research findings. *British Medical Journal, 317*(7150), 72–75.

Hopkins, K. D., Glass, G. V., & Hopkins, B. R. (1995). *Basic statistics for the behavioral sciences* (3rd ed.). Toronto: Allyn & Bacon.

Lincoln, Y. S., & Guba, E. G. (1985). *Naturalistic enquiry*. Newbury Park, CA: Sage Publications.

Neyman, J., & Pearson E. S. (1933). The testing of statistical hypotheses in relation to probabilities a priori. *Mathematical Proceedings of the Cambridge Philosophical Society, 29*, 492–510. doi:10.1017/S030500410001152X

Pedhazur, E. J. (1997). *Multiple regression in behavioral research* (3rd ed.). Toronto: Holt, Rinehart and Winston, Inc.

Popper, K. (1972). *The logic of scientific discover*. London: Hutchinson & Co. Ltd.

Rogers, E. M. (1962). *Diffusion of innovations*. New York, NY: The Free Press.

Rogers, E. M. (2003). *Diffusion of innovations* (5th ed.). New York, NY: The Free Press.

Ryan, B., & Gross, N. C. (1943). The diffusion of hybrid seed corn in two Iowa communities. *Rural Sociology, 8*, 15–24.

Sage Publications. (n.d.). *Sage journals psychological science*. Retrieved from http://pss.sagepub.com/

Sahlberg, P. (2011). *Finnish lessons*. New York, NY: Teachers College Press, Teachers College, Columbia University.

Shattock, M. (2006). Policy drivers in UK higher education in historical perspective: "Inside out," "outside in" and the contribution of research. *Higher Education Quarterly, 60*(2), 130–140.

Sprinthall, R. C. (2011). *Basic statistical analysis* (9th ed.). Toronto: Allyn & Bacon.

Trow, M. (2003). In praise of weakness: Chartering, the University of the United States, and Darmouth College. *Higher Education Policy, 16*(1), 9–27.

BONNIE STELMACH

2. ISSUES WITH EVIDENCE IN CONSTRUCTIVIST/
INTERPRETIVIST EDUCATIONAL RESEARCH

Concerns with evidence in research are neither new nor circumscribed by discipline (Chandler, Davidson, & Harootunian, 1994). But as Denzin and Giardina (2006, 2008) have argued, what counts as "fact", "truth", "evidence", and how social science research is judged is entangled in a political agenda that overvalues objectivism and the scientific method. In *Qualitative Inquiry and the Politics of Evidence* (2008), they argue the "evidence-based research movement" is the "elephant in the living room" (p. 11), squeezing out research that does not conform to quantitative criteria and employ experimental methodologies. In education, this evidence movement is carried by multiple monikers: data-based decision making (Kowalski & Lasley II, 2009), research-based practice (Hammersley, 2005), scientifically based research (SBR) (Denzin, Lincoln, & Giardina, 2006), evidence-based practice (EBP) (Kowalski, 2009), evidence-based policy-making (Sanderson, 2003), and, indexing *No Child Left Behind,* "Bush science" (Lather, 2004, p. 19).

The qualitative research community has rallied against the evidence-based research movement with epistemological and theoretical defenses; new criteria of trustworthiness (Guba, 1981), novel forms of verification (Morse, 2006), checklists for rigor (Barbour, 2001; Beck, 2009), and appeals to adopt the term "evidence" as a floating signifier contingent upon professional judgment (Staller, 2006) are among the arguments against the "epistemological essentialism" (Koro-Ljungberg & Barko, 2012, p. 257) claimed to be the fulcrum of the evidence-based movement. At the same time, some scholars contend the qualitative community contributes to the incredulity because of diverse and emerging methodologies (Cheek, 2007; Morse, 2006), and lack of paradigmatic unity (Rolfe, 2006). Despite the claim that the so-called paradigm wars of the 1980s have settled (Denzin & Lincoln, 2011), qualitative research is precariously positioned when it comes to the current evidence-based movement. One cannot ignore the ongoing privileging and depriviliging of research approaches, but my aim here is not to put a poker in this political fire. Rather, my concerns are these: First, to identify and clear-up sources of confusion regarding the use of "constructivist" and "interpretivist" to argue that concerns with evidence derived from such studies are founded on mistaken epistemological assumptions about these approaches; second, to consider how the processes of collecting data and creating evidence in non-experimental studies matters to questions of evidence;

P. Newton & D. Burgess (Eds.), The Best Available Evidence, 19–32.

and, finally, to consider the potential and limitations of what we commonly call qualitative research for educational improvement. To achieve my second objective, I borrow from Sandelowki and Barroso's (2002) list of problems associated with finding findings in qualitative research as a conceptual guide. I culminate my discussion by considering the challenge of transferability and generalizability, and how this impacts upon the potential for qualitative data to contribute to educational improvement. My goal is to give what we broadly conceive of as "qualitative" research a chance in the evidence-based movement in educational research, notwithstanding some cautionary notes.

Why This Discussion Matters

Defenses for qualitative approaches in educational research have been developing in response to a matrix of government and non-profit initiatives that champion "scientific" research using randomized control trials (RCTs) and other experimental methodologies (Denzin & Giardina, 2008). The United States has arguably been an engine in this movement. The Campbell Collaboration developed in 2000 promotes systematic reviews of education research for scientific validity in a similar way the earlier established Cochrane Collaboration does for health research. The mandate of the Campbell Collaboration is augmented by the *Education Sciences Reform Act of 2002*, which promotes "scientifically based", "rigorous, systematic and objective methodology to obtain reliable and valid knowledge relevant to education activities and programs" (Section 18.i). The National Board of Science, the Institute of Education Sciences, and What Works Clearinghouse (WWC) are pistons pumping the evidence machine.

The United States is by no means blazing this ideological trail, for the United Kingdom has its Research Assessment Exercise (2008) and for Australia, the Australian Qualifications Framework (2013). Canada escapes national judicial treatment of this issue because education belongs to provincial jurisdiction. We are, however, not immune. The Council of Ministers of Education (CMEC), which provides national leadership for education, clearly displays our provinces' preoccupation with their global ranking in the Programme for International Student Assessment (PISA). Further, the phrase "data-driven decision making" and its derivative terms is ubiquitous on provincial education ministry websites and documents. Given the girth of this trend toward making education a more exact science, one might expect constructivist and interpretivist research to be declining. This is not the case.

Using "school administration" as a search term in ProQuest Dissertation and Theses, which stores documents from universities in North America and Europe, I took a cursory glance at the incidence of Master's theses and doctoral dissertations reporting to use qualitative, constructivist, or interpretivist approaches, as indicated in abstracts or table of contents. I explored the time frame 1975–1985 wanting to explore this idea before the interpretive turn associated with the publication of *Naturalistic Inquiry*. The first 25 doctoral dissertations were primarily from American universities, and tipped the balance toward quantitative studies by 16 to 9. The decade following, 1986–1996, the distribution of 25 looked like this: 12 qualitative; 11 quantitative, and 2 mixed-method. Concerned with a more contemporary picture, I searched documents posted between 2000 and 2013, considering the legislation of *No Child Left Behind,* and the drive of the science agenda that ensued. Indeed, the landscape has shifted: 22 qualitative; 2 quantitative—a dramatic turn away from objective methodologies.

Interested in how things looked in my back yard, I conducted similar searches for the University of Saskatchewan where I was—at the time of writing—a faculty member in the Department of Educational Administration, and University of Alberta, my alma mater and current university. I used larger samples when searching the University of Alberta (see Table 1), but was disappointed to find the search results limited when I attempted this for the University of Saskatchewan. For example, my search for documents between 1975 and 1985 had one result only. Out of 22 results in the search of University Saskatchewan theses and dissertations completed during the time period 1986–1996, 15 reported to be qualitative, 4 quantitative, and 3 were mixed method. Between 2000 and 2013, based on 40 results, 92.5% (n=37) studies were described as qualitative, 5% (n=2) were described as quantitative, and 2.5% (n=1) used mixed method. Admittedly, the search results do not warrant comparison among these data, but reflect a trend in the use of qualitative methods since the 1990s noted by others (Elmore & Woehlke, 1996). The increase in academic journals and publications focusing on qualitative research also testify to this trend. Accounting for this shift exceeds the scope of my project here, but the patterns noted highlight the importance of this discussion. If it is the case that more graduate programs are supporting constructivist and interpretivist research, it behooves those who mentor graduate students to seriously consider how their work can contribute to school improvement. If much of the research in educational administration shared with schoolteachers and leaders is based on qualitative evidence, we must be clear about what evidence of this nature can and cannot do.

Table 1. Percentage theses and dissertations combined employing quantitative, qualitative and mixed method at the University of Alberta

	Quantitative	Qualitative	Mixed method
1975–1985 (n=25)	52% (n=13)	40% (n=10)	8% (n=2)
1986–1996 (n=50)	20% (n=10)	80% (n=40)	0
2000–2013 (n=100)	21%	76%	3%

DEFINING INTERPRETIVIST/CONSTRUCTIVIST RESEARCH

Constructivism and interpretivism are commonly understood as paradigms within which research is conducted. They are cousins by their epistemological and ontological heritage. There is, however, considerable variation in how they are presented, and Crotty (1998) would argue, *misrepresented*. This has implications for how we think about evidence in studies of this nature; therefore, before proceeding with the main discussion, it is worth straightening out some confusion.

Lincoln and Guba's (1985) seminal work, *Naturalistic Inquiry,* made qualitative and quantitative research a household distinction. In their original paradigm table they delineated the epistemological and ontological assumptions among positivist, post-positivist, constructivist, and critical theory (Lincoln, Lynham, & Guba, 2011). Others have adapted and extended their typology. For example, Prasad's (2005) paradigm includes interpretive, critical, and "post"-traditions (e.g. postmodernism). Carr and Kemmis (1995) distinguish among positivist, interpretive, and critical. Mertens' (2010) adaptation includes postpositivism, constructivism, transformative, and pragmatic. Merriam (2009) summarizes the perspectives in terms of positivist/ postpositivist, interpretivist/constructivist, critical, and postmodern/poststructural. While qualitative research is characterized as affording liberties to a researcher to "[make] sense of the underlying philosophical influences in his or her own way" (Merriam, p. 8), the proliferation of paradigms and variations in language use muddies what it intends to clarify. In fact, those who suggest interpretivism and constructivism are interchangeable (Merriam), or fuse "constructivist/interpretivist/ qualitative perspective[s]" oversimplify and create problems for how we understand evidence in studies conducted using these perspectives.

The primordial issue lies in aligning constructivism and interpretivism with qualitative research, and postpositivism with quantitative research. Doing so epistemologically polarizes quantitative and qualitative research (Crotty, 1998). According to Crotty, most research texts categorize research in this way, ignoring that historically research dubbed "qualitative" has employed positivist approaches, and that quantification is an important aspect of how we qualitatively understand our world. How, then, do we understand constructivist, interpretivist, and qualitative research?

What is often reported as "constructivist" research according to Crotty (1998) is based on social constructionism, stemming from Berger and Luckmann's (1966) treatise that reality is socially constructed. This concept has shifted through multiplicity of use over time and in various disciplines (Haslanger, 2012). Fundamental to Berger and Luckmann's theoretical outlook is the idea that the subjectivist understanding of the world does not discount that there is an objective element to it. Objects themselves exist (objectivism). We come to understand them through collective negotiation and interaction (subjectivism). Citing Merleau-Ponty, Crotty explains: "The world and objects in the world are indeterminate. They may be pregnant with potential meaning, but actual meaning emerges only when consciousness engages with them" (p. 43). Constructionism, then, implies that "meaning is not discovered but constructed" (Crotty, p. 42). Meaning is both objective and subjective. It is objective because things do exist in the world, but it is subjective because things in themselves are meaningless until we make sense of them. This is true of the natural and social world. Yet, it is often assumed that the natural world is outside of subjective apprehension and lends itself to objective methodologies, and the social world has no objective reality and therefore is understood subjectively.

If social constructionism is the view that all knowledge depends on human practices, and is constructed and transmitted through interaction between individuals and the world, what do we mean by *constructivism*? Again, Crotty's (1998) explanation is helpful. Constructivism refers to an individualistic position, emphasizing the unique experience of individuals. He suggests this term is best used to describe the individual's sense-making in the world. That world itself, however, is a social construction. To believe the world is purely constructed in our minds is to subscribe to von Glasersfeld's (2010) position of radical constructivism. This viewpoint leaves no room for objectivism, and relies on Cartesian dualism. In my reading of educational research claiming to be constructivist, constructs such as *teacher* and *school* are themselves uncontested. Their existence is a social construction; therefore, constructivism is not the paradigmatic assumption per se, but an assumption about the source of the data. Such studies are qualitative by virtue of the methods used and the nature of the data (e.g. interviews, photos) that set them apart from experimental research.

Interpretivism is sometimes conflated with constructivism and applied as a paradigm. On this point, again Crotty (1998) departs, for he describes interpretivism as a theoretical perspective rather than an epistemology. Associated with qualitative data, interpretivism is often mistaken for subjectivism. Crotty unravels this with clarity, and is worth citing at length:

> Researchers claiming to be phenomenological talk of studying experience from the "point of view" or "perspective" of the subject. What these researchers are interested in as "everyday" experience, experience as people understand it in everyday terms. If they talk at all of "phenomenon", it is either used interchangeable with "experience" or presented as an essence distilled from everyday accounts of experience ... the phenomenology of the phenomenological movement is a first-person exercise. (pp. 83–84)

In the above Crotty is pointing to the transformation that phenomenology has undergone. When researchers claim to conduct studies within an interpretive paradigm, and they call their approach phenomenology, they are discounting the "objective character and critical spirit, so strong in the phenomenological tradition" (p. 85). This tradition—the phenomenology of Husserl—rests on objectivist assumptions, assuming that there is an "essence" to a phenomenon and that it can be captured through interpretation. This ultimately is a postpositivist assumption (Rolfe, 2006). Hermenuetics as it developed within biblical studies holds a similar assumption that language and its structure must be interpreted to get at the essence of meaning. So again, research that considers individual perceptions of phenomena and interpretations of experiences is not epistemologically anchored to subjectivism. Rather, it is more helpful to understand that the manner in which the data are created and analyzed requires intersubjective transactions.

Social constructionism and interpretivism are assumed to have no place in the evidence-based movement because the findings of such research are influenced by the subjectivity of participants and researcher. The critique of and defense for this kind of research has been based on epistemology, and misplaced assumptions that there is nothing objective about our social world, and nothing subjective about our natural world. If we accept Crotty's (1998) explanation, it is clear that the epistemological tension is unfounded, and that the anti-science discourse of the politics of evidence campaign is itself an orthodoxy worth contesting (Seale, 2004). The qualitative-quantitative binary is misleading, and it may make more sense to speak of experimental versus non-experimental research.

But non-experimental research is not off the evidence hook. I contend it is the manner in which data are collected and analyzed, and the ambiguity of how final interpretations or results came to be that contribute to suspicion around non-experimental research. How we treat qualitative data makes a difference to whether and how they are accepted as evidence. I focus the next section on this matter.

A CONCEPTUAL FRAMEWORK

Sandelowski and Barroso (2002) analyzed 99 qualitative studies of women with HIV infection to gain insight into how findings are created and reported. Their concern was the "communication of challenges arising from the very effort to synthesize qualitative findings and the reasons behind procedural, analytic and interpretive moves taken to synthesize a set of findings" (p. 213). Although their study was based on nursing scholarship, the key problems they identified with finding findings are applicable to qualitative studies regardless of discipline. Data, data analysis, theme, and pattern are taken-for-granted in the vernacular of non-experimental research in any discipline. Condensing Sandelowski and Barosso's list of concerns, two key questions frame my discussion about evidence:

1. How do qualitative data become evidence?
2. How do themes or patterns represent evidence?

The Question of Data and Evidence

Evidence is about building the case for conclusions (Freeman, deMarrais, Preissle, Roulston, & St. Pierre, 2007). "Data are not evidence" (Miller, 2003, p. 41). Data only *become* evidence when we have a model for how this takes place (Miller & Fredericks, 2003). What counts as data is contingent upon the inquiry itself.

Research questions and research objectives set the boundaries for data (Chandler, Davidson, & Harootunian, 1994). Thus, in 75 pages of interview transcripts one could claim there are 75 pages of data, but not everything that is in the transcripts counts as evidence. Through the process of analysis, researchers must filter and sort data that are relevant to the inquiry before shaping them into forms of evidence.

Morse (2006) argued, "we must focus on the type and role of data, and develop appropriate strategies for ensuring quality" (p. 99). She describes data as direct (or descriptive), semidirect, and indirect. Direct data provide a description of a phenomena, collected through methods such as surveys. Semidirect data are comprised of narratives and perceptions provided in participants' reports. This type of data, Morse argued, tolerates error because of the fallibility of human perception. Finally, indirect data are inferential and abstract, based on nonverbal signs and symbols in language. Indirect data are not concerned with questions of accuracy, but rather whether the data are supported among others for the development of theory. This typology suggests that data are units of information that can be assembled as evidence according to the function they play and how an inquiry is framed. Evidence is never free of context, and is inherently biased because it is generated for a purpose (Davies, 1999).

Similarly, evidence is not a monolithic term. Miller (2003) differentiated between evidence *of* a claim, and evidence *for* a claim. Evidence *of* is a weaker claim. It entails looking for all positive instances of something. For example, if we claim that teachers experience increased levels of stress, we might point to absenteeism rates, or the number of teachers requesting stress or medical leave as evidence of this claim. In this example, absenteeism and requests for leave are among many other potential pieces of evidence that may warrant a claim regarding teacher stress. Thus, absenteeism and requests for leave are *sufficient* conditions for the claim, but not *necessary*. Evidence *for* provides for a necessary condition, and constitutes a stronger claim. In the case of teacher stress, perhaps high rates of teacher complaints about workplace conditions could be the necessary condition, and therefore considered evidence for claiming teacher stress. When one claims evidence of something, there is a possibility for a rival interpretation. Absenteeism and request for leave may be related to conditions outside of the work environment. On the other hand, when one claims evidence for something, rival interpretations are ruled out. In both instances, the data become confirming evidence in varying degrees of strength according to whether an inquiry aims to find sufficient conditions for interpretations, or sufficient *and* necessary.

From the above, we can conclude it is not sufficient to present qualitative data in a research report as if the data speak for themselves. The retelling of stories through lengthy quotes has been defended as a non-intrusive way to represent participants; however, as Sandelowski and Barosso (2002) argued, the lack of interpretation and/ or a theoretical framework results in data devoid of explanatory power. Additionally, it matters to the utility of research whether we claim data are evidence *of* something or they are evidence *for* something. In evidence-based educational research, we must be clear about the strength and nature of the claims we make to ensure findings are not applied inappropriately. The development of policy, for example, requires evidence of the necessary conditions for a desirable state; evidence *of* claims speaks to contextual conditions only, and not necessary ones. Given Miller's (2003) distinction, it is the type of evidence that matters to the purpose in[for?] which it will serve, not simply whether or not evidence is claimed.

The Question of Patterns and Themes

Guba and Lincoln (1985) have argued that there is no such thing as pure data or raw data and that the process of analysis involves reconstructing constructions made by those participating in research. Justifying claims comes with demonstrating appropriate data generation, as well as demonstrating systematic analysis with reference to a question or argument (Lincoln, 2002). What typically is offered is detailed explanation of coding rather than justification for how one assigns pieces of data to particular codes (Sandelowski & Barosso, 2002; Freeman, deMarrais, Preissie, Rouston, & St. Pierre, 2007). For example, the researcher must be able to explain how in the process of generating categories or patterns, one decided from transcripts that certain linguistic elements were sufficient for the creation of the category (Miller, 2003). How qualitative analysis confirms a claim is paramount, and the first step is to explicate the decision making in coding processes.

Along the same vein, Sandelowski and Barosso (2002, p. 217) asked: "On what basis were things presumed to fall into a pattern?" Is a pattern or theme reliant on frequency? Is a theme based on multiple meanings or motif? Do data become a pattern when the pattern typifies other participants (intersubjective pattern)? Or is a pattern thematic for that participant alone (intrasubjective pattern)? Are patterns and themes demonstrations of convergence or divergence? If data cannot speak for themselves, neither does it suffice to say that themes were constructed or that they emerged from the data. Researchers must clarify what criteria were applied to the data that were coded into patterns, and how the data were prioritized into themes.

Two common methods for demonstrating that one's interpretations are reliable are member check and triangulation (Guba & Lincoln, 1985). Member check typically involves sharing interview transcripts with participants who are asked to validate the findings. The presumption is that their participation in the transcripts will lead to the elimination of significant errors that may impact upon the quality of the data (Mero-Jaffe, 2011). Guba (1981) contended member check was the single most important action that "goes to the heart of the credibility criterion" (p. 85). Member check, however, is a process that is fraught with problems such as power issues and different values. On a practical level, a researcher's aim when doing member check(s) may be to ensure the data resonate with the participant, but participants may aim to reduce embarrassment regarding their articulation, or to garner sympathy on a specific issue (Koelsch, 2013). Member check assumes participants have an "unadulterated viewpoint" (p. 170). Hagens, Dobrow, and Chafe (2009) found that sharing transcripts with participants did very little to improve the quality of the data, and in fact, resulted in the loss of valuable data that participants deleted. Further, if member check is limited to interview transcripts rather than the report of findings and interpretations, its contribution to thematic confirmation is specious.

Triangulation is similarly lauded as a security check on interpretations of qualitative data. Barbour (2001) posits the heavy reliance on triangulation in research grant applications "testifies both to the respect accorded to this concept and to its perceived value in demonstrating rigour" (p. 1117). In theory, he argues, triangulation is laudable, but in practice, data collected through different methods cannot be compared directly. When parallel databases are created, there are no grounds for refutation, only corroboration. It is through negative cases that a data set can be shaped into the form of a theme. Moreoever, triangulation assumes a positivist point of corroboration, whether we mean theoretical triangulation, source or method triangulation as Guba (1981) proposed. Thus, the discussion is not about whether or not to triangulate, but rather, "what can be claimed by doing so" (Whiteley, 2012, p. 257). Triangulation still begs the evidence question.

Even if researchers execute and elaborate their methods of qualitative data collection and analysis diligently, non-experimental educational researchers must contend with the question of utility (Pawson, Boaz, Grayson, Long, & Barnes, 2003). In the final section I outline the challenges to generalizability, and the potential for findings based on qualitative data to contribute to educational improvement.

CHALLENGES TO GENERALIZABILITY AND TRANSFERABILITY, AND THE POTENTIAL FOR EDUCATIONAL RESEARCH

There is no escaping the critique that claims derived from qualitative data are not generalizable. This accounts for the lack of recognition and status of qualitative studies within the evidence-based movement in education. The qualitative camp dodges this critique by offering trustworthiness as a more suitable alternative, and arguing that generalizability is an undesirable goal in the social realm. Guba's (1981) comprehensive criteria for establishing trustworthiness in naturalistic inquiry—credibility, transferability, dependability, and confirmability—have long since been accepted in the qualitative community as the standards for rigor. Instead of rallying against generalizability as a standard for qualitative research, I interrogate generalizability itself to question its exalted status vis-à-vis transferability in educational research. Given that qualitative research is prevalent in educational studies in spite of the attempt to make it scientific, what is the value and use of a corpus of research that relies on transferability?

The evidence-based movement is rooted in the study of medicine, and premised on projectable causal connections. We can trust that a heart works similarly regardless of the human body in which it inhabits (ignoring environmental factors, of course). Starving a heart of oxygen will cause it to stop pumping. It makes sense to say this knowledge is generalizable. But do causal claims in education have the same limitless scope? Schools, classrooms, students and teachers are not anatomical units distilled from contextual factors. If a randomized control trial isolates a causal connection, the scope of the causal claim is still in question. Cartwright (2013) suggests, causal claims can mean one of three things: it works "somewhere", "widely" or will work "here" (p. 97). Thus, "what we identify as a cause seldom is enough on its own to produce the targeted effect" (p. 99). Small class size, for example, may be identified as the cause for improved student achievement in one school, but unless the "support factors" exist in another school, a policy of small class size may be ineffective. Lack of qualified teachers, for example, may render such a policy detrimental. This idea has prompted others to suggest that qualitative research is a necessary antecedent to randomized control trials so that context and support factors can be discerned (Torrance, 2008). As Cartwright noted, "if we lack the information that underwrites an induction, we do not have strong reason to suppose that the conclusion of that induction is true" (p. 106).

Further, generalizability assumes research questions and the application of evidence are value-neutral. The kind of knowledge necessary to inform policy may be defined in one way from the policy-makers' perspectives or the stakeholders' viewpoint, and still another from the researchers' point of view. The desired outcome is also a matter of judgment (Hammersley, 2005). Parent involvement, for example, has received considerable attention in the research world and policy arena, yet, there is a palpable divide between teachers' interest in working with parents and policy mandates to include parents in educational matters (Schecter & Sherri, 2009). My own research on this topic confirmed that teachers are more likely to buffer themselves against perceived intrusion of parents than to work collaboratively with them (Stelmach, 2004, 2006). The effects of policy are highly mediated by local circumstances, rendering claims about the positive effect of parent involvement on student outcomes futile. Evidence, even if it is generalizable, is subjected to human judgment. Furthermore, the application of strategies that work requires the consent of those to whom it will be applied. The evidence-based movement in education is premised on rational choice theory, but human beings are not only rational beings (Humphries, 2003). Evidence is accepted and applied in the same fashion, whether it is deemed generalizable is irrelevant.

If we accept the above critique of generalizability, we are left with the notion that educational research is, at best, subject to the conditions of transferability. Transferability leaves the judgment about the applicability of research evidence to the consumer, and it is the responsibility of the researcher to provide contextual information to support this assessment. Geertz (1973) called this contextual information "thick description." If meeting the transferability criterion is contingent upon individual research consumers assessing its value for their specific contexts, how can qualitative research findings be useful in large-scale, systematic educational improvement?

Metcalfe and Lynch (2002) proposed that social inquiry should produce actionable knowledge and critical heuristics that serve as rules of thumb for exploring boundaries. Practitioners know that context matters to the success of any strategy; a reading strategy may work with one set of students but not with another, and the same strategy may be successful one day, but not the following week. Practitioners are constantly evaluating and assessing strategies within context, and evidence from qualitative studies may inform, but not dictate their practice. Metcalfe and Lynch suggested, "good knowledge is … as much about appreciating justified perspectives as it is about seeking universal truths for human behavior" (p. 75).

A common argument against generalizability is that multiple realities characterize our social world (Guba, 1981). It may be the case that human behavior is not completely predictable or controlled, but it is equally extreme to suggest that human behavior defies understanding. If my discussion of social constructionism and interpretivism has merit, we can accept that there are certain things about human behavior we can understand. Most people will flinch and protect themselves if you throw something at them, for instance. Children will respond to positive feedback, and so on. Qualitative research, rather than being predictive or an uncontested answer, may contribute to our understanding of educational matters through assemblage (Gordon, 2007; Koro-Ljungberg & Barko, 2012; Marcus & Saka, 2006). Research may enrich our understanding without foreclosing on answers. In this way, qualitative research has an advantage over so-called objective knowledge, which treats evidence as "an endpoint for research indicating a closure and the end of a text, interpretation and dialogue" (Koro-Ljungberg & Barko, p. 256).

But transferability has its limitations. The proclaimed virtue of qualitative research is that it affords in-depth examination of phenomena. Because breadth is sacrificed, however, it raises questions about utility in large-scale educational reform:

> The argument has been that educational research…is too often conceived and conducted as a "cottage industry," producing too many small-scale, disconnected, noncumulative studies that do not provide convincing explanations of educational phenomena or how best to develop teaching and learning. (Torrance, 2008, p. 508)

As noted earlier, I reviewed close to 300 theses and dissertations to characterize the research landscape. One study was described as longitudinal. Consequently, the above critique is warranted. There may be practical reasons why longitudinal research is seldom conducted in education—stress on research sites, the exploration of educational issues that require immediate response, the need for currency—but rather than lament what we do not have, it makes sense to acknowledge that much educational research makes limited claims. Miller (2003) contended that "subjective evidence" is not inferior, but rather makes claims for an individual group at a particular point in time. What matters is how qualitative analysis confirms a claim, rather than for how far the claim extends. One might argue that because schools exist at the nexus of political, social, and economic shift, tentative, or time-bound evidence is what matters most. This may not satisfy those concerned with large-scale educational reform, but on this front, the battle may never be won.

So where do we go from here? Qualitative inquiry has suffered attack on grounds that privilege objectivism over subjectivism, and assume a separate and distinct epistemology for methodologies associated with qualitative and quantitative research. I have argued the protean nature of research terminology has contributed to this misleading assumption. Educational research based on qualitative methodologies must be conducted in a manner that clarifies how claims are made; what constitutes a theme is a critical, but often taken-for-granted element. It is the *manner* in which a claim is made from qualitative data that matters, rather than whether the claim itself can stand up to a doctrine of generalizability (Miller, 2003). Educational evidence based on qualitative data has its place in informing debates, engaging intellectualism, and enriching the experience of school and teaching. It remains unpredictable. It is more fruitful to defend evidence derived from qualitative data on the basis of what it can do, rather than what it cannot. Schwandt's (2006) proposal to redirect the opposition that ensues between qualitative and quantitative camps by accepting that educational research has multiple agendas may be a worthwhile resolution. He asks qualitative researchers to be "less concerned with always defining [their research] in opposition to some way of investigating the sociopolitical world and more concerned with embracing a genuine heterogeneous conception of social inquiry" (p. 809). In the "what works" vernacular, continuing to characterize qualitative research against quantitative approaches does not work.

REFERENCES

Australian Qualifications Framework. (2013). *What is the AQF?* Retrieved from http://www.aqf.edu.au/aqf/about/what-is-the-aqf/

Barbour, R. S. (2001). Checklists for improving the rigour in qualitative research: A case of the tail wagging the dog? *British Medical Journal, 322,* 1115–1117.

Beck, C. T. (2009). Critiquing qualitative research. *Association of Peri-Operative Registered Nurses, 90*(4), 543–554.

Berger, L., & Luckmann, T. (1966). *The social construction of reality: A treatise in the sociology of knowledge.* New York, NY: Penguin Putnam.

Carr, W., & Kemmis, S. (1995). *Becoming critical: Education; knowledge and action research.* London: Hyperion Books.

Cartwright, N. (2013). Knowing what we are talking about: Why evidence doesn't always travel. *Evidence & Policy, 9*(1), 97–112.

Chandler, J., Davidson, A. I., & Harootunian, H. (Eds.). (1994). *Questions of evidence: Proof, practice, and persuasion across the disciplines.* Chicago, IL: University of Chicago Press.

Cheek, J. (2007). Qualitative inquiry, ethics, and politics of evidence: Working within these spaces rather than being worked over by them. *Qualitative Inquiry, 13*(8), 1051–1059.

Crotty, M. (1998). *The foundations of social research: Meaning and perspective in the research process.* London: SAGE.

Davies, P. (1999). What is evidence-based education? *British Journal of Educational Studies, 47*(2), 108–121.

Denzin, N. K., & Giardina, M. D. (Eds.). (2006). *Qualitative inquiry and the conservative challenge.* Walnut Creek, CA: Left Coast Press.

Denzin, N. K., & Giardina, M. D. (Eds.). (2008). *Qualitative inquiry and the politics of evidence.* Walnut Creek, CA: Left Coast Press.

Denzin, N. K., & Lincoln, Y. S. (2011). The discipline and practice of qualitative research. In. N. K. Denzin & Y. S. Lincoln (Eds.), *The sage handbook of qualitative research* (pp. 1–20). Los Angeles, CA: Sage Publications.

Denzin, N. K., Lincoln, Y. S., & Giardina, M. D. (2006). Disciplining qualitative research. *International Journal of Qualitative Studies in Education, 19*(6), 769–782. doi:10.1080/09518390600975990

Elmore, P. B., & Woehlke, P. I. (1996, April 8). *Research methods employed in American Educational Research Journal, Educational Researchers and Review of Educational Research, 1978–1995*. Paper presented at the Annual Meeting of the American Educational Research Association, New York, NY.

Education Sciences Reform Act of 2002 H.R. 3801. Retrieved from http://ies.ed.gov/pdf/PL107-279.pdf

Freeman, M., deMarrais, K., Preissle, J., Roulston, K., & St. Pierre, E. A. (2007). Standards of evidence in qualitative research: An incitement to discourse. *Educational Researcher, 36*(1), 25–32.

Geertz, C. (1973). *The interpretation of cultures: Selected essays*. New York, NY: Basic Books.

Gordon, M. (2007). Living the questions: Rilke's challenge to our quest for certainty. *Educational Theory, 57*(1), 37–52.

Guba, E. G. (1981). Criteria for assessing the trustworthiness of naturalistic inquiries. *Educational Communications and Technology Journal, 29*(2), 75–91.

Hagens, V., Dobrow, M. J., & Chafe, R. (2009). Interviewee transcript review: Assessing the impact on qualitative research. *BMC Medical Research Methodology, 9*, 47. Retrieved from http://dx.doi.org/10.1186/1471-2288-9-47

Hammersley, M. (2005). The myth of research-based practice: The critical case of educational inquiry. *International Journal of Social Research Methodology, 8*(4), 317–330.

Haslanger, S. (2012). *Resisting reality: Social construction and social critique*. Oxford: Oxford University Press.

Hatch, J. A. (2006). Qualitative studies in the era of scientifically-based research: Musings of a former QSE editor. *International Journal of Qualitative Studies in Education, 19*, 403–407.

Humphries, B. (2003). What *else* counts as evidence in evidence-based social work? *Social Work Education, 22*(1), 81–91.

Institute of Education Sciences. (n.d.). Retrieved from http://ies.ed.gov/

Koelsch, L. E. (2013). Reconceptualizing the member check. *International Journal of Qualitative Methods, 12*, 169–179.

Koro-Ljungberg, M., & Barko, T. (2012). "Answers," assemblages, and qualitative research. *Qualitative Inquiry, 18*(3), 256–265.

Kowalski, T. J. (2009). Evidence and decision making in professions. In T. J. Kowalski & T. J. Lasley II (Eds.), *Handbook of data-based decision making in education* (pp. 3–19). New York, NY: Routledge.

Kowalski, T. J., & Lasley II, T. J. (Eds.). (2009). *Handbook of data-based decision making in education.* New York, NY: Routledge.

Lather, P. (2004). This is your father's paradigm: government intrusion and the case of qualitative research in education. *Qualitative Inquiry, 10*(1), 15–34.

Lather, P., & St. Pierre, E. A. (2013). Post-qualitative research. *International Journal of Qualitative Studies in Education, 26*(6), 629–633. doi:10.1080/09518398.2013.788752

Lincoln, Y. S. (2002, November). *On the nature of qualitative evidence.* Paper presented at the meeting of the Association for the Study of Higher Education, Sacramento, CA.

Lincoln, Y. S., & Guba, E. G. (1985). *Naturalistic inquiry.* Newbury Park, CA: Sage.

Lincoln, Y. S., Lynham, S. A., & Guba, E. G. (2011). Paradigmatic controversies, contradictions, and emerging confluences, revisited. In. N. K. Denzin & Y. S. Lincoln (Eds.), *The sage handbook of qualitative research* (pp. 97–128). Los Angeles, CA: Sage.

Marcus, G., & Saka, E. (2006). Assemblage. *Theory, Culture, & Society, 23*(2–3), 101–109.

Mero-Jaffe, I. (2011). 'Is that what I said?' Interview transcript approval by participants: An aspect of ethics in qualitative research. *International Journal of Qualitative Methods, 10*(3), 232–247.

Merriam, S. (2009). *Qualitative research: A guide to design and implementation.* San Francisco, CA: Jossey-Bass.

Mertens, D. M. (2010). *Research and evaluation in education and psychology: Integrating diversity with quantitative, qualitative, and mixed methods* (3rd ed.). Los Angeles, CA: Sage.

Metcalfe, M., & Lynch, M. (2002). A critique of generalizability in interpretive research. *Australian Journal of Information Systems, 10*(2), 70–75.

Miller, S. (2003). The nature of "evidence" in qualitative research methods. *International Journal of Qualitative Methods, 2*(1), 39–51.

Miller, S., & Fredericks, M. (2003). The nature of "evidence" in qualitative research methods. *International Journal of Qualitative Methods, 2*(1), 2–27.

Morse, J. M. (2006). Insight, inference, evidence, and verification: Creating a legitimate discipline. *International Journal of Qualitative Methods, 5*(1), 93–100.

National Board for Education Sciences. (2010). *Director's final proposed priorities for the Institute of Education Sciences*. Retrieved from http://ies.ed.gov/director/board/priorities.asp

Pawson R., Boaz A., Grayson L., Long A., & Barnes C. (2003) *Types and quality of knowledge in social care*. London: Social Care Institute for Excellence.

Prasad, P. (2005). *Crafting qualitative research: Working in the postpositivist traditions*. Armonk, NY: M. E. Sharpe.

Research Assessment Exercise. (2008). *About us*. Retrieved from http://www.rae.ac.uk/aboutus/

Richards, L., & Morse, J. M. (2013). *Readme first for a user's guide to qualitative methods* (3rd ed.). Los Angeles, CA: Sage.

Rolfe, G. (2006). Validity, trustworthiness and rigour: Quality and the idea of qualitative research. *Journal of Advanced Nursing, 53*(3), 304–310.

Sandelowski, M., & Barroso, J. (2002). Finding the findings in qualitative studies. *Journal of Nursing Scholarship, 34*(3), 213–219.

Sanderson, I. (2003). Is it 'what works' that matters? Evaluation and evidence-based policy-making. *Research Papers in Education, 18*(4), 331–345.

Schecter, S. R., & Sherri, D. L. (2009). Value added? Teachers' investments in and orientation toward parent involvement in education. *Urban Education, 44*(1), 59–87.

Schwandt, T. (2006). Opposition redirected. *International Journal of Qualitative Studies in Education, 19*(6), 803–810. doi:10.1080/09518390600979323

Seale, C. (2004). Quality in qualitative research. In C. Seale, G. Gobo, J. F. Gubrium, & D. Silverman (Eds.), *Qualitative research practice* (pp. 409–419). Thousand Oaks, CA: Sage.

Staller, K. M. (2006). Railroads, runaways, & researchers: Returning evidence rhetoric to its practice base. *Qualitative Inquiry, 12*(3), 503–522.

Stam, M., Miedema, W., Onstenk, J., Wardekker, W., & ten Dam, G. (2014). Researching how and what teachers learn from innovating their own educational practices: The ins and outs of a high-quality design. *International Journal of Qualitative Studies in Education, 27*(2), 251–267. doi:10.1080/09518398.2012.758789

Stelmach, B. (2006). *The role of parents in school improvement: Secondary school parent and student perspectives* (Unpublished doctoral dissertation). University of Alberta, Canada.

Stelmach, B. (2004). Unlocking the schoolhouse doors: Institutional constraints on parent and community involvement in a school improvement initiative. *Canadian Journal of Educational Administration and Policy, 31*. Retrieved from http://www.umanitoba.ca/publications/cjeap/issuesOnline.html

The Campbell Collaboration. (n.d.). *Background*. Retrieved from http://www.campbellcollaboration.org/background/index.php

The Cochrane Collaboration. (2013). *About us*. Retrieved fropm http://www.cochrane.org/about-us

Torrance, H. (2008). Building confidence in qualitative research: Engaging the demands of policy. *Qualitative Inquiry, 14*(1), 507–527.

U.S. Department of Education. (2002). *Education Sciences Reform Act. H.R. 3801*. Retrieved from http://www2.ed.gov/policy/rschstat/leg/PL107-279.pdf

von Glasersfeld, E. (2010). A radical constructivist view of meaning and the problem of communication. *Studies in Meaning, 3*–8.

What Works Clearinghouse. (n.d.). *About us*. Retrieved from http://ies.ed.gov/ncee/wwc/aboutus.aspx

Whiteley, A. (2012). Supervisory conversations on rigour and interpretive research. *Qualitative Research Journal, 12*(2), 251–271.

PAUL NEWTON AND DAVID BURGESS

3. EXPLORING TYPES OF EDUCATIONAL ACTION RESEARCH[1]

Implications for Research Validity

Although the field of educational action research has been the subject of countless articles emanating from both critics and advocates, we have yet to arrive at a satisfactory conclusion with respect to the efficacy and credibility of educational action research as a research approach. In this chapter we attempt to uncover the key features of action research and explore the effect of those features on the knowledge claims of research products and processes. In particular, we address the issue of validity claims within action research. Second, we suggest that much of action research, although predicated on notions of emancipatory research, is, in fact, not always primarily emancipatory in nature. Educational action research can be classified as emancipatory, practical, or knowledge building, and, as such, the conception of validity ought to reflect the different modes of research. Finally, we argue that for action research to contribute to a knowledge base about teaching, it must be open to scrutiny by a research community, and to withstand scrutiny, it must be rigorous. We suggest that rigor can be ensured by reconceptualizing validity as contingent on the mode of research being used.

Origins and Foundations of Educational Action Research

Educational action research owes much to Lewin (1946) and Collier (1945). Not only was the evocative prefix and prescription of "action" coupled with research by them in response to challenges they saw in improving group relations, but so, too, in the case of Lewin, was the form of research linked to schools, teachers, parents, and students. Out of Lewin's advocacy of a hermeneutic process based on standards of practice and with his and Collier's specific interests in the resolution of social, economic, and political injustices found in schools and other public institutions, a bridge between the worlds of research and philosophy was erected. Where Collier defined action research as participatory research in which the layperson defines a need and engages the structures that provide scaffolding, however, Lewin's work arguably broke ground for critical approaches in research. As such, debates engaged by the body of critical theory have subsequently encompassed action research and its various progenies (see, for example, descriptions of debates over Habermasian

P. Newton & D. Burgess (Eds.), The Best Available Evidence, 33–46.
© 2008 International Journal of Qualitative Methods. Reprinted with permission.

and Gadamerian hermeneutics in the context of teacher research in Brown & Jones (2001) and more provocative social change advocated in the work of Freire (1970), Giroux (1998), and McLaren (1998) on critical pedagogy).

Lewin's (1946) work has emerged as the predominant representative of the concept, and his inclusion of schools as a key venue for action research means that school-based and teacher research that follows the structural requirements explored in Lewin's writing, as well as the contributions of others to the development of the method, is its progeny.

Criticisms of Educational Action Research

Action research in schools has not been without its detractors. Cordingley (2000) suggested that teachers "were attracted to research that was relevant and enabled them to do their tasks more effectively and/or more efficiently" (p. 1). In other words, teachers prefer research that addresses issues that are practical in nature. Yet the mismatch between the practical problems identified as important to teachers and the use of emancipatory action research approaches requires some explanation. True emancipatory research approaches are a "tough sell" in schools as these approaches demand that practitioners take a hard look at the structures and social arrangements that dominate segments of the population, arrangements that they (teachers) might function to reinforce (see, for example, Pajak & Green, 2003). Brown and Jones (2001) provided a critique of action research that succinctly questions the critical nature of such approaches.

> Such an approach…has the potential to lead not to the unlocking of complexity but to the elucidation of rigid preconceptions which serve only to confirm injustices of the "found" world. Hitherto, action research has assumed a reality which can be uncovered and then altered in some way or improved upon for emancipatory purposes. This however begs key questions about where our ideas of what counts as "improvement" come from. How can the researcher both "observe" reality as well as being part of it and thus be implicated in its continual creation and recreation? These issues are much more complex than action research has acknowledged so far. (p. 5)

Similarly, Heydenrych (2001) stated that action research ought not to involve simply reflecting on practice and finding ways to improve performance. It ought to focus on examining those practices and arrangements within education that are commonly accepted and universally justified and then problematizing them. As Noffke (1997) articulated,

> Despite the concern with social issues and even social transformation on the part of academics writing about action research, there have been few examples of practitioners engaged in efforts to link their practices with efforts focused on gender and racial inequality. (pp. 329–330)

In what ways have the foci of action research projects been directed, if not to emancipatory ends? Lytle (2000) suggested that although action research has tended to focus on matters of classroom pedagogy, it often problematizes "the nature and purposes for reading, writing, and talking in school" (p. 699) and, through this, maintains an emancipatory focus. In other words, educational action research often links the improvement of practice with emancipation.

More recently, action research has been linked to staff development and professional develop- ment (see, for example, Parsons, McRae, & Taylor, 2006). "Action research, though, is often employed primarily as a form of in-service education or staff development. In these approaches, efforts to redefine professional roles in education, particularly that of the teacher, are evident" (Noffke, 1997, p. 323). Noffke, however, has cautioned that such instrumental uses of action research are problematic: "Seeing action research as a means for professional development raises a complex set of questions related to issues of power: Who and what is being 'developed' and by whom, and, most important, in whose interests?" (p. 334). In addition, she identified the manner in which action research, professional development, and school improvement are increasingly being linked: "Within these contexts, action research as a form of staff development centered on areas for improvement is an increasingly visible aspect of school reform initiatives" (p. 326).

Similarly, Lytle (2000) recognized the use of action research as a mechanism to address larger institutional and societal goals. "Universities, school districts, state education departments, and national reform networks have begun to attach some form of teacher inquiry to all manner of teacher education and professional development, school reform, and curricular improvement" (p. 694). The implications for action research as an institutionally directed (rather than emergent) mode of inquiry seem obvious. The purposes of action research are clearly moving away from locally determined improvement initiatives. In this case, action research is focused on the improvement of practice as its primary purpose. Anderson, Herr, and Nihlen (1994) posed this question over a decade ago. "It remains to be seen whether this movement will lead to empowerment or be co-opted as the latest teacher in-service scheme by a top-down reform movement" (p. 8).

Self-directed action research approaches coupled with external accountability measures (as experienced in education systems in Canada, the United States, the United Kingdom, New Zealand, and Australia) represent an uneasy partnership. If such collegial professional learning and action research approaches serve a social legitimizing function within schools or function to achieve organizational ends, there exists no antithesis to the dominant discourse of accountability and large-scale, high-stakes testing-directed policies and practices. Brown and Jones (2001) suggested that action research, in its currently conceived form, serves to reinforce this dominant discourse. "Presently, practitioners have a tendency to expect the research task to tell them 'how it is' so that they can then plan new strategies for the creation of new outcomes" (p. 169). Indeed, the most influential school improvement fad in

North America (at the time of writing), professional learning communities (PLCs), identifies action research as "the engine of improvement" (DuFour & Eaker, 1998, p. 25). This is troubling in that these authors have defined improvement targets as "clear, measurable performance standards" (p. 102). Although their work suggested that many factors contribute to effective schools, the authors maintain that action research used to achieve gains relative to performance standards are key to the learning community. This vision of action research lies far from the type of research envisioned by Lewin (1946) and others. It is our contention that the conceptualization of action research proffered by DuFour and Eaker is frequently exercised in North American schools. Put in another way, we suggest that purposes of research under the guise of school improvement are not emancipatory; rather, they might very well serve to reinforce a dominant discourse in educational policy.

Research Purposes and the Types of Action Research

Resolving these contested perspectives on educational action research is no easy task. White (1999) described three modes of research: explanatory, interpretive, and critical. Each of these modes is influenced by a corresponding philosophical position and logic. "Explanatory research is heavily influenced by the positivist tradition in the philosophy of science" (p. 3). Interpretive research is fundamentally concerned with discovering meaning within a social phenomenon, while critical research is concerned with affecting political, social, or personal change. White's modes of research owe much to the work of Habermas (1987), who referred to types of human interest that are knowledge constitutive. That is, the manner in which knowledge is acquired or the extent to which knowledge claims can be justified is dependent on the arena of human action. If the arena of human action is technical, then empirical and hypothetical-deductive modes of inquiry are appropriate. If it is practical (i.e., social knowledge), then interpretive or hermeneutic approaches are warranted. If it is emancipatory in nature, critical approaches are appropriate.

Berg (2001) suggested that there are three modes of action research: (a) technical/ scientific/collaborative, (b) practical/mutual collaborative/deliberative, and (c) emancipating/enhancing/critical science. Each mode has a distinct goal. The technical/scientific/collaborative mode has as its goal "to test a particular intervention based on a pre-specified theoretical framework" (p. 186). The practical/mutual collaborative/deliberative mode "seeks to improve practice-and-service delivery" (p. 186). The emancipating/enhancing/critical science mode can "assist practitioners in lifting their veil of clouded understandings, and help them to better understand fundamental problems by raising their collective consciousness" (p. 187).

The authors above suggested that there are distinct approaches to educational action research that are dependent on the goals and purposes of the inquiry. These distinctions are significant, and, as we suggest later in this paper, the type or mode of action research ought to direct how we can conceptualize validity and how we can justify our knowledge claims. For the purposes of this paper, we identify these three modes as (a) a knowledge-generating mode, (b) a practical (improvement of practice) mode, and (c) an emancipatory mode. These modes are commensurable with those offered by Berg (2001), White (1999), and Habermas (1987) but resonate more with us in understanding the nature of inquiry in educational institutions.

New Paradigm Argument

Before we speak of validity in action research, it is prudent to explore claims of scholars in action research that it represents a new paradigm and therefore requires a new understanding of the testing of truth claims.

> Concurrent with this spread and growth has been an intensified debate about whether teacher research is a new *paradigm*, a new *genre* of research that is part of a wider social and political movement, or even qualifies, epistemologically and methodologically, as *research* at all. (Lytle, 2000, p. 694, emphasis in original)

Does action research represent a new and incommensurable research paradigm? We cannot make sense of this question easily, for in establishing whether research belongs to a new paradigm, we must justify this claim from within an existing paradigm that we are reasonably sure exists. Huberman (1996) characterized the teacher-researcher claims that their research represents a new paradigm as follows:

> The argument for the new paradigm goes something like this: Our values and biases dictate many of our methods and findings: our knowledge is purely situation specific and socially constructed, and so there are many plausible "truths," corresponding to the many a priori assumptions and methods of investigation. (p. 127)

We are left with two options: Either practitioner action research is a new paradigm or it is not. We do not intend to conclusively determine the answer to this question here, and, as Denzin and Lincoln (2005) suggested, it is not possible to do so in any case as "these beliefs can never be established in terms of their ultimate truthfulness" (p. 183). However, Lincoln and Guba (2005) have concluded that even if practitioner action research represents a new paradigm, it is commensurable with qualitative research. As such, we propose that techniques for ensuring validity of qualitative research must similarly apply.

The question remains, then, one of commensurability rather than paradigmatic exclusivity. If the argument were presented that action research is not commensurable with other research methods, then a systematic justification of epistemic claims about knowledge exclusivity to the domain/paradigm of action research akin to that explored in the 1980s by, among others, Guba and Lincoln (1982) is required. For our purposes, and in the absence of such an argument positing the incommensurability of action research, we proceed from the assumption that it is appropriate to apply qualitative research's requirement for validity to action research.

What, then, is validity in action research? Many qualitative researchers have rejected validity as a useful concept within qualitative approaches. They have instead sought alternatives for ensuring the quality of the research and the justification of truth claims. Heikkinen, Huttunen, and Syrjälä (2007) emphasized the importance of arriving at some measure of "goodness" of action research. Although they take a pragmatist perspective on the quality of action research, focusing on the notion of "workability" of the results of action research, the importance of ensuring quality is central to their argument: "We certainly should not take lightly the question of quality assessment" (p. 7). Similarly, Moghaddam (2007) suggested that "validity refers to the reasons we have for believing truth claims" (p. 236). As we argue later in this paper, how we might align approaches to validity that provide reasons for believing in the truth claims we developed as part of our research process becomes a central concern for action researchers. This conception of validity is highly dependent on the nature of the truth claims being generated. As we argue later in the paper, the three purposes of educational action research reflect three different types of truth claims and, consequently, require different types of validity.

Feldman (2007) articulated this concern for the nature of truth claims and tackled the notion of validity from an ontological/epistemological position. He suggested that qualitative researchers have attempted "to seek alternatives to the use of validity as an indicator of the quality of their work" (p. 22). He argued that the quantitative origins of the concept of validity have been viewed as incongruent with, in particular, constructivist epistemologies. "Many if not most qualitative researchers reject the realist epistemology upon which the definition of validity appears to be based" (p. 22). Feldman, however, is somewhat critical of the alternatives that have been proffered by the qualitative research community. He argued that alternative conceptualizations of validity such as "credibility, persuasiveness, verisimilitude and others…tend to focus on the quality of the report rather than the quality of the research" (p. 22). He called for a conception of validity that takes a middle road between naïve realism and constructivism and argued for

a more realistic view of realism…[in which] it is possible to construct knowledge about the world that has some correspondence with a reality separate from ourselves, and that that knowledge can be tested to see how well it corresponds to reality. (p. 23)

In an argument similar to the one we intend to propose in this paper, he suggested that

there is much that is in an action research report that we can accept based on criteria such as credibility, persuasiveness and verisimilitude, but there are other claims, such as how and what to teach, for which I, for one, would like to see some evidence that it is an accurate representation. (p. 24)

The conceptualization of validity that we offer later in this paper addresses some of Feldman's concerns regarding the differing claims embedded within action research.

Potential Risks of not Attending Adequately to Validity

The tenets of action research articulate a concern for the welfare of research participants and the objects of research (if we can use that term). However, it is not clear that action research taking place daily in schools has given a sufficient accounting of such factors as anonymity, coercion, and confidentiality. Indeed, many of the research projects we have witnessed in schools do not require an ethical review. Most educational action research projects never see the light of scrutiny with respect to ethical standards of research. Action research projects that are developed as part of a graduate studies program or facilitated by an academic researcher will have been subjected to this scrutiny, but these types of projects are in the minority of all of the educational action research projects that have been developed (Noffke, 1997). The risks inherent in overlooking or disregarding ethical protocols do not require further explanation here; however, we cannot leave it at that. Clearly, the ethical features of the research must be attended to. We recommend that school districts establish research offices whose job it is, in part, to ensure that action research projects adhere to minimal standards of ethical conduct. In many action research studies, the researchers themselves are the objects of study. Certainly, this situation helps to mitigate some of the risk involved, but, for example, coercion of teachers into action research projects is one ethical concern that requires further investigation. Furthermore, in cases where the "objects" of the research projects are children, the risk must be considered to be at least moderate.

The second concern is one more fundamental to the nature of action research. This is a concern with the capacity of teacher researchers to ensure that selected modes of inquiry are appropriate to the research problem, that research approaches can reasonably be assumed to produce desired research outcomes, and that teacher researchers can assess whether they have, in fact, achieved the desired outcomes for the research process. Huberman (1996) argued that teacher research (as it is not, he believes, a new research paradigm and has no unique system for justifying teacher research knowledge claims) borrows knowledge justification approaches from qualitative research: "We are bringing some fairly classic techniques of qualitative research to bear on the teaching experience, techniques used more and more routinely by people in the academy, and ones requiring methodical training and practice" (p. 128).

To illustrate the problematic nature of some educational action research approaches, we call on a recent experience in a school with which we are familiar. We believe this is not an atypical account of the practice of action research in schools. In this school the teaching staff members were directed to conduct research and a planning process to address low levels of achievement in the skill of estimating in arithmetic calculations through a standardized mathematics exam. The staff entered into an action research process in which they used a pretest-intervention-posttest strategy. They took the data from the previous year's standardized assessment as pretest data, developed and implemented new teaching strategies for teaching estimating through an action research approach, and used the current year's standardized assessment as their posttest measure. It goes without saying that there were numerous flaws in their design, not least of which was the fact that the sample of pupils was low (fewer than 10 pupils) and (of course) different pupils were administered the posttest than those who took the pretest.

How can we understand the validity of such claims in action research? Kelly and Gluck (1979, cited in Stringer, 1999) stated that the efficacy of action research projects must be evaluated based on emotional and social terms. That is, it must examine the pride and dignity of participants, among other things. In the case we have outlined, the school staff reflected on the research project and determined that it was successful because they achieved their targets, all teachers felt included in the process, and teachers felt that they had improved their collective ability to teach estimating. Although this may be true, however, obviously it cannot be assumed that the new instructional strategies had any impact on student learning. In other words, the evidence for success of this intervention was less than compelling. Similarly, when action research that is truly emancipatory (i.e., directed toward the reduction of pupil marginalization, etc.) is evaluated in terms of the pride and dignity (etc.) of the teachers through the process, it neglects the intended outcome of assessing the pride and dignity of the objects of the research (pupils). In this case, the evidence of emotional and social outcomes experienced by teachers is not compelling evidence that the action research process is effective for students.

Maturity of Educational Action Research

To judge the maturity of a method or practice is naturally a contestable concept and one that is arguably difficult to define. Discussion of what exactly constitutes mature research is minimal at best. In the area of research and development for gambling policy studies, it has been suggested that mature research is inclusive of mixed-methods, long- and short-term study, and the use of contrary arguments in any concluding discussion (Yaffee & Brodsky, 1997). The majority of educational action research does not produce artifacts for public or academic consumption, artifacts that might enjoy public or academic scrutiny (Noffke, 1997). We would be therefore justified calling into question the maturity of research conducted in a field where the majority of research engaged exists within a vast morass of gray.

Research in psychology and educational psychology since the 1960s suggests that epistemic belief systems mature through developmental, and distinguishable, stages (Schommer-Aikins, 2004). To this end, research, rooted in epistemic belief of the observer (and in the case of action research, observed, if a distinction may be drawn), must similarly mature. Participatory research is particularly capricious when cast in this light, however, as collective maturity might be at issue, yet research that claims a methodology, participatory or otherwise, but fails to demonstrate methodological consistency throughout the life of the research project is arguably less mature than research produced through consistency (Evers & Lakomski, 2000). Alternatively viewed, research that becomes incorporated into a "body of knowledge" (as opposed to being lost or shown to be invalid via scrutiny) might be claimed to hold maturity as the measure of maturity in this case is favorable peer review (see the arguments of Chew & Relyea-Chew, 1988).

Some have suggested that exploratory research offers to provide vitality within a field (Dietterich, 1990). Such exploratory research nicely fits within the central domain of action research as envisioned by Lewin (1946) and Collier (1945); that is, such forms of research are "usually driven by specific problems in specific domains" (Dietterich, 1990, p. 5) and are cyclical in their development. Yet exploratory research is not in itself an indicator of immaturity, nor is it an indicator of maturity. Rather, maturity is reflected in the degree to which the knowledge gained adds to a body of knowledge and receives longevous and favorable peer review (see also Bird, 2007).

The related notion of the "goodness" of research has been explored in some greater depth. In psychology, Salmon (2003) has articulated a need within his field of study to identify characteristics of good research. He suggested that key among these characteristics is an openness to scrutiny. Good research invites the reader to "expose the coherence of the finished work to scrutiny" (p. 26). Open, forthright exposure of research results to an open peer review, then, appears consistent with notions of maturity detailed above. Salmon's argument places responsibility for inciting scrutiny with the researcher. We can infer from it that scrutiny leads to coherence, and we further theorize that coherence leads to incorporation into a body of knowledge.

Similarly, and perhaps most significant, Anderson and Herr (1999) referred to dialogic validity as key to ensuring the goodness of educational action research. We suggest that dialogic validity is a central validity type for all three action research modes. As they have suggested, practitioner peer review serves to ensure the goodness and dissemination of the knowledge generated from educational action research projects.

Conceptions of Validity in Action Research

Although we recognize that considerable debate has occurred with respect to validity in practitioner research, we suggest that many of the frameworks for establishing validity are incomplete. We propose that validity is contingent on the modes of action research; that is, the mode of action research determines the configuration of validities to assess the knowledge claims of the action research project. The validities identified by Anderson and Herr (1999) are particularly appealing for this purpose. They suggested that action research adhere to outcome, process, democratic, catalytic, and dialogic validities. Briefly, *outcome validity* refers to the extent to which outcomes of the research are successful. Put another way, outcome validity refers to the extent to which the outcomes of the research match the intended purposes of the research. *Process validity* focuses on "the much debated problem of what counts as 'evidence' to sustain assertions" (p. 16). This validity is concerned with the efficacy of the research approach in addressing the research problem. *Democratic validity* is concerned with "the extent to which research is done in collaboration with all parties who have a stake in the problem under investigation" (p. 16). *Catalytic validity* refers to the ability of the research process to transform the participants, deepen the understanding of the participants, and motivate participants to further social action. *Dialogic validity* is akin to the peer review process in academic research. In practitioner research, however, it is suggested "that practitioner researchers participate in critical and reflective dialogue with other practitioner researchers" (p. 16).

We argue that Anderson and Herr's (1999) contention that "all of these 'validity' criteria for practitioner research are tentative and in flux" (p. 16) is only partially correct. Each of the action research modes identified earlier in this paper (knowledge generating, practical, and emancipatory) are predicated on the differing goals and epistemologies of each mode. It follows that each action research mode makes somewhat different knowledge claims and therefore relies on somewhat different configurations of validity.

In Table 1 we illustrate how the three modes of action research rely on different primary and secondary validities to assess their knowledge claims. Although all of the validities identified by Anderson and Herr (1999) are present in the illustrated model, the suggestion that some are primary and some are secondary is significant. If we can accept that there are different modes with different primary goals, purposes, and epistemologies, then it follows that the manner in which knowledge claims are assessed is contingent on those factors. Primary validities answer the question, To what extent has the primary goal of the action research mode been achieved? Secondary validities ensure that the research project falls within the domain of educational action research. Primary validities alone are not sufficient to ensure that the research project does not belong to some other research or nonresearch tradition that does not share the epistemological and ontological features of action research. For example, in the case of an action research project in the emancipatory mode that is not assessed using its primary validities, we cannot be certain that the project has been successful in achieving its purpose. On the other hand, such a project that has not been assessed using the emancipatory mode's secondary validities cannot be assumed to be action research at all. In such a case, the project might conform to primary validities and be merely activism or social transformation but not necessarily research. Similarly, action research of the knowledge-generating or practical modes might achieve their stated purposes yet not be action research at all. Without attending to secondary validities, we cannot be sure that these varieties of research are not another form of inquiry or social process. Dialogic validity (as discussed previously in this paper), in our view, is central to assessing the goodness of the research and in disseminating the knowledge generating from such action research projects.

Table 1. Action research modes and corresponding validities. Adapted from Anderson and Herr (1999)

Action research mode	Primary validity	Secondary validity	
Knowledge generating	Outcome validity	Democratic validity	Dialogic validity
	Process validity	Catalytic validity	
Practical (improvement of practice)	Catalytic validity	Process validity	
	Outcome validity	Democratic validity	
Emancipatory	Democratic validity	Process validity	
	Catalytic validity	Outcome validity	

Anderson and Herr's (1999) contention that validity criteria "are tentative and in flux" (p. 16) is insufficient for ensuring that the assertions made through action research are warranted. Such a contention puts the onus on the action researchers themselves to choose from among the validity alternatives. Without further clarification, action researchers are left to their own devices to determine which validities are "valid." In many cases democratic validity has been overused and misused as a warrant for claims. In such cases there is the potential of abuse of the action research process in reinforcing the dominant discourse in educational reform. Without a robust and well- structured approach to validity, educational action research is susceptible to a number of pathologies. For example, action research that focuses only on democratic validity has the potential to be used to manipulate research participants and to build contrived consensus for a predetermined educational reform agenda (for a philosophical discussion of this general point, see Burgess, 2008). Similarly, action research that focuses solely on outcome validity represents a form of pragmatism that ignores the important moral and political dimensions of teaching and of the research process.

It is our hope that the preceding framework will further refine the notion of validity in action research and will assist educational researchers to successfully engage in a meta-inquiry about the nature of their research. Identifying whether an action research project has as its purpose the emancipation of marginalized populations, the improvement of practice, or the building of knowledge about teaching will necessitate the establishment of approaches to validity and rigor that align with those purposes. This type of meta-inquiry is an absolute requirement if action research is to evolve into a mature form of research.

CONCLUSION

As Huberman (1996) stated, "Teachers collect, analyze, and interpret data; and they are meant to do it carefully, systematically, and rigorously" (p. 132). It is Huberman's contention that educational action research does not appear revolutionary. If this is, in fact, the case, the examination of action research must focus on those features that ensure rigor and warrant knowledge claims. It is our contention that we have been derailed far too long by questions of new paradigms and epistemologies at the expense of the generation of new knowledge and understandings of education. It is now time to set aside such infertile arguments and turn our attention back to systematic creation of knowledge through rigorous action research. As Huberman succinctly put it,

> Teacher researchers will have to move from a multiplicity of cogent, provocative, and promising ideas to a leaner, more internally coherent set of terms and interpretive frames. They will also need a less woolly body of evidence for the descriptions, interpretations, and explanations for grounding those frames. (p. 137)

We suggest that we need not be disheartened, that action research is ready to attain the level of a mature research approach within a qualitative research paradigm. We have argued in this paper that attending to rigor and validity is a critical last step for this research approach. One of the criticisms leveled at action research is its lack of incorporation into a body of knowledge about teaching. We suggest that this particular criticism points to a lack of research rigor, or more accurately, a lack of an accounting of research rigor within action research projects. A systematic approach to ensuring the validity of knowledge claims in the three different modes of action research will go a long way toward the incorporation of action research into a body of knowledge about teaching.

Feldman (2007) suggested,

> Because of the moral and political aspects of action research, we are compelled to ask whether the results of our inquiries are valid. … If that knowledge is to be trusted and put to use in these larger contexts, then there must be reason for other teachers, students, administrators, policy-makers and parents to believe and trust that knowledge. (pp. 29–31)

In Feldman's view, the knowledge that we build as action researchers is dependent upon the validity of the outcomes of the research. The brute pragmatism that is found in, for example, declarations of "best practice," or the naïve contrived consensus represented in the anecdote presented in this paper are the result of an incomplete conception of validity in action research. An action research process that reconceptualizes validity as contingent upon the mode of research being used promises to move action research toward a form of research that builds knowledge, improves practice, and attends to the moral, political, and emancipatory dimensions of teaching and research.

DEREK STOVIN

4. NARRATIVE, INSIGHT, AND EFFECTIVE DECISION MAKING IN EDUCATION

The truth about stories is that's all we are.

(Thomas King, 2003 Massey Lectures)

Narrative approaches to research are now common. Although narrative approaches are an alternative to the hegemonic empirically based tradition that Clandinin and Connelly (2000) called "a 'grand narrative' of social science inquiry" (p. xxv), narrative researchers no longer need to defend their approach as "legitimate" from attacks by critics who question its validity. Fittingly, Dodge, Ospina, and Foldy (2005) declared "the 'narrative turn' [as] already influential in the social sciences" (p. 286). It is now widely understood that narrative research falls within the qualitative, interpretive paradigm and that its focus on personal stories can lead to a rich and deep understanding of a different kind than is produced through other approaches to evidence. That is, one can gain a unique understanding of the thoughts, beliefs, and feelings of individuals through the stories of their lived experiences at a particular time and place, thereby acquiring a vantage point from which one may also gain insight into the context of that experience. Consequently, a narrative method of inquiry is an appropriate choice whenever there is significant interest in the experience of an individual (Ellis, 2006). It is also an appropriate choice if one wishes to acquire multiple understandings of a particular social milieu, which is a desire and an openness that is a necessary condition for consistently wise and effective decision making in organizations.

Despite the increased attention to, and influence of, narrative research, it tends to be used less often in so-called "applied policy" areas and remains particularly underutilized in educational decision making. For example Bess and Dee (2008), while considering effective policy and practice in post-secondary administration, wrote that "the positivist position is most commonly followed ... [because] it lends itself most easily to rapid decision making and action, even if flawed" (p. 471). This tendency, along with the willingness to accept the risks associated with potentially flawed decision-making processes, is striking given that our ultimate concern (and ethical duty) as educators—whether at the public school or the tertiary level—lies in the *experience* our students have through the educational institutions with which we are entrusted. Further, at the public school level certainly, our decision making with regard to students and their educational experiences must be guided by what is in *the best interests of the child* (United Nations, 1989), not by administrative expediency.

P. Newton & D. Burgess (Eds.), The Best Available Evidence, 47–61.

If, on the other hand, the bias in educational decision making toward positivism is generally an unconscious one (i.e. systemic and normative, not just convenient), it is also quite perplexing since the conscious choice in education to focus on the subjective qualities of individual experience is not a novel one. Rather, Dewey (1938) famously sought to draw educators' and the public's attention to a "progressive" pedagogy that aimed to create an enjoyable experience within educational environments that encourage and actively engage individual students instead of the harsh and stifling status-quo imposed on all. It is scarcely believable that otherwise knowledgeable educational leaders could be ignorant of Dewey's progressive school of educational thought and not have some appreciation of the importance of maintaining a focus on the subjective quality of experience.

> Bess and Dee (2008) elaborated that, in the effort to avoid the delay and administrative conflict that may threaten [decision-making] efficiency, ... the danger is that organizational leaders may [come to] accept positivist theories without question ... [thereby foregoing the] alternative paradigms [of] social constructionism and postmodernism, [which] offer checks and balances against the perpetuation of the status quo. (p. 471)

In other words, while the use of alternative paradigms may not increase decision-making *efficiency*, their intentional use will improve decision-making *effectiveness*. The purpose of this chapter is, therefore, to draw the attention of educational decision makers and others interested in educational policy issues toward the possibilities offered by one important alternative approach – that of narrative research. It is also intended to provide encouragement and practical support for individuals to make the conscious choice to counterbalance the positivist bias in educational decision making. To that end, in what follows I will introduce the narrative approach to research, provide some examples of its application in educational policy contexts, and conclude with a discussion of its potential to contribute to effective decision making in educational organizations.

The Narrative Approach to Research

There are two overarching types of narrative research in the literature. The first is typically called a "Narrative Review" or "Narrative Synthesis" and is, essentially, a type of literature review. It is similar in nature to a "Meta-Analysis" that is often performed within the empirical tradition and parallels the scientific method (Kavale, 2001).[1] According to Mostert (2004), meta-analysis is a "powerful technique that provides very useful answers for theory, policy, and practice. In terms of uncovering meta-answers to questions of intervention efficacy, it continues to be useful for theorists and practitioners alike" (p. 114). However, meta-analysis is not infallible and is not appropriate for every research interest. Meta-analyses are limited by the expertise of the analyst, the amount of information reported in the primary studies, the comingling of different research designs, and publication biases

(Spaulding, 2009).[2] Further, a meta-analysis tends to leave the impression that its results are definitive, which can be misleading (Mostert, 2001), and is especially problematic where the audience may not have the background in quantitative methods necessary to interpret the findings critically.

In contrast, narrative syntheses analyze the details of individual studies, including qualitative studies, to draw overall conclusions related to a research question or set of questions (Spaulding, 2009, p. 9).

> They serve to analyze the strengths and weaknesses of primary studies in detail, rather than refute or support general findings; attempt to make sense of divergent research findings around a similar research hypothesis; provide a summary of what is already known; allow researchers to uncover patterns and consistencies across studies; allow researchers to place more weight on studies using valid designs and reporting more complete data; and finally, narrative syntheses allow researchers to draw meta-conclusions. (Spaulding, 2009, p. 9)

A narrative synthesis is, therefore, an appropriate choice when the desire of the researcher is to take a close look at the details of all types of studies within a defined body of research. It is also an option where standard meta-analysis techniques are not possible because primary research results are not transformable into the necessary data type. Clearly, then, a narrative synthesis can be an excellent starting point for an educational decision maker wishing to gain insight into an area of interest where a substantial body of research exists.

Spaulding (2009) made a strong case for making greater use of the narrative synthesis type of research in the area of special education, and the argument easily extends to education more broadly. It is, however, the second type of narrative research that I will focus on in the remainder of this chapter and, following Bess and Dee (2008), the type of research with which I am most concerned about its underutilization in educational decision making. This second type can be called, generally, "Narrative Inquiry" and, unlike narrative synthesis, it is direct research. It almost always involves conversational interviews and often includes other activities such as the researcher as participant, the creation of artifacts by participants, document analysis, ethnographic observation, autobiography, career history, and storied photography to name a few. A fundamental characteristic of narrative inquiry is a genuine holistic interest in the storied experience of a particular individual (Ellis, 2006). A primary goal of narrative inquiry is to produce a particular type of story that enables the reader to come to a rich and deep understanding of an individual's experience in a specific social context, including the thoughts, beliefs, feelings, and meanings ascribed to that experience.

> Through narrative, one can appreciate embodied knowing: what an experience *feels* like in a subjective and close way, rather than what it *looks* like in an objective and dispassionate way; one can learn facts as well as social impacts; one can be moved towards action rather than simply understanding

(Girard, 2006). These benefits are crucial for an applied profession such as nursing (Diekelmann, 2003). (McAllister et al., 2009, p. 157)

Other professionals, such as teachers, lawyers, and doctors can, of course, also reap the same benefits. For example, narrative inquiry has been used as a way to improve the practice and cognitive self-awareness of beginning medical doctors (Clandinin & Cave, 2008) and of beginning teachers (Clandinin & Connelly, 1987).

Constructivist Foundations of Narrative Inquiry

Because narrative inquiry seeks to develop both the storied experiences of particular individuals and a storied interpretive account of those experiences, it is further distinguished from other research approaches in the sense that narrative becomes both the object and the method of inquiry (Clandinin & Connelly, 2000). According to Ellis (2006), "Gadamer (1989) … clarified that knowledge is the product of human activity, and meaning or knowledge is created rather than found" (p. 112). In narrative inquiry, the researcher and participant reach a deeper level of understanding through the creative process of constructing a narrative. For this reason, Dodge et al. (2005) wrote that "narrative inquiry has its roots in what philosophers of science call a 'constructivist epistemology,' a theory of knowledge that suggests we know the world not by objectively observing an external reality, but by constructing how we understand it with others" (p. 289). This epistemological and methodological approach has implications at both the level of the researcher and the participant.

For the participant, the task is to construct their knowledge of their past and/or current experience, which is often best accomplished through stories. Ellis (2006) cited Mishler (1986), Carr (1986), and Sarbin (1986) to support the claim that "research participants can best reveal their sense-making and experience narratively" (p. 112). It is not imperative that the participant recall events and details with perfect accuracy as though they are declaring objective facts. It is important to remember that we, as narrative researchers, are interested in *gaining insight* from learning the deeply held beliefs, thoughts, feelings, assumptions, and interpretations that a participant uses to guide their actions and decisions. These are embedded within a participant's story in a consistent way even if the details of the story may change somewhat if told in a different time or place. An implication, then, for the participant is that they are actively engaged in the research and committed to the creation of their storied experience rather than, say, passively answering a priori questions from a researcher-determined interview script.

An important implication for researchers is that they, too, are participating in the construction of their own knowledge through the questions that they ask, the topics that they choose to initiate and follow-up on, and their preconceptions that they uncover, examine, reconstitute, and apply to the specific research project. Guba and Lincoln (1994) stated that "the aim of inquiry is *understanding and reconstruction* of the constructions that people (including the researcher) initially hold, aiming toward consensus but still open to new interpretations as information and sophistication improve" (p. 113).

Because of these implications for the researcher and the participant, the primary task of narrative research is considered to be the "co-construction" of knowledge.[3] Some other implications, resulting fundamentally from narrative inquiry's primary location within the social-constructivist paradigm, must also be highlighted. First, the researcher is not a disinterested, objective observer of facts from a distance—as a positivist method will normally assume. In other words, "the concept of the aloof researcher has been abandoned" (Denzin & Lincoln, 1994, p. 11). In contrast, the researcher is "in" the research by participating in the construction of knowledge—a knowledge that is elaborated in a "rich" and "thick" discursive format. This is because, according to Guba and Lincoln (1994), in the constructivist paradigm "realities are apprehendable in the form of multiple, intangible mental constructions, socially and experientially based, local and specific in nature, … and dependent for their form and content on the individual persons or groups holding the constructions" (p. 110). This means that narrative researchers do not attempt to "bracket" themselves out of the research. Instead, they bring all that they can of themselves, carefully, to contribute to the research. Second, and relatedly, the results of the research are not "generalizable" in the sense often assumed by positivistic empirical research. The results are neither reported as statistically significant, for example, nor with an estimate of their predictive power. The results do, however, contribute to a deepening of understanding and the gaining of insight into specific experiences, which may be transferable depending upon the degree of similarity between varying contexts. Finally, the research results are not "repeatable." This is self-evident, as a different researcher working with the same participant would necessarily co-create a different narrative. Indeed, just as a reader will learn (and experience) new things from re-reading literature at a different stage in life, even the same researcher-participant pair will likely interpret the stories in different ways when they are reconsidered at a future point in time (and may have co-created a different narrative if the research had been done at a different point in time).

Hermeneutical Foundations of Narrative Inquiry

While true that narrative inquiry falls predominantly within the social constructivist paradigm, Ellis (1998) notes that it is also important for us to remember other early influences contributing to the emergence of narrative inquiry as a formal research method. According to Ellis (1998), "any discussion of interpretive inquiry ought to start with a review of three themes present in hermeneutics since Schleiermacher's work in 1819" (p. 15). The three themes Ellis (1998) identified are: (a) the creative and holistic nature of interpretative research; (b) a continuous "back and forth" movement between "part and whole" visualized as the "hermeneutical circle"; and (c) the important role of language as both a facilitating and limiting factor (pp. 15–16).

With respect to the first theme, Ellis (2006) explained that the researcher needs to bring everything that they know to the act of interpretation. This will include personal experience, belief systems, and familiarity with related literature, theory, and practice. It is important, however, that the researcher approach interpretation holistically. This means that although the researcher is employing their knowledge, skills, and beliefs creatively to construct a holistic understanding of what the participant means, the researcher "refrains from imposing [taxonomies or classification systems] reductively" (Ellis, 2006, p. 115). Further, "such research often necessitates as much attention to the past as to the present" (Ellis, 2006, p. 113). It is often helpful for the researcher to construct a narrative in order to pull everything together in a way that the reader can understand the participant's experiences and deeper beliefs in a meaningful way.

The second theme related to hermeneutics places emphasis on the part-whole relationship. In order to gain some understanding of the whole, one must be knowledgeable about its parts. But in order to understand the significance of the parts, one must have an understanding of the whole. Hermeneutical theory recognizes this back and forth continuous movement as being necessary for interpretation. As one moves back and forth from part to whole to part again, one's understanding increases and new insight is gained. This is conceived of and communicated as the hermeneutical circle. It is important to note that "no interpretation is possible until interpretation has begun" (Scruton, 1982, p. 202). Similarly, Ellis (1998) noted that one "makes the path by walking it" (p. 16). One of the strengths, then, of this type of research is that it explicitly acknowledges that the interests of researchers are likely to change as they walk the hermeneutical path and gain sophistication in the area of knowledge that they are co-constructing with a participant.

The role of language is the focus of the third theme. Language is a crucial aspect of hermeneutics as it both limits and enables interpretation. Language is present in, and affects the interpretation of, both the researcher's and the participant's experiences. It also differs depending upon one's cultural, social, geographical, and historical location. Different words, phrases, and usage patterns will carry different meanings in different contexts and these differing meanings will not always be obvious. For these reasons, the researcher has to become very self-aware about their choice of language—both during the interview process and the writing process. For example, the participant may adopt the language or choice of expression that the interviewer is using rather than express their experience in their own words with the "fuller" meaning that those words carry. It is, in part, for this reason that Ellis (2006) recommends using open-ended questions when interviewing. "Open-ended questions identify a topic for discussion, but do not provide any direction for the discussion" (Ellis, 2006, p. 117). Another benefit is that open-ended questions, asked with genuine interest and care, will often generate stories in a participant's own words that carry even greater meaning for interpretive research.

Evaluation of Interpretive/Narrative Research

Central to the evaluation of the outcomes from an interpretive research project is the understanding that it is an assessment process quite different from an "objective" validation common within the empirical research tradition. Fundamentally, "to evaluate an [interpretive] account, one should ask whether the concern which motivated the inquiry has been advanced" (Ellis, 1998, p. 30). Ellis (1998) built on Packer and Addison (1989) to provide six questions useful in evaluating an interpretive inquiry:

1. Is it plausible?
2. Does it fit with other material we know?
3. Does it have the power to change practice?
4. Has the researcher's understanding been transformed?
5. Has a solution been uncovered?
6. Have new possibilities been opened up for the researcher, research participants, and the structure of the context? (pp. 30–31)

It is also important to realize that different qualitative methods have developed differing tendencies with respect to evaluation/assessment. Narrative interpretive inquiry, for example, uses evaluation criteria that are related to the above six interpretive criteria but appear in a slightly different form depending upon the type of narrative research one chooses. At the root, however, one must understand that evaluating an interpretive account is like judging the "goodness" of a hammer—its goodness is related to its suitability for the task at hand (Heidegger, 1927/1962, cited in Packer & Addison, 1989, p. 291). Like a sledgehammer chosen to drive spikes or a ball-peen hammer chosen for metalwork, "a good interpretive account is one that advances the practical concerns with which we undertake an interpretive inquiry, and one that works well with the other activities we are engaged in" (Packer & Addison, 1989, p. 291). With the constructivist paradigm comes the understanding that there can be no absolute certainty. And without certainty, "there is no technique, no interpretation—free algorithm or procedure with which we can evaluate an interpretation. As Rosen (1987, p. 143) puts [sic] it: 'There are no canons by which one can usefully restrict legitimate from illegitimate readings'" (Packer & Addison, 1989, p. 290). So we must choose our evaluative strategies carefully to fit the specific interpretive task while, at the same time, be able to accept that the post hoc evaluation of narrative research will not yield certainty.

Examples of Applied Narrative Research in the Educational Context

Despite the rise in prominence of a narrative approach to research, it has not been widely adopted in the field of education for applied program and policy analysis or for other evaluation and assessment purposes. In this section, in order to illustrate some of the advantages and possibilities that a narrative approach offers to practicing educators and educational leaders, I am including four brief examples of its use in educational environments that I have located in the extant literature.

In *Teaching Narratives: A Source for Faculty Development and Evaluation*, Wood (1992) explains that

> as a supervisor of teachers … I have struggled to find an effective means of faculty evaluation and supervision, particularly for experienced teachers. I have worked with a clinical supervision model and a number of other approaches … including a variety of checklists, self-evaluations, and professional goal setting. I have tried peer coaching, student evaluations, and videotaping. All of these approaches have benefits, yet I have become increasingly dissatisfied with their limitations. (p. 535)

Wood (1992) offers the belief that the clinical observation process is subject to the law of diminishing returns and is, therefore, less effective for experienced teachers. She wanted to design an evaluation and supervision program that would contribute to their professional development by encouraging reflection, facilitating the articulation of insights gained, and planning a wider application of these insights (p. 537). Wood (1992), therefore, designed a nine-phase evaluation program that was voluntary for teachers and based on "autobiographical narratives of their own learning and teaching experiences" (p. 537). Wood (1992) chose this approach because "I became increasingly frustrated by the fact that teachers' voices were not a central part of what I was hearing and reading about educational reform. I began to notice more and more that teachers' insights and experiences seemed to be excluded from educative discourse" (p. 538).

This narrative autobiographical approach to teacher evaluation (i.e., more accurately, professional growth), yielded excellent results.

> By putting teachers' experiences at the center of the evaluation process, … a vehicle [is provided] to help teachers view their work seriously as grounds for conscious theory making, problem-solving, and decision making … Some [teachers] gained profound insights that changed their fundamental approach … [while others] set more modest goals … [but] whatever the level of change … I found that experienced teachers responded to it more seriously and positively than they did to the clinical supervision model. (Wood, 1992, p. 550)

In addition, the process helped Wood (1992) to refine her own sense of what characterizes good teaching practice and, indeed, instilled a sense of amazement at how these teachers "negotiate all the exigencies and contradictions of real classroom life" (p. 548).

An innovative use of a narrative approach for program and policy evaluation was employed by Xu and Liu (2009). In this case the authors were interested in determining why assessment for learning (AFL) teaching methods were generally not being implemented in colleges in China. More specifically, they wanted to explore why AFL was not being used by teachers of courses in English as a foreign language, despite policies requiring the use of this approach to teaching. Xu and Liu (2009) believed that a narrative approach was appropriate, in part, because "teacher knowledge is not something objective and independent of the teacher that may be learned and transmitted but is rather the sum total of the teacher's experiences" (p. 497).

Xu and Liu (2009) used the concept of "sacred" stories and "secret" stories to frame their analysis, where "sacred stories and secret stories are told by the authorities and teachers, respectively, [and] are analytically distinctive" (p. 498). In other words, "sacred stories represent the *you should* type of knowledge prescribed by the authority, whereas secret stories stand for teachers' *I should* knowledge that is embodied in their actual practices" (p. 504). What they found was that a teacher's practice (their secret story) changes based on his or her experiences in relation to the complex conditions in which they teach. Three of these conditions, drawing upon Clandinin and Connelly (1996), are temporality, sociality, and place. For example, "teachers' decision making and actual practice of assessment are mediated by the power-laden relationship in the interpersonal landscape (sociality)" (p. 508). Further, Xu and Liu (2009) found that teachers need "space and resources to develop their own interpretations and adjustments … to their students' learning" (p. 509) due to the context-dependent nature of teaching. In this case, then, a narrative research approach gave detailed and rich information about policy implementation, as well as solid advice for making changes to programs in order to increase their effectiveness.

At the secondary school level, Jones, Segar, and Gasiorski (2008) used narrative inquiry to explore the effectiveness of a required service-learning program. The authors note that service learning programs are becoming more common at both the high school and tertiary levels in the hopes of "promoting civic engagement and continued community involvement … [but] no studies investigate how a statewide service-learning requirement influences students' future intentions to serve in college or beyond" (p. 5). Jones et al. (2008) decided, therefore, to explore new college students' experiences in their high school service-learning programs. The authors were struck by the inability of the students to convey a compelling story related to their service. Jones et al. (2008) explained that their "participants were resisting what they perceived as the forced nature of the requirement, not the idea of service-learning or community service [itself]" (p. 13). Their results also suggested that it was not just the forced nature of the programs that were problematic, but also the way the programs were structured in the school context. A strength of a narrative approach, however, is that it can reveal more sophisticated results than other methods. For example, in this case, the findings can be described as "mixed results." In other words, some positive experiences were described, such as helping students to feel good about themselves, to further develop their work ethic, to become more responsible, and to learn to work more effectively with others (Jones et al., 2008, p. 13). So, "although the goal of qualitative inquiry is not generalizability, the results of this study hold the potential to influence policy and practice" (Jones et al., 2008,

p. 13). Some policy recommendations from this case were that college students should be approached more directly for participation in voluntary service-learning and should be supported in applying self-reflection skills. Also, perhaps more importantly, they need to be engaged in service that is meaningful for them, which occurs most often when the service is related to students' identity development.

A final example offered here is from a doctoral dissertation by Barbee (2009) that explored through a narrative approach the perceptions of young educators about their formal teacher induction program. The experiences of beginning teachers have long been a source of concern in the field of education, and the issues are far from being resolved. Barbee's (2009) research investigated how the program influenced new teachers' professional growth, including "determining how the induction program shaped teachers in their pedagogy, culture, and personal level of comfort in the profession and district" (p. iv). Barbee's participants included both teachers who remained in the district and those who left. Barbee (2009) concluded that, instead of easing the transition into regular teaching, the induction program "increases the level of tension and stress at the beginning of the teacher's career" (p. v). All of the participants "expressed some frustration, and even confusion, about certain expectations that did not match between [the school] building and district, or that were not clearly spelled out to them" (p. v). Barbee (2009) outlined several steps that the district could take to improve communications with beginning teachers, recommended the implementation of "a more specific and useful mentor program" (p. v), and suggested that the induction process be tailored to meet the varied needs of different groups of teachers.

The Potential of Narrative for Improving Decision Making

As indicated in the introduction to this chapter, narrative approaches to research can provide insight into an area of interest by interpreting the experience of an individual in a particular context that is communicated through a co-constructed personal story.

> Narrative research captures both the individual and the context. That is, it focuses on how individuals assign meaning to their experiences through the stories they tell. According to Carter (1993), "the richness and nuances of experiences cannot be expressed in definitions or abstract propositions". They can only be demonstrated through storytelling. In this sense, Gudmundsdottir (1997) considers the narrative approach as an interpretive research method that attempts to make sense of and interpret phenomena in terms of the meaning people bring to them. The understanding of interpretive research shifts the focus to the concept of voices, "basically an interaction between the individual's beliefs and experiences and past, present, and future external voices" (Moen et al., 2003). Such narratives contribute to provoking, inspiring and initiating discussions and dialogues that are crucial for reflection on practice and its development. (Carter, 1993; Farhat, 2010, p. 394)

By choosing individual storytellers carefully and approaching the conversational interviews in the right way, decision makers can gain access to voices that are not present in other types of research. "The narrative movement has ... grown to include teaching, research and practice-based strategies, each designed to hear those whose voices may have been silent or silenced, and to understand people's experience from a close, rather than distanced, point of view" (McAllister et al., 2009, p. 157). Choosing to pay attention to the silenced voices of experience is particularly important in human service areas, where at root it is the experience of the patient, client, or student that matters most—and is the primary variable that can be influenced by leaders to increase the likelihood of having or extending organizational success into the future.

> For these reasons, Dodge et al. (2005) believe that the narrative turn has opened up new pathways for research that focus on *interpreting* social events and understanding the intentions and meanings of social actors, rather than just explaining and predicting their behavior. In public administration, this research often focuses on the stories that people in public institutions tell about their work, illuminating diverse dimensions of public institutions and their administrative and policy problems. (p. 286)

To illuminate something is to make the unseen seen, the invisible visible, or to put something in one's line of sight. Narrative research can be used by organizational decision makers to gain such advantage, or insight, in at least four different ways: (a) to supplement current, often positivistic, approaches; (b) as an antecedent to other approaches; (c) simultaneously, as a complement to other approaches; or (d) on its own, as a solitary approach.

The first approach is, perhaps, the most easily imagined and invites the least controversy. Survey questionnaires, for example, often include 'open-ended' questions asking for participants' opinions and researchers then interpret the resulting prose, often either providing rich detail to support their other quantitatively-based survey interpretations or providing helpful insight into some aspect of the survey topic. The National Health Service in England recently began encouraging open-ended feedback (in addition to Likert scale prompts) from patients about their hospital experiences and publishes it online in a moderated format. Lagu, Goff, Hannon, Shatz, and Lindenauer (2013) used these "online narrative reviews" (p. 7) to examine "the scope [and] content of the narrative feedback ... and to determine how narrative feedback might complement other forms of publicly reported quality data" (p. 8). They found that the open-ended responses cover similar areas of interest to the usual satisfaction surveys "but also include detailed feedback that would be unlikely to be revealed by such surveys" (p. 7). It is important to note, however, that the use of open-ended questions in surveys is not novel. Further, the research carried out by Lagu et al. (2013) is not really a narrative approach as described above but, rather, a discourse analysis. The reason for drawing attention to this type of research is to emphasize that it can be easily expanded into narrative inquiry if it is designed to allow contact with survey participants. In other words, the initial responses can serve to indicate who might be a good participant for a given topic of interest.

The second use of narrative research is as an antecedent to other research. There may, for example, be little known about a particular area of research or what is thought to be known may be unsatisfactory such that a researcher has little confidence in being able to credibly determine a semi-structured interview tool to use, design a Likert scale based questionnaire, or choose an empirical model to estimate. In this situation, seeking understanding through conversations with knowledgeable insiders may be the only reasonable way to proceed and to hopefully avoid the so-called "blind alleyways" that both positivistic and qualitative researchers sometimes end up exploring. Martin Trow (1974/2010), a famous higher education theorist, employed this method almost exclusively (although it was not, to my knowledge, referred to as narrative research but, rather, as his "unique" research style). Narrative research as an antecedent cannot only, therefore, be expected to provide substantive results, it can also be expected to direct future research of any type in a less ad hoc way. It is foundational research.

Third, it can be complementary research. That is, it can be engaged in for simply increasing one's general knowledge related to an area of research interest without an expectation of how it specifically will be useful. Despite a lack of specificity here, this type of activity should be considered necessary, since if an area is of sufficient legitimate interest to demand other qualitative and quantitative research, then one should want to learn as much as possible about the broad topic. And, likely, there will be a "payoff" with respect to the initial research regardless. For example, one of my earliest research projects employed what would today be called a mixed methods approach (Stovin, 1999). It was, essentially, a case study of a research centre in terms of its output, processes, and organizational structure. The primary method was quantitative in nature, employing a multi-variable, panel data regression analysis. However, at the outset of the research, I also engaged in open-ended interviews with key scientists to gather qualitative data and to better understand the organizational context. Luckily these senior scientists took the opportunity to tell me stories about their careers and the internal history of the research centre. What could not have been foreseen was that this complementary narrative approach not only provided me with a broader understanding of the topic, it also happened to provide me with the information necessary for making a correct interpretation of the so-called "hard" data and discern a "break point" that would otherwise have gone unnoticed.

Finally, in some circumstances, a narrative approach may be the only one that is needed for effective decision making. If a program of interest is rather small, for example, then all participants can be included in the study and the large amount of data that the narrative approach generates will not be onerous. This was the case for Schwind, Zanchetta, Aksenchuk, and Gorospe (2013), who wished to evaluate an international placement program that formed part of three nursing students' practicums. In other cases a researcher may want to sample selectively because certain individuals may hold specialized knowledge. For example, in an applied research project I co-led a few years ago we invited heavy end-users to discuss[4] and demonstrate their experiences with a new online interface and asked them to talk out loud while being video recorded performing routine tasks. This approach was chosen so that we would hopefully discover any immediate "red flags" that might have been overlooked and, at the same time, perhaps gain a better sense of priorities for future development from a user's perspective and their embodied knowledge. While we might have gained knowledge of the former using other approaches, we could not have gained the latter.

CONCLUSION

Returning to the quotation from Thomas King at the top of the chapter, when we come to the understanding that we (as individuals or groups of individuals) *are* the stories that we tell, we realize the importance of capturing, re-imagining, and interpreting these stories. We need to do so consciously, explicitly, and with serious intent if we are to learn from them and draw lessons for action from them. In other words, we realize the need to engage in narrative inquiry. If wise and effective decision making requires a deep and holistic understanding (i.e. "knowledge"), if it requires insight or, better yet, multiple insights, then there is no way but this.

NOTES

[1] A meta-analysis is an empirical technique that combines findings and information from numerous previous studies in an area of interest to test research questions using a larger data set to arrive at new or strengthened results.

[2] The use of the term publication bias in the context of meta-analytic technique refers to its exclusion of results from sound qualitatively based research as well as the tendency for quantitative studies that do not produce a high enough level of statistical significance to not be published. The latter situation is problematic because if the information was reported it could turn out to be significant once aggregated appropriately.

[3] I prefer to use the term "understanding" rather than knowledge, as knowledge implies a certainty that is not attainable within a constructivist paradigm and does not allow for multiple, simultaneously held interpretations of a particular situation.

[4] As part of the discussion, we encouraged participants to tell the story of their prior experiences with the organization and its related technologies.

REFERENCES

Barbee, B. (2009). *A qualitative study of a local district teacher induction program and itsperception by young educators* (Unpublished doctoral dissertation). University of Kansas, the Department of Teaching and Leadership, Kansas, KS.

Bess, J., & Dee, J. (2008). *Understanding college and university organizations: Theories for effective policy and practice*. Sterling, VA: Stylus.

Carr, D. (1986). *Time, narrative, and history*. Bloomington, IN: Indiana University Press.

Clandinin, J., & Cave, M. (2008). Creating pedagogical spaces for developing doctor professional identity. *Medical Education, 42*, 765–770.

Clandinin, J., & Connelly, M. (1987). *Narrative, experience and the study of curriculum*. Edmonton: Alberta Advisory Committee for Educational Studies.

Clandinin, J., & Connelly, M. (1996). Teachers' professional knowledge landscapes: Teacher stories – Stories of teachers – School stories – Stories of schools. *Educational Researcher, 25*(3), 24–30.

Clandinin, J., & Connelly, M. (2000). *Narrative inquiry: Experience and story in qualitative research*. San Francisco, CA: Jossey-Bass.

Denzin, N., & Lincoln, Y. (Eds.). (1994). *Handbook of qualitative research*. Thousand Oaks, CA: Sage.

Dewey, J. (1938/1997). *Experience and education*. New York, NY: Touchstone.

Dodge, J., Ospina, S., & Foldy, E. (2005, May/June). Integrating rigor and relevance in public administration scholarship: The contribution of narrative inquiry. *Public Administration Review, 65*(3), 286–300.

Ellis, J. (1998). Interpretive inquiry as a formal research process. In J. Ellis (Ed.), *Teaching from understanding: Teacher as interpretive inquirer*. New York, NY: Garland.

Ellis, J. (2006, Fall). Researching children's experience hermeneutically and holistically. *Alberta Journal of Educational Research, 52*(3), 111–126.

Farhat, N. (2010). College students' end-of-semester assessment of instructors' performance: Students' narratives are the best interpretive research tool that validates the survey questionnaire results. *International Journal of Information and Operations Management Education, 3*(4), 392–416.

Guba, E., & Lincoln, Y. (1994). Competing paradigms in qualitative research. In N. Denzin & Y. Lincoln (Eds.), *Handbook of qualitative research*. Thousand Oaks, CA: Sage.

Jones, S., Segar, T., & Gasiorski, A. (2008, Fall). "A double-edged sword": College student perceptions of required high school service-learning. *Michigan Journal of Community Service Learning, 15*(1), 5–17.

Kavale, K. (2001). Decision making in special education: The function of meta-analysis. *Exceptionality, 9*(4), 245–268.

King, T. (2003). *The truth about stories: A native narrative*. Toronto, ON: House of Anansi Press Inc. CBC Massey lectures series.

Lagu, T., Goff, S., Hannon, N., Shatz, A., & Lindenauer, P. (2013). A mixed-methods analysis of patient reviews of hospital care in England: Implications for public reporting of health care quality data in the United States. *The Joint Commission Journal on Quality and Patient Safety, 39*(1), 7–15.

McAllister, M., John, T., Gray, M., Williams, L., Barnes, M., Allan, J., & Rowe, J. (2009). Adopting narrative pedagogy to improve the student learning experience in a regional Australian university. *Contemporary Nurse, 32*(1–2), 156–165.

Mishler, E. (1986). The analysis of interview-narratives. In T. Sarbin (Ed.), *Narrative psychology: The storied nature of human conduct* (pp. 233–255). New York, NY: Praeger.

Mostert, M. (2001). Characteristics of meta-analysis reported in mental retardation, learning disabilities, and emotional and behavioral disorders. *Exceptionality, 9*(4), 199–225.

Mostert, M. (2004). Face validity of meta-analysis in emotional and behavioral disorders. *Behavioral Disorders, 29*(2), 89–118.

Packer, M., & Addison, R. (1989). Evaluating an interpretive account. In M. Packer & R. Addison (Eds.), *Entering the circle: Hermeneutic investigation in psychology*. Albany, NY: SUNY Press.

Sarbin, T. (1986). Introduction and overview. In T. Sarbin (Ed.), *Narrative psychology: The storied nature of human conduct* (pp. ix–xviii). New York, NY: Praeger.

Schwind, J., Zanchetta, M., Aksenchuk, K., & Gorospe, F. (2013). Nursing students' international placement experience: An arts-informed narrative inquiry. *Reflective Practice, 14*(6), 705–716.

Scruton, R. (1982). *A dictionary of political thought*. New York, NY: Harper and Row.

Spaulding, L. (2009). Best practices and interventions in special education: How do we know what works? TEACHING *Exceptional Children Plus, 5*(3), Article 2. Retrieved October, 2013, from http://escholarship.bc.edu/education/tecplus/vol5/iss3/art2

Stovin, D. (1999). The microeconomic determinants of technological change: A case study of the Crop Development Centre. Unpublished Master's thesis, University of Saskatchewan, Saskatoon, Canada.

Trow, M. (1974/2010). Problems in the transition from elite to mass higher education. In *General report on the conference on future structures of post-secondary education* (pp. 55–101). Paris: OECD. (Reprinted in M. Burrage (Ed.), *Martin Trow: Twentieth-Century higher education, elite to mass to universal*. Baltimore, MD: The Johns Hopkins University Press)

United Nations. (1989, November). *Convention on the rights of the child*. Retrieved August, 2013, from http://advocate.gov.ab.ca/home/Youth_Rights.cfm

Wood, D. (1992). Teaching narratives: A source for faculty development and evaluation. *Harvard Education Review, 62*(4), 535–550.

Xu, Y., & Liu, Y. (2009). Teacher assessment knowledge and practice: A narrative inquiry of a Chinese college EFL teacher's experience. *TESOL Quarterly, 43*(3), 493–513.

5. VALUES, VIRTUES, AND HUMAN CAPABILITIES

A Positive Perspective on Educational Improvement

:ment and how we might measure
)est of our human experiences in
rning—the core work of schools.
of a future education where the
s own flourishing as a first step
ommunity may flourish, as well.
literature in positive psychology
sent our conceptual model of
)ticing, fostering, and sustaining
t well-being may be one of the
communities.

)NAL IMPROVEMENT

:ions are typified by greed,
-minded focus on winning.
. Imagine that members of
st, anxiety, self-absorption,
awsuits, contract breaking,
/ interactions and social
archers investigating these
ing, reciprocity and justice,
chieving profitability, and
:e of contrast, now imagine
re typified by appreciation,
ilness. Creating abundance
s. Imagine that members of
iiness, resilience, wisdom,
ationships and interactions
respect, and forgiveness.
vorth living. Imagine that

Waterstones

```
Waterstones
Blackett Street
Newcastle
NE1 7JF
0191 261 7757
SALE TRANSACTION

BEST AVAILABLE EVID          £39.00
9789463004367
Transfer S&S Card            3.0 stamps
Balance to pay               £39.00
Visa Debit                   £39.00

WATERSTONES PLUS CARD
CARD NUMBER:      **** **** **** 3436
Your Current Balance         £0.00
Qualifying spend             £39.00
Starting Stamps total             0
Stamps earned in this transaction 3
Manual Stamps added               3
Current Stamps total              6
Stamps collected so far on this card
```

```
*** CARDHOLDER COPY ***

P:W3433413      T:****1909
M:***00752
       21/08/2018 14:38:01
```

scholarly researchers emphasize theories of excellence, transcendence, positive deviance, extraordinary performance, and positive spirals of flourishing. (Cameron, Dutton, & Quinn, 2003, p. 2)

We use this quotation as a starting point for reimagining educational improvement and how we might measure schools in ways that encourage and privilege the best of our human experiences in and through the fulfilling work of teaching and learning—the core work of schools. We have been inspired by the ideas, and assumptions embedded in this question, as reflected in our current research and writing on the potential of positive school improvement (Cherkowski & Walker, 2012, 2013a, 2013b, 2013c, 2014). As an underpinning to our own positive organizational scholarship we are guided by a similar question:

What if we imagine that the primary role of teachers is to learn how to thrive as educators and, in so doing, to continually co-explore and facilitate all means by which everyone in their learning communities flourishes most of the time? (Cherkowski & Walker, 2013a)

As we carry out research with educators, the answers we find as we delve more deeply into the positive organizations and positive psychology research encourages our continued exploration of new ways to think about how to assess the success of our various educational enterprises.

As we have said, the constructs of happiness and well-being have garnered significant global attention as ways for us to mark the status of human rights, national well-being, and our levels of innovation and prosperity (as well as our struggling and suffering). Research evidence in positive scholarship suggests that a focus on human capacities, such as flourishing, compassion, resilience, and optimism in schools yields important insights on new ways of raising and enriching the capacity of our education efforts. Teachers, and other school leaders, are the central players in students' educational experiences and have significant roles to play in the beneficial outcomes and impacts from these experiences. In our writing, we have considered the influence of opening the aperture of our viewing lenses to what is good, positive, and life-enhancing in schools, in students and in their teachers to create new and generative models of educational improvement. We imagined that this use of positive organizational research perspectives could enhance the possibilities of our honouring the fullness of the human experience in schools for educators and their students. Further, we wondered about becoming more wide-awake to new ways of measuring positive organizational climates and the facilitative elements for flourishing in diverse school communities; such that we are better able to foster and sustain the benefits. In this chapter, we describe the landscape of positive organizational research and provide an overview of our ongoing research and our emerging model of flourishing in schools as a starting point for assessing educational improvement from a positive perspective.

CURRENT CONTEXT OF SCHOOL IMPROVEMENT

As we have previously said, school improvement initiatives tend to function from a deficit-orientation as researchers and practitioners earnestly work to fix and change what is wrong, lacking, dysfunctional or detrimental to students and their families (Cherkowski & Walker, 2014). Much has been learned about how to improve schools through the use of these gap-focused lenses and so we encourage continued work in this form of school improvement. We do all we can to ensure children are getting the best educational experiences possible and so, of course, the determination of gaps and finding problems to be solved can be efficacious, and this is certainly a noble and well-intentioned approach. At the same time, we have suggested that there ought to be a shift in the balance of our attention toward focusing on what is working well and fostering more vitality, joy, compassion, kindness, creativity, and other virtuous behaviours and capabilities. This positive shift to focusing on robust and nourishing aspects of human experience in the context of schooling is vital for improving our efforts to improve education. In the next section, we describe several catalysts that have helped to shift how we think about educational improvement by re-focusing on the moral purpose of education, using positive research views from psychology and organizational studies, applying alternative approaches to social and human development—and by exploring the possibilities that emerge when our perspectives are shifted toward more positive research frameworks for studying school organizations and the people who animate them.

THE MORAL PURPOSE OF EDUCATION: A CATALYST FOR SHIFTING
HOW WE THINK ABOUT EDUCATIONAL IMPROVEMENT

Education is a moral endeavour. The purpose of schooling is tied to larger ideals about how best to prepare young people for the future. Educators and policy makers forecast what kind of world these students will inhabit and regularly consider how school learning communities might best ensure that these young citizens have the capabilities and capacities to flourish as persons, find gainful employment, and contribute to the common good of civil society. However, some might argue that schooling can be too narrowly focused and overly instrumentalist. Critics have suggested that schooling ought to provide a broad set of experiences to develop and equip students for actualizing fuller human potentials through education (Noddings, 2005; Starratt, 2005; Walker, 2010). As we think about the purposes of education and the role of schools in providing for these purposes, we suggest that a shift in our thinking toward larger questions will serve us well: What kinds of people are being served? What kind of communities and societies are we aiming to co-construct with our students? What kinds of capacities, capabilities, and mindsets might we cultivate in schools, such that help all members of the school community to live and learn well together—now and into the future?

The current and common pretext for improvement of schools seems too narrowly focused on economic benefits of education. We join with others who might suggest that the moral purpose of education is far larger, deeper, and more important than merely raising test scores or ensuring a good supply of well-prepared workers for the increasingly complex economies of our world (Noddings, 2003; Ravitch, 2010; Starratt, 2004). What if we were to assume that one of the goals of education for all of the students was to develop an awareness of and capabilities for flourishing—their own and others? Indeed, this goal would align with the timeless human quest for developing the habits and dispositions for a life characterized by civility, virtue, and a commitment to contributing to the common good. As we have described in our writing, these ideals have been explored in the humanities and other disciplines, with current views describing an evolution away from our tribal roots of fighting for our survival toward developing societies based in cooperation, empathy, and compassion (Armstrong, 2006, 2011; Rifkin, 2009; Wheatley, 2005). Current approaches to schooling rarely reflect the promise for greater cooperation, empathy and compassion. Rather, there seems to be a decreasing emphasis on schooling as a vehicle for individual and collective moral growth and an increasing emphasis on school as a vehicle for individual pursuit with a focus on test scores as an important measure of success (Apple, 2010; Hayward et al., 2007). We have noted how Richard Layard, an economist, suggested that a better balance might be reached between these two extreme views of the purpose of school in which, as a society, we are "less obsessed with [school] rankings than at present. For our fundamental problem today is a lack of common feeling between people—the notion that life is a competitive struggle" (p. 163). For Layard and others, schools ought to provide a learning environment that balances individual competitive pursuits with striving to contribute to the common good and serving others.

The encouragement of moral growth amongst young people as one of the key goals for schooling has been a central theme in much of the writing and research in educational leadership (cf. Begley, 1999; Greenfield, 2004; Hodgkinson, 1991). Starratt (2007) argued that teachers and other school leaders have a moral obligation to provide authentic learning experiences for all students as a way of engaging them, through their present schooling experiences, to develop over time into the kinds of caring, authentic and educated citizens for which we hope. Authentic learning opportunities would be designed so that students experience, in developmentally appropriate ways, what it means to be an active citizen of a pluralistic democratic school community; a design that would start from students' personal experiences and lead outward toward reflecting on their own personal moral agendas of becoming more clear about their true selves and, at the same time, reflecting on the public implications of their roles as contributors to the relationships that make up their social and natural worlds. The subject matter and course content becomes the vehicle for authentic learning. Starratt explained how schools could be the practice places for how to learn to live well together. However, teachers, and other school leaders, are often "accustomed to view the learning agenda of the school as an end in itself, rather than as a means for the moral and intellectual filling out of learners as human beings" (Starratt, 2007, p. 167). Shifting the perspective by using a new lens through which we view the purpose of schooling might give the space for imagining anew the purpose of school and the power of education. We see the potential in a positive organizational perspective for new thinking about how to create environments that foster and promote a more full human experience through schooling for students and their teachers.

POSITIVE PSYCHOLOGY AND POSITIVE ORGANIZATIONAL SCHOLARSHIP: NEW LENSES FOR VIEWING EDUCATIONAL IMPROVEMENT

Two emerging fields of study offer insights on new ways of researching the organizational, interpersonal, and individual aspects of schooling—positive psychology and positive organizational scholarship (POS). We anchor much of the theoretical framework for our research in these two research fields. Positive psychological research highlights how attending to strengths and positive outlooks, as opposed to a deficit-model of thinking, can increase resilience, vitality, and happiness and can decrease stress, anxiety, and depression (Lyubomirsky, 2007; Petersen et al., 2005). We have argued that these findings have implications for how we imagine the teaching and learning that goes on in schools and for thinking about the benefits of focusing on what works, what goes well, and what brings vitality to people in school organizations (Cherkowski & Walker, 2013a, 2013b, 2014). There are few studies that have used a positive organizational perspective to examine educational contexts. Given the benefits and advantages of attending to organizational health (Lencioni, 2012), positivity and happiness in the workplace (Achor, 2011), we aim to help fill this gap with research on the etiology and dynamics of flourishing in schools. In psychology, flourishing is defined as optimal ways of functioning characterized by goodness and wholeness (Fredrickson & Losada, 2005; Gable & Haidt, 2005) often resulting in resilience, self-fulfillment, contentment, and happiness (Haybron, 2008; Martin & Marsh, 2006; Rassmussen, 1999). Based on the positive research literature and on our early research findings with school leaders (Cherkowski & Walker, 2013c), we currently define flourishing in schools as the confluence of forces, factors, and dynamics that contribute to a sense of thriving in three domains of the school organization: subjective well-being, generative leader mindsets and adaptive community dispositions. With our ongoing research, we aim to increase the understanding of how it is that certain schools and people in schools flourish.

Positive psychological research findings indicate that developing positive outlooks, habits, and mental models rather than a deficit-model approach of trying to repair the negative and destructive ones is beneficial for increasing individual well-being (Achor, 2011; Bakker & Schaufeli, 2008; Ben-Shahar, 2008; Keyes, Fredrickson, & Park, 2012; Seligman, 2002; Seligman & Csikszentmihalyi, 2000) by increasing resilience, vitality, and happiness and decreasing stress, anxiety, and depression (Lyubomirsky, 2007; Petersen et al., 2005). Similarly, evidence from positive organizational research shows that paying attention to capacities such as happiness, resilience, optimism, and compassion in the workplace can lead to benefits such as improvements in organizational commitment, professional learning, innovation, and overall organizational health. POS scholars recognize the negative aspects and challenges of organizations and yet place an intentional research focus on the strengths, virtues, and positive human capacities of those within organizations (Carr, 2004). Recent findings show that emphasizing high quality connections at work can increase individual and team resiliency (Dutton & Heaphy, 2003; Stephens et al., 2013), and expressing and receiving compassion at work is linked to increased retention and organizational commitment (Lillius et al., 2008). In their meta-analysis of positive psychological behaviours at work, Luthans and Youseff (2007) found that positive psychological capital (representative of hope, optimism, resilience, and efficacy) is a strong predictor of other positive organizational outcomes such as commitment, performance and organizational citizenship. Other studies have examined diversity in organizations with a focus on positive leadership (Youseff & Luthans, 2013) and positive organizational change (Stevens et al., 2008). We have said that we need to start thinking of organizations as potential vehicles for bringing more compassion, courage, love, and care to the world (Cooperrider, n.d.). This may be an inspiring, and arguably idealistic, perspective within which to view the potential for schools to reclaim their role as essential contributors to building just and caring communities; however, we see how the research findings in these two fields of positive research can transfer to the work of teaching and learning that goes on in schools and can provide strong learning for establishing a more full model of school well-being.

WE MEASURE WHAT WE PAY ATTENTION TO: APPRECIATIVE APPROACHES TO EDUCATIONAL IMPROVEMENT

Schools have long been charged with the task of increasing student learning as measured by results on achievement tests. Teachers are responsible to the system for increased measurement (measurism) of test scores as well as for the number of children who achieve (closing the gap, raising the bottom, sustain the high achievement). In our Western societies, we tend to value what we can measure. Organizationally, we remain largely in a problem-solving paradigm where we recognize and then aim to fix problems based on measureable outcomes. In this paradigm, the focus is on deficits and problems: what is keeping us from excelling, as we think we should. To create school environments where students and teachers take risks necessary to engage in authentic learning that can move them towards moral growth and development of a fuller range of human capacities and capabilities, we suggest that a positive organizational perspective focused on generative, life-giving paradigms can shift the thinking away from deficiencies and toward abundance.

Shifting our focus to pay attention to that which we wish to increase in meaning, value, and frequency is at the heart of appreciative processes for transformational change. A selective list of the basic principles of appreciative inquiry illustrates the shift in thinking needed to embrace the constructive capacity for positive transformation within our schools: In every society, organization, or group, something works; what we focus on becomes our reality; reality is created in the moment, and there are multiple realities; it is important to value differences; the language we use creates our reality (Coghlan, Preskill, & Tzavaras Catsambas, 2003; Whitney & Trosten-Bloom, 2010). Although appreciative inquiries have been carried out with success in schools and school districts (*cf.*, Bushe, 2007) there has not be a widespread use of this generative approach despite its promise for developing and sustaining a positive climate and culture in schools from a strengths-based perspective. In this next section, we provide an overview of three approaches to measuring success and achievement to illustrate the possibilities for conceiving of alternative approaches to measuring a broader understanding of success in schools.

ALTERNATIVE MEASURES OF SUCCESS: CAPABILITIES, HAPPINESS, AND VALUES

How do we measure the prosperity of a society? Is it only through economic indicators, or are there others way to notice how well life is being lived by those who make up the society? We have found philosopher Martha Nussbaum's argument for using broader measures that include an understanding that human dignity is inherent in measurements of a life well-lived through thinking about the capabilities that ought to be freely developed for all people in a society helpful for reflecting on this question. Nussbaum (2011) developed a list of ten basic capabilities that moves the standard economic approach by which societies measure their well-being (e.g., measuring GNP) toward a more holistic understanding of well-being that "defines achievement in terms of the opportunities open to each person" (p. 14). From this human development perspective, Nussbaum suggested that policies that are "truly pertinent to a wide range of human situations means attending to diverse factors that affect the quality of a human life—asking in each area, 'what are people (and that is each person) actually able to do and to be'" (p. 14). The ten central capabilities provide a baseline measure for thriving: living a normal life span; having good health; being able to move freely from place to place; being able to use senses, to imagine, think and reason, being able to have attachments, to love and be loved, to form conceptions of good and engage in critical reflection, to be able to affiliate with others and engage in respectful social activities, living with concern and respect with the world of nature, being able to laugh, play and enjoy, and being able to have some control over one's environment (political and material) (p. 34). Her list of central capabilities clearly suggests that economic prosperity is only one piece of quality of life for which individuals strive. Nussbaum conceded that conflicts among and between the capabilities are inevitable when crafting policies that affect people's lives, but that the responsibility for policymakers is to find ways to ensure that the minimal threshold of each capacity be maintained so as to ensure a basic level of human dignity for all citizens.

Happiness is another indicator used to measure quality of life. For example, in the country of Bhutan, efforts to measure levels of gross national happiness have created a more widespread international interest in measuring the happiness and well-being of citizens as an indicator of success, rather than only economic indicators of prosperity. The Canadian Index of Well-Being (n.d.) and various Gallup polls (n.d.) target a more holistic measure of success and achievement in life, such as happiness, health, social connections, as well as economic achievement. Although there are no agreed upon tests or standards for determining a life well-lived, the increased attention toward understanding how to improve well-being has broadened the set of indicators to include many elements that might at first glance seem immeasurable. This points to a growing awareness of the benefits of widening the aperture for viewing success, vitality, and achievement.

Finally, organizational health has been proposed as a broad measure of success for businesses (Lencioni, 2012). Healthy organizations are measured primarily by how well-aligned their values are to their actions. A poorly aligned organization will likely suffer from negative politics at work, poor morale, and a poor bottom line. From decades of research and practice, Lencioni noticed that in healthy organizations, integrity (defined as wholeness of values, vision, and action) is essential, and that expressed values must be authentic and sufficiently inspiring to carry over or transfer into the words, deeds, and attitudes of everyone within the organization. Organizational health is possible when leaders do the hard work of clarifying their own values, ensuring these align with organizational values, and building trust in relationships so that the work of clarifying and aligning values can happen at all levels of the organization. Although the profits in business tend to increase as organizations gain greater clarity and alignment of why they exist and how they behave as they live out their core values, Lencioni suggested that profits are rarely the goal of organizational health and are more often an indicator of healthy organizations.

In schools, the traditional measures of educational success have been academic—grades, attendance, graduation. A group of Canadian education activists, *People for Education*, are inquiring into the possibility of including measurements of other areas of life that are important to our human dignity, but that are not necessarily captured in current measures for improvement (People for Education, 2013). With their work, they aim to establish a wider set of indicators of school success that might include measurement of physical and mental health, social and emotional development, citizenship and democracy, creativity and innovation, and school climate and supports. These broad categories reflect the belief of an expansive view of schooling for human development. We have noted elsewhere (Cherkowski & Walker, 2014) how educational programs such as the Penn Resiliency Program and the Strath Haven Positive Psychology Curriculum, two longstanding efforts (almost 20 years), are designed to promote student well-being through positive education (Seligman, 2011, pp. 81–84) and to better understand the processes that enhance well-being. We also described the Geelong Grammar School Project as another example of how to embed positive education into the culture of a school (Seligman et al., 2009, pp. 302–307). In general, however, the current model of education tends to mirror a more traditional view of schooling as a means of academic achievement as the end goal of gaining work for economic prosperity.

We began this chapter by asking: What might schools look like if greater attention were paid to the well-being of all school community members? Nel Noddings (2003) suggested, in her book on happiness in schools, that if we were serious about preparing all students for a full and meaningful life as contributing and engaged citizens, we would concentrate on much more than the few academic subjects and skills required for university entrance. We would design our schools to honour and prepare for many more of the skills, aptitudes, and interests needed to be an engaged, informed, and—indeed—passionate members of society, including, but not limited to, the skills and requirements necessary for gainful employment. How might we structure our schools in a way that embraces a more full meaning of humanity, beyond test scores in academic subjects and what might this provide for our students and their teachers? What might schools look like if we asked, as a starting point, questions like these? Again, what if we imagine that the primary role of teachers is to learn how to thrive as educators and, in so doing, to continually co-explore and facilitate all means by which everyone in their learning communities flourishes most of the time?

WELL-BEING: A NEW GUIDEPOST FOR EVALUATING EDUCATIONAL IMPROVEMENT

Focusing on the human capabilities, capacities, and potentials (Scheffler, 1985; Sen, 2009; Nussbaum, 2011) of the school organization—attending to the human flourishing of teachers and other school leaders—may provide new opportunities for developing sustainable learning communities in schools. Through our ongoing research on flourishing in schools, we have developed a conceptual model for examining school organizations and the people within them from a positive organizational research perspective (Figure 1). The model elaborates three domains of attention for thinking about flourishing in schools: adaptive community; subjective well-being; and generative leader mindsets. We assumed that professional virtues, such as compassion, hope and trust, influence and interact in and through these domains to foster and sustain flourishing in schools. In the next section, we present the flourishing model as a possible template for noticing, fostering and sustaining the well-being of schools, with the assumption that well-being may be one of the guideposts in assessing schools as healthy learning communities.

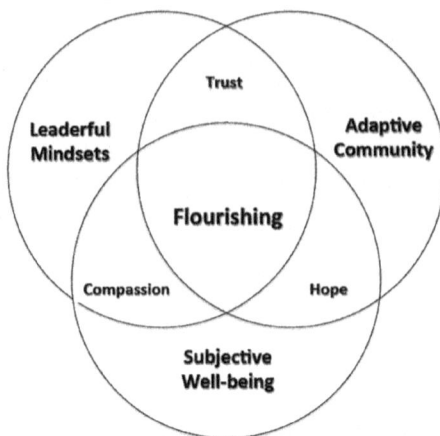

Figure 1. Model for flourishing in schools

ADAPTIVE COMMUNITY: RELATIONSHIPS AT WORK

Humans are a social species—we are meant to live, to work, and to play together in social contexts. Learning to be in relationships with others is a developed skill. Historically, teaching has been described as a lonely job, where individual teachers carry out their work in their classrooms, isolated from one another (Lortie, 1975). With the growing trend to develop schools as learning communities for attaining school improvement goals, creating opportunities for teachers to work together in professional relationships—in the form of collaboration, shared reflection, and shared decision making—is an important aspect of school organizing. Coupled with this is the growing need to understand how to foster climates for improved professional learning (Hargreaves & Fullan, 2012).

We have described how research on leadership for change in organizations from a developmental psychology perspective has been successfully transferred for use in schools where principals learned about and then practiced implementing strategies for creating challenging, but emotionally safe, climates for improving professional learning for teachers (Cherkowski & Walker, 2014). We see that findings from positive organizational research may have similar transferability for supporting professional learning and development in school organizations. For example, individual and group resiliency has been found to increase as the capacity to constructively express emotions is nurtured in work relationships (Stephens et al., 2013). This idea of resiliency is echoed in our concept of adaptive community where teachers and other school leaders would be encouraged and supported in learning how to communicate openly and effectively with colleagues, to disagree respectfully, to develop healthy work teams and to disband teams that are no longer working well, to provide and receive compassion and care at work, to draw out passion, fun, and joy in themselves and in others at work. Using practices developed from research in positive psychology (*cf.* Seligman, 2011) to encourage personal professional growth at work could become an innovative approach to improving professional learning for teachers and other school leaders.

GENERATIVE LEADER MINDSETS: CONNECTING LEADING TO MEANING

Finding ways to make meaning from our experiences is a capacity unique to humans, and can help us to feel that we belong and contribute to something greater than ourselves—an important element in personal well-being (Lyubmorsky, 2007; Seligman, 2011). While teachers may intuitively know that their contribution to their students, in the long run and in the big picture, has meaning, we see how attending to their role as a generative leader through developing capacities and dispositions for this mindset could provide more immediate feelings of contribution and well-being through the work of teaching and learning. Our ideas about generative leader mindsets reflect the research-based awareness that sustainable school improvement requires leadership at all levels of the school (Elmore, 2000; Hargreaves & Fullan, 2012; Slater, 2008), and the research findings from positive psychology that indicate that well-being increases with autonomy and a positive sense of achievement (Seligman, 2011).

It is common in leadership literature to talk about the importance of creating visions for the organization and developing mission statements that evoke a sense of commitment to the moral purpose of the organization. From a positive organizational perspective, teacher leadership, for example, could be explored from a perspective of flourishing through developing deeper understanding of the impact of creating personal meaning through teachers' and other school leaders' work in schools. The generative leader mindset domain emphasizes the personal and professional benefits of attending to personal visions for flourishing through work, and these can generate momentum for positively influencing others toward developing their own sense of leadership (Quinn, 2004).

Robin Sharma writes business fables to help explain the corporate world. In his book, *The Leader Who Had No Title* (2010), a young bookstore clerk undertakes a great learning journey with a magical mentor to come to understand that leadership is a role available to all, and that through pursuing personal leadership in all aspects of our work, we can transform any job into a meaningful career that serves others and bring enormous personal satisfaction. And, of course, the profits will likely follow. There is much to be learned from thinking about the power and potential of transforming classrooms and schools through developing capacities and habits of mind that reflect a personal leadership approach to creating meaningful work. Robert Quinn (1996) similarly wrote about the potential for transformation in self, and then others, when work becomes an opportunity for personal professional development. We suggest that classrooms and schools can serve as similar places of personal and professional transformation through developing positive climates that support meaningful personal growth (for examples, see Kegan & Lahey, 2009) toward increasing personal leadership mindsets in schools.

SUBJECTIVE WELL-BEING: POSITIVE EMOTION AND FLOW AT WORK

Diener and Seligman (2004) described well-being as "peoples' positive evaluation of their lives, which includes positive emotion, engagement, satisfaction, and meaning" (p. 1). We developed our model with an aim to extend ideas of well-being in schools beyond the research on student well-being and academic achievement (Berkowitz & Bier, 2005; Cohen, 2001; Elias & Arnold, 2006; Greenberg et al., 2003), teachers' well-being linked to student achievement (Jennings & Greenberg, 2009; Zins et al., 2004) and research on the mindful management of stress (Roeser et al., 2013). From findings in positive psychology, we understand that a focus on positive emotions in one aspect of life can contribute to increasing capacities and capabilities in other areas of their lives (Fredrickson et al., 2008), meaning that increasing positivity in the workplace can have generative, life-giving, and beneficial effects across many levels of the workplace.

Mikhaly Csikszentmihalyi is credited as one of the founding scholars of positive psychology. One of the constructs he researches is "flow," a psychological state of joy produced from engagement in an activity in which individuals demonstrate an intense and focused concentration, a sense of losing track of time, a loss of self-consciousness, a feeling of control of one's actions and environment, and high levels of intrinsic satisfaction (Csikszentmihalyi, 1997; Nakamura & Csikszentmihalyi, 2003; Seligman, 2011). Studying the state of flow is a relatively new area of scholarship and much of the research in education settings has focused on adolescents. For example, researchers have studied the conditions necessary for flow to occur among gifted children (Fredrickson et al., 2010), and the positive affects when adolescents experience flow (Shernoff et al., 2003). In a large Canadian study on student engagement, *What Did You Do in School Today Project* (2009), researchers used Csikszentmihalyi's flow theory to measure levels of intellectual engagement of Canadian students in math and language arts.

Few studies examine the positive organizational aspects of subjective well-being for teachers, beyond those that measure the effects of using mindfulness programs to attend to stress and burnout (*cf.* Roeser et al., 2013). However, we see the potential for growth and development in examining teachers' commitment to professional learning, happiness at work, and the levels of flow that they are able to experience through their work as a chance to learn new ways of thinking about teacher engagement at work. Using positive research perspectives for phenomena such as well-being as a guidepost for educational experiences and educational improvement opens a wider space for thinking about the learning climate that may be fostered for teachers and other school leaders.

FINAL THOUGHTS: HOSTING PROFESSIONAL VIRTUES FOR
FLOURISHING AS EDUCATIONAL IMPROVEMENT

To reiterate, an appreciative, generative, and positive approach to school improvement might start with the magnitude of presence of the professional virtues that can host flourishing: compassion, trust, and hope. Trust has long been researched in educational leadership, and findings show that increased trust links to an improved learning climate in the school (e.g., Bryk & Schneider). With colleagues, we have written extensively about the role of trust in school, from the perspective of principals and their trust brokering roles (Kutsyuruba, Walker, & Noonan, 2011; Kutsyuruba, Walker, & Noonan, 2010; Noonan, Walker, & Kutsyuruba, 2008; Walker, Noonan, & Kutsyuruba, 2011). Our research with Canadian principals confirms the essential nature of this construct in leader-constituent relationship, its fragility and the importance of restoring broken trust and remediating betrayal where this has occurred. The research points to the mediating or brokering role of school administrators who may be called upon to help restore relationships and rebuild trust amongst those in the their learning communities. The stewardship of trusting relationships is critical to the functioning good-will within a school setting. Likewise, the construct of hope is fundamental to the moral purposing and negotiation of life in schools. In our work, we boldly echo the declaration that fostering hope is the first and last task of a school leader (Walker, 2006; Walker & Atkinson, 2010). There are many versions of hope. We suggest that a warranted hope that embodies an adaptive confidence in the prospects for future well-being and a sense of collective efficacy are vital for generative school climates.

Research findings indicate that compassion responses in the workplace can increase affective commitment and positive emotions at work (Lillius et al., 2008), can lead to quicker recovery in the face of traumas suffered at work (Cameron & Caza, 2004), are linked to high-quality connections at work (Lillius et al., 2011), and can create a virtuous cycle in the workplace (Dutton et al., 2002). Research on compassionate leadership indicates that a leader's willingness to show concern for members' pain has a positive influence on other members expressing their pain in healthy ways with their colleagues (Kanov et al., 2004). Finally, researchers have found that organizations that support and encourage individual expressions of compassion, build capacities for collectively noticing, feeling, and responding to pain (Dutton et al., 2006; Frost et al., 2000). These findings are relevant for the work of teachers. We are living in a time of rapid change and great uncertainty. As teachers are also faced with increasing complexity and uncertainty in their work, understanding how to notice and alleviate pain, stress, and suffering through extending and receiving compassion to self and others at work would seem an important capability to foster and support among learning community members.

We sense that the time is right to imagine a future education where the primary role of the teacher is to ensure her or his own flourishing as a first step toward ensuring that all members of the learning community may flourish as well. As we think about how to develop broader measures and signposts for educational improvement, we appreciate arguments that education must move beyond an instrumental approach to increase grades and test scores, and instead, to provide an authentic learning experience that leads to developing among all students the social habits for contributing to the democratic public good. We suggest that these authentic learning experiences extend to teachers, school leaders, and community members and can be elicited within positive environments that encourage and support the wholeness of the human experience through attending to the flourishing of those within schools.

REFERENCES

Achor, S. (2011). *The happiness advantage: The seven principles of positive psychology that fuel success and performance at work.* New York, NY: Crown Business.

Apple, M. (Ed.). (2010). *Global crises, social justice, and education.* New York, NY: Routledge.

Armstrong, K. (2006). *The great transformation: Beginnings of our religious traditions.* New York, NY: Alfred A. Knopf.

Armstrong, K. (2011). *Twelve steps to a compassionate life.* New York, NY: Alfred A. Knopf.

Bakker, A. B., & Schaufeli, W. B. (2008). Positive organizational behavior: Engaged employees in flourishing organizations. *Journal of Organizational Behavior, 29*(2), 147–154.

Begley, P. T. (Ed.). (1999). *Values and educational leadership.* Albany, NY: State University of New York.

Ben-Shahar, T. (2008). *Happier.* Maidenhead, Berkshire, England: McGraw-Hill.

Berkowitz, M., & Bier, M. C. (2005). *What works in character education: A research-driven guide for educators.* Washington, DC: Character Education Partnership. Retrieved from http://www.character.org/resources/ceppublications/

Bushe, G. (2007). *The appreciative inquiry into learning at the Metropolitan School District: Unleashing a culture of creative engagement.* A report prepared for the Metropolitan School District, Toronto, ON.

Cameron, K. S., & Caza, A. (2004). Introduction: Contributions to the discipline of positive organizational scholarship. *The American Behavioral Scientist, 47*(6), 731–739.

Cameron, K. S., Dutton, J. E., & Quinn, R. E. (Eds.). (2003). *Positive organizational scholarship.* San Francisco, CA: Berrett-Koehler.

Canadian Index of Well-Being. (n.d). Retrieved from https://uwaterloo.ca/canadian-index-wellbeing/

Carr, A. (2004). *Positive psychology: The science of happiness and human strengths.* New York, NY: Routledge.

Cherkowski, S., & Walker, K. (2012, May 26–June 2). *Flourishing communities: Advancing a positive framework for school improvement.* A paper presented at the 81st Congress of the Humanities and Social Sciences, University of Waterloo, Guelph, ON.

Cherkowski, S., & Walker, K. (2013a). Living the flourishing question: Positivity as an orientation for the preparation of teacher candidates. *Northwest Journal of Teacher Education, 11*(2), 80–103.

Cherkowski, S., & Walker, K. (2013b). Schools as sites of human flourishing: Musing on an inquiry into efforts to foster sustainable learning communities. *Canadian Journal of Educational Administration and Foundations, 23*(2), 139–154.

Cherkowski, S., & Walker, K. (2013c, April 27–May 1). *Flourishing leaders: Enriching human capacity development in schools.* A paper presented at the American Educational Research Association, San Francisco, CA.

Cherkowski, S., & Walker, K. (2014). Flourishing communities: Re-storying educational leadership using a positive research lens. *International Journal of Leadership in Education: Theory and Practice, 17*(2), 200–217.

Cohen, J. (Ed.). (2001). *Caring classrooms/intelligent Schools: The social emotional education of young children (Social and Emotional Learning, 2).* New York, NY: Teachers College Press.

Coghlan, A. T., Preskill, H., & Tzavaras Catsambas, T. (2003). An overview of appreciative inquiry in evaluation. *New directions for evaluation, 2003*(100), 5–22.

Cooperrider, D. L. (n.d.). *Appreciative inquiry commons.* Retrieved November 19, 2015, from http://appreciativeinquiry.case.edu/

Cooperrider, D. L., & Whitney, D. (2001). A positive revolution in change: Appreciative inquiry. *Public Administration and Public Policy, 87*, 611–630.

Csikszentmihalyi, M. (1997). *Finding flow: The psychology of engagement with everyday life.* New York, NY: BasicBooks.

Diener, E. (2000). Subjective well-being: The science of happiness and a proposal for a national index. *American Psychologist, 55*(1), 34–43.

Diener, E., & Seligman, M. (2004). Beyond money. *Psychological Science in the Public Interest, 5*(1), 1–31.

Drago-Severson, E. (2009). *Leading adult learning: Supporting adult development in our schools.* Thousand Oaks, CA: Corwin.

Dutton, J. E., & Heaphy, E. (2003). The power of high quality connections. In K. Cameron, J. E. Dutton, & R. E. Quinn (Eds.), *Positive organizational scholarship* (pp. 263–278). San Francisco, CA: Berrett-Koehler.

Dutton J. E., Frost P. J., & Worline, M. C. (2002). Leading in times of trauma. *Harvard Business Review, 80*, 54–61.

Dutton, J. E., Worline, M. C., Frost, P. J., & Lillisu, J. (2006). Explaining compassion organizing. *Administrative Science Quarterly, 51*(1), 59–96.

Dweck, C. (2006). *Mindset. The new psychology of success: How we can learn to fulfill our potential.* New York, NY: Random House.

Eaker, R., & Keating, J. (2009). Deeply embedded, fully committed: Leaders transform Washington District into a professional learning community. *Journal of Staff Development, 30*(5), 50–55.

Elias, M. J., & Arnold, H. (Eds.). (2006). *The educator's guide to emotional intelligence and academic achievement.* Thousand Oaks, CA: Corwin.

Fredrickson, B. (2008). Promoting positive affect. In M. Eid & R. Larsen (Eds.), *The science of subjective well-being* (pp. 449–468). New York, NY: Guildford.

Fredrickson, B., Cohn, M., Coffey, K., Pek, J., & Finkel, S. (2008). Open hearts build lives: Positive emotions, induced through loving-kindness meditation, build consequential personal resources. *Journal of Personality and Social Psychology, 95*(5), 1045–1062.

Fredrickson, B. L., & Losada, M. F. (2005). Positive affect and the complex dynamics of human flourishing. *American Psychologist, 60*(7), 678–686.

Frost, P., Dutton, J., Worline M., & Wilson, A. (2000). Narratives of compassion in organizations. In S. Fineman (Ed.), *Emotions in organizations* (pp. 25–45). London: Sage.

Fullan, M. (2006). *Turnaround leadership.* San Francisco, CA: Jossey-Bass.

Fullan, M., & Hargreaves, A. (2012). *Professional capital: Transforming teaching in every school.* New York, NY: Teachers College Press.

Gable, S., & Haidt, J. (2005). What (and why) is positive psychology? *Review of General Psychology, 9*(2), 103–110.

Gallup. (n.d.). *Gallup.* Retrieved November 19, 2015, from http://www.gallup.com/

Greenberg, M. T., Weissberg, R. P., Utne O'Brien, M., Zins, J. E., Fredericks, L., & Resnik, H. (2003). Enhancing school-based prevention and youth development through coordinated social, emotional, and academic-learning. *American Psychologist, 58*, 451–466.

Greenfield, W. D. (2004). Moral leadership in schools. *Journal of Educational Administration, 42*(2), 174–196.

Haybron, D. (2008). Happiness, the self and human flourishing. *Utilitas, 20*(1), 21–49.

Hayward, K., Pannozzo, L., & Colman, R. (2007, August). *Developing indicators for the educated populace domain of the Canadian index of wellbeing.* A report prepared for the Atkinson Charitable Foundation, Toronto, Canada.

Hodgkinson, C. (1991). *Educational leadership: The moral art.* Albany, NY: SUNY.

Jennings, P. A., & Greenberg, M. T. (2009). The prosocial classroom: Teacher social and emotional competence in relation to child and classroom outcomes. *Review of Educational Research, 79*, 491–525.

Kanov, J., Maitlis, S., & Worline, M. C. (2004). Compassion in organizational life. *American Behavioral Scientist, 47*(6), 808–827.

Kaser, L., & Halbert, J. (2009). *Leadership mindsets: Innovation and learning in the transformation of schools.* New York, NY: Routledge.

Kegan, R., & Lahey, L. L. (2009). *Immunity to change: How to overcome it and unlock potential in yourself and your organization.* Boston, MA: Harvard Business Press.

Keyes, C., Fredrickson, B., & Park, N. (2012). Positive psychology and the quality of life. In C. Keyes, B. Fredrickson, & N. Park (Eds.), *Handbook of social indicators and quality of life research* (pp. 99–112). Dordrecht, The Netherlands: Springer.

Kutsyuruba, B., Walker, K., & Noonan, B. (2010). The ecology of trust in the principalship. *Journal of Educational Administration and Foundations, 21*(1), 23–47.

Kutsyuruba, B., Walker, K., & Noonan, B. (2011). Restoring broken trust in the work of school principals. *International Studies in Educational Administration, 39*(2), 81–95.

Layard, R (2005). *Happiness: Lessons from a new science.* London, England: Penguin.

Lencioni, P. (2012). *The advantage: Why organizational health trumps everything.* San Francisco, CA: Jossey-Bass.

Lilius, J. M., Worline, M. C., Dutton, J. E., Kanov, J., Maitlis, S., & Frost, P. J. (2011). Understanding compassion capability. *Human Relations, 64*, 873–899.

Lillius, J. M., Worline, M. C., Maitlis, S. Kanov, J., Dutton, J. E., & Frost, P. (2008). The contours and consequences of compassion at work. *Journal of Organizational Behaviour, 29*, 193–218.

Lortie, D. (1975). *Schoolteacher.* Chicago, IL: Chicago University Press.

Luthans, F., & Youseff, C. M. (2007). Positive organizational behavior in the workplace: The impact of hope, optimism and resilience. *Journal of management, 33*(5), 774–800.

Lyubomirsky, S. (2007). *The how of happiness: A scientific approach to getting the life you want.* New York, NY: Penguin.

Martin, A. J., & Marsh, H. W. (2006). Academic resilience and its psychological and educational correlates: A construct validity approach. *Psychology in Schools, 43*(3), 267–281.

Nakamura, J., & Csikszentmihalyi, M. (2003). The motivational sources of creativity as viewed from the paradigm of positive psychology. In *A psychology of human strengths: Fundamental questions and future directions for a positive psychology* (pp. 257–269). Washington, DC: American Psychological Association.

Noddings, N. (2003). *Happiness and education.* Cambridge, UK: Cambridge University.

Noddings, N. (2005). *The challenge to care in schools: An alternative approach to education.* New York, NY: Teachers College Press.

Noonan, B., Walker, K., & Kutsyuruba, B. (2008). Trust in the contemporary principalship. *Canadian Journal of Educational Administration and Policy, 85*(2), 1–17.

Nussbaum, M. (2011). *Creating capabilities: The human development approach.* Cambridge, MA: Belknap.

People for Education. (2013). *Broader measure of success: Measuring what matters. A report.* Retrieved June, 2013, from http://www.peopleforeducation.ca/measuring-what-matters/get-informed

Peterson, C., Park, N., & Seligman, M. E. (2005). Orientations to happiness and life satisfaction: The full life versus the empty life. *Journal of Happiness Studies, 6*(1), 25–41.

Quinn, R. (1996). *Deep change: Discovering the leader within.* San Francisco, CA: Jossey Bass.

Quinn, R. (2004). *Building the bridge as you walk on it: A guide for leading change.* San Francisco, CA: Jossey Bass.

Rassmussen, D. (1999). Human flourishing and the appeal to human nature. *Social Philosophy and Policy, 16*(1), 1–43.

Ravitch, D. (2010). *The death and life of the great American school system: How testing and choice are undermining education.* New York, NY: Basic.

Rifkin, J. (2009). *The empathic civilization: The race to global consciousness in a world in crisis.* New York, NY: Penguin.

Roeser, R. W., Schonert-Reichl, K. A., Jha, A., Cullen, M., Wallace, L., Wilensky, R., ... Harrison, J. (2013). Mindfulness training and reductions in teacher stress and burnout: Results from two randomized, waitlist-control field trials. *Journal of Educational Psychology, 105*(3), 787–804. doi:10.1037/a0032093

Scheffler, I. (1985). *Of human potential: An essay in the philosophy of education.* Boston, MA: Routledge & Kegan Paul.

Seligman, M. (2002). *Authentic happiness: Using the new positive psychology to realize your potential for lasting fulfillment.* New York, NY: Free Press.

Seligman, M. (2011). *Flourish: A visionary new understanding of happiness and well-being.* New York, NY: Free Press.

Seligman, M., & Csikszentmihalyi, M. (2000). Positive psychology: An introduction. *American Psychologist, 55*(1), 5–14.

Seligman, M., Ernst, R., Gillham, J., Reivich, K., & Linkins, M. (2009). Positive education: Positive psychology and classroom interventions. *Oxford Review of Education, 35*(3), 293–311.

Sen, A. (2009). *The idea of justice.* London: Allen Lane.

Sergiovanni, T. J. (1993, April). *Organizations or communities? Changing the metaphor changes the theory.* A paper presented at the Annual Meeting of the American Educational Research Association, Atlanta, GA.

Shernoff, D., Csikszentmihalyi, M., Schneider, B., & Shernoff, E. S. (2003). Student engagment in high school classrooms from the perspective of flow theory. *School Psychology Quarterly, 18*(2), 158–176.

Sharma, R. (2010). *The leader who had no title: A modern fable on real success in business and in life.* New York, NY: Free Press.

Slater, L. (2008). Pathways to building leadership capacity. *Educational Management, Administration, and Leadership, 36*(1), 55–69.

Starratt, R. J. (2004). Leadership of the contested terrain of education for democracy. *Journal of Educational Administration, 42*(6), 724–731.

Starratt, R. J. (2005). Cultivating the moral character of learning and teaching: A neglected dimension of educational leadership. *School Leadership and Management, 25*(4), 399–411.

Starratt, R. J. (2007). Leading a community of learners: Learning to be moral by engaging the morality of learning. *Educational Management Administration & Leadership, 35*(2), 165–183.

Stephens, J. P., Heaphy, E. D., Carmeli, A., Spreitzer, G. M., & Dutton, J. E. (2013). Relationship quality and virtuousness: Emotional carrying capacity as a source of individual and team resilience, *Journal of Applied Behavioral Science, 49*(1), 13–41.

Stevens, F. G., Plaut, V. C., & Sanchez-Burks, J. (2008). Unlocking the benefits of diversity: All-inclusive multiculturalism and positive organizational change, *Journal of Applied Behavioral Science, 44*, 116–133.

Walker, K. (2006). Fostering hope: A leader's first and last task. *Journal of Educational Administration, 44*(6), 540–569.

Walker, K., & Atkinson, M. (2010). Warranted hope. In R. Couto (Ed.), *Political and civic leadership: A reference handbook.* Thousand Oaks, CA: Sage.

Walker, K., Noonan, B., & Kutsyuruba, B. (2011). The fragility of trust in the world of school principals. *Journal of Educational Administration, 49*(5), 471–494.

Walker, M. (2010). A human development and capabilities 'prospective analysis' of global higher education policy. *Journal of Education Policy, 25*(4), 485–501.

Wheatley, M. (2005). *Finding our way: Leadership for an uncertain time.* San Francisco, CA: Berrett-Koehler.

Whitney, D., & Trosten-Bloom, A. (2010). *The power of appreciative inquiry: A practical guide to positive change* (2nd ed.). San Francisco: CA: Berrett-Koehler.

Youssef, C. M., & Luthans, F. (2013). Positive leadership: Meaning and application across cultures. *Organizational Dynamics, 42*(3), 198–208.

Zins, J., Weissberg, R., Wang, M., & Walberg, H. J. (Eds.). (2004). *Building academic success on social and emotional learning: What does the research say?* New York, NY: Teachers College Press.

SCOTT TUNISON

6. THE CARTOGRAPHY OF SUCCESS

Mapping the Education Data Terrain toward Ethical
Practice for Continuous Improvement

While data-driven decision making in the education sector is sometimes held up by skeptics as the flavour of the month, "recent clarion calls for educational accountability have dramatically changed the landscape of PK-12 public education … the most recent evolution [of which has led to] the standards-based accountability movement" (Crum, 2012, p. 3). In any case, the process of using data to make decisions in the classroom and administrative offices is by no means new.

> Teachers have [always] used a wide range of data sources … to make judgments about their students' understandings … school administrators routinely have used data to make managerial and operational decisions. What is new, however, is that *data are now inextricably coupled with accountability*. (Mandinach & Honey, 2008, p. 2; emphasis added)

The coupling of data-driven decision making with the "accountability movement" in many jurisdictions in United States, Great Britain, and Canada, among other places, has tainted the acceptance and implementation of data-driven decision-making processes. The media are rife with "horror stories" in which data have been used as cudgels to browbeat already struggling schools and districts with teacher sanctions and school closures in the name of accountability.

Nonetheless, *accountability* and *data-driven decision making*, as constructs, should not be construed as expletives. To realize the improvements in our education systems we desire, we must find ways to incorporate data into our decision-making processes—not for external accountability *per se* but to inform, from within, our progress toward continuous improvement (Mandinach & Gummer, 2013).

The core education-sector accountability questions are: (a) for what is the sector accountable, and (b) to whom? Datnow and her colleagues (2011) opined, "Children do get left behind and groups of students, especially those from low-income and minority backgrounds, are often failed by our school systems" (p. 10). Moreover, as pointed out by Black and Wiliam (2010),

> Present policies in the U.S. and many other countries treat the classroom as a black box. Certain inputs from the outside—pupils, teachers … standards, tests with high stakes, and so on—are fed into the box. Some outputs are supposed

P. Newton & D. Burgess (Eds.), The Best Available Evidence, 81–98.

to follow: pupils who are more knowledgeable and competent, better test results ... and so on. But what is happening inside the box? How can anyone be sure that a particular set of new inputs will produce better outputs if we don't at least study what happens inside the box? (p. 81)

Raising the lid of the black box requires data collection, analysis, and mobilization—skills that have not traditionally been part of college and university pre- or in-service teacher training (Crum, 2012). Furthermore, with the ever-evolving data analysis and visualization tools being created for the educational realm, building a framework for ethical data processes for the education sector could not be more important or timely.

Formalised data-driven practice (often called evidence-based practice) has a long history and clear ethical standards—particularly in academia, medicine, and business. Universities and colleges are guided by research ethics policies and review boards; stock markets are governed by securities commissions; many professions (e.g., medicine, law, education, etc.) follow codes of ethics, and governments themselves are directed by ethical standards of various kinds.

Writ large, data practices are typically assumed to be conducted in an ethical manner—*until* inappropriate data practices come to light. As pointed out by the National Forum on Educational Data Ethics (2010),

Ethics ... rarely get much [explicit] attention until someone behaves in an unethical manner ... [for example] business ethics become headline news when financiers put their own personal interests ahead of their clients' financial well-being [and] sports ethics arouse public debate when an athlete is accused of steroid use, cheating, or gambling. (p. 1)

DEVELOPING A CARTOGRAPHY OF ETHICAL DATA PRACTICES

To avoid the potential negative consequences of improper and/or unethical data use and reap the benefits of educational data-driven decision-making (ED³M) initiatives, "the process must be well-thought out and executed" (Crum, 2012, p. 4). The National Forum on Educational Statistics documents underscore the importance of developing an ethical data framework.

Although the world is full of good people, ethical behavior does not just happen automatically ... When an individual's interest is at stake, people may be tempted to engage in unethical behavior—to knowingly manipulate or misrepresent statistics to make a point; misuse data for personal gain; or convince themselves that privacy and confidentiality requirements don't need to be observed ... by establishing standard procedures for collecting data, generating and reviewing reports, releasing publications, and communicating with the public, organization[s] limit the opportunities for inappropriate behavior. (NFES, 2010, p. 2)

This chapter charts a course through three seminal data ethics frameworks to yield an ethical data practices map explicitly designed for the education sector. Specifically, it examines the implications these frameworks have for policy, practice, and leadership in the education sector.

Orienting Ourselves—Physical Features of the Landscape

There are many ways to navigate new terrain. From the earliest times, people have used the physical characteristics of their environment to guide their travels. Astronomic phenomena (e.g., stars, moon, sun, etc.), landscape and environmental features (e.g., valleys and mountains, rivers and streams, particular rocks and trees, etc.), the natural world (e.g., migration of animals and birds, plant growth characteristics, etc.), and community history (e.g., traditional ceremonial and hunting grounds), have helped travelers to get their bearings and divine their direction.

While documenting the landscape, cartographers make a plethora of decisions such as: (a) the means of documentation (e.g., pictograph, piles of stones along the path, tree bark notches, a map, etc.), (b) landscape features to include, and (c) the level of detail required. For example, while a mountain is a major landmark visible from a great distance, travelers typically require trailmarkers along the path both to keep them on the "right track" and to encourage them to persist on their journey.

The last two decades has witnessed a convergence of thinking and action related to the ethics of data collection, analysis, and mobilization in Canada—especially with Aboriginal peoples. From these processes, two major landmarks for academic data-related work in Canada have become clear: (a) *Tri-Council Policy Statement: Ethical Conduct for Research Involving Humans* (TCPS) and (b) "Ownership, Control, Access, and Possession." Since I focus in this chapter on ED^{3}M, the United States' National Forum on Education Statistics' *Forum Guide to Data Ethics* (FGDE) has been incorporated into this cartographic guide to ED^{3}M, as well.

Furthermore, as is the case with most effective maps, these key *Cartography of Success* landmarks also have trail-markers leading up to them. These trail-markers provide additional detail for travelers and are also described in the sections that follow.

Tri-council policy statement: Ethical conduct for research involving humans (2014). The Tri-Council Policy Statement (TCPS) is, perhaps, the most important landmark for ethical ED^{3}M processes in Canada. It governs research practices for Canada's federally funded research agencies (i.e., the Canadian Institutes of Health Research, the National Sciences and Engineering Research Council of Canada, and the Social Sciences and Humanities Research Council of Canada) and represents tremendous insights developed collaboratively with stakeholder groups across the country.

The TCPS is founded on three core principles. These include: (a) respect for persons; (b) concern for welfare; and (c) justice. Furthermore, it also has five navigational trail-markers including: (a) risk-benefit balance; (b) privacy and confidentiality concerns; (c) fairness and equity; and (d) respectful relationships.

Each principle and trail-marker, as described below, provides essential information for the journey toward this particular landmark and, of course, is central to the overall cartographic process.

TCPS core principles. *Respect for persons.* Respect for persons recognizes the inherent worth of all human beings. It shines light explicitly on individuals' and communities' autonomy and the importance of *full and informed consent.*

This principle points to data collectors' and users' commitments to accountability and transparency—especially when involving "vulnerable" individuals. In the education sector, data collectors and users (e.g., teachers, administrators, Ministries of Education) must ensure that the individuals involved are clear about: (a) the purposes of the assessments and/or data collection, (b) the intended uses of the information, and (c) the foreseeable risks and benefits that may accrue from participation.

Concern for welfare. This principle denotes the importance of identifying the potential impact of research on participants and ensuring that individuals have sufficient information to assess the potential benefits and risks associated with participation. Key welfare considerations include: (a) privacy, (b) control of information, (c) use of information, (d) the balance between risks and benefits, and (e) individual and collective harm.

Justice. Justice, the third TCPS core principle relevant to this map, highlights the importance of treating everyone involved in a project fairly and equitably— not necessarily equally. "Differences in treatment or distribution are justified when failures to take differences into account may result in the creation or reinforcement of [existing or future] inequities" (TCPS, 2014, p. 8).

A critical aspect of the equity/equality duality is the extent to which those involved are "vulnerable". In this context, vulnerability refers to situations in which individuals or groups (a) who may have limited capacity or access to social goods such as rights, opportunities, and power, and/or (b) whose circumstances cause them to be vulnerable or marginalized may need to be afforded special attention in order to be treated justly. Following this definition of vulnerability, nearly all children and youth as well as many families, teachers, and communities in the education sector are vulnerable. In fact, this landmark is the foundation upon which this entire map has been developed.

TCPS Trail-markers. The TCPS includes several trail-markers that make explicit the path for ethical research in Canadian contexts. Specifically, its markers define the path researchers must follow for a research project to be considered "ethical". The following sections outline the key data-related markers defined by the TCPS.

Risks and benefits. One of the most critical data-related trail-markers is defined by risk-benefit calculations. This calculation is the ratio between the risks (defined as the intersection between the potential significance or seriousness of the harm and the likelihood the harm will occur) and the potential benefits associated with participation.

For the purposes of marking the path for ethical data practices, data handlers must consider the following when making the risk-benefit calculations:

- Risks and benefits may not be perceived in the same way by everyone involved;
- Purpose, intended use(s) of the data, and context (both of individual and group) must be clear at the outset;
- Possession and access to the data; and
- Dissemination of findings to those from whom the information was gathered.

Privacy and confidentiality. In the context of ethical data practices, the privacy and confidentiality has two key markers: (a) the extent to which an individual (or group) is identifiable in the data and (b) the potential harm that might result in being identified. This applies to all personal information.

Data come in several forms—varying in the likelihood that the individual from which the information was collected may be identified. For the purposes of this *Cartography*, key categories for personal information were considered. In broad terms, the student and his or her family should have a reasonable expectation of confidentiality and the "system" has an obligation to maintain the integrity of that promise of privacy.

Various pieces of legislation—both provincially and federally—govern privacy practices. Having said that, as pointed out in the TCPS, the duty of confidentiality must be balanced against the best interests of the individual or group (e.g., disclosure of abuse, self-harm, and illegal activity *or* assessment results collected by one professional and shared among others for the overall improvement of educational programming at the individual or group level, etc.). However, the core question remaining here is: *Who determines the best interests?*

Fairness and equity. Research suggests that student achievement improves when educators and educational authorities collect and use data effectively. Confrey (2008) pointed out that "data-driven decision making based on sufficient … data, [they can be] a powerful route to fairer and more effective [instructional] practice" (p. 32). Kowalski and his colleagues (2008) argued that "educators who use data to make decisions … [should] develop purposeful questions that assist them … [to] explore [and improve instructional practice] in the classroom" (p. 101). This research is grounded in the belief that data help both the learner and the learning facilitator (e.g., classroom teacher, principal, consultants, etc.) know where one is on her or his learning journey *right now* and how learning can improve and/or progress *in the future.*

Respectful relationships and reciprocity in creating ethical data dialogue. Research does not take place in a vacuum. The policy statement reinforces that research—specifically data collection, interpretation, and dissemination—is a process of negotiation and collaboration between the researcher and the research subject or "researchee" (broadly defined).

Ownership, control, access, and possession (OCAP). OCAP, the second key landmark for this *Cartography of Success*, shines a direct light on research data-related practices with First Nations, Inuit, and Métis peoples. Concomitantly with the work on the first TCPS, the National Steering Committee of the First Nations and Inuit Regional Longitudinal Health Survey (RHS), coined the principles of "OCA" referring to the locus of ownership and control of data as well as the manner in which access to the data are governed. Since then, an additional principle, possession of data, has become part of the lexicon. Now commonly referred to as "OCAP"; these trail-markers recognize "the First Nations' way" (First Nations Centre, 2007, p. 2) and have led to "an increase in First Nations research capacity and a widely shared core value of self-determination" (p. 4).

OCAP is "not a doctrine or a prescription. [Rather] it is a set of principles in evolution" (Schnarch, 2004, p. 81). OCAP principles (or trail-markers) stress "the importance of the community having control over not just the data, but also, how it is used, and what actions are taken and by whom" (Patterson, Jackson, & Edwards, 2006, p. 52). OCAP also raises the profile of community collaboration in data processes at each level and, at the same time, provides clear trail-markers for navigating the trail of ethical data practices.

Finally, when OCAP principles are honoured effectively, data – and the knowledge generated from those data – are mobilised toward some useful purpose that benefits both the participating communities and the individuals themselves. In other words, it is not good enough just to find out, we must also do something in response to what is learned. Each OCAP trail-marker is described in the sections that follow.

Ownership. Ownership marks "the relationship of a First Nations community to its cultural knowledge/data/information" (Schnarch, 2004, p. 81). Specifically, it makes explicit that all knowledge resides with both the community and the individuals who make up that community. In other words, "the community or group owns information collectively in the same way that an individual owns their personal information" (Schnarch, 2004, p. 81).

While collective local ownership of knowledge is a fundamental principle of ethical research, the concept need not be applied in a literal sense. The principle of ownership is less concerned with the physical location of knowledge than it is with the knowledge itself—including the active involvement of the community in managing the knowledge.

Control. The principle of control points to the right of the community to be actively involved in everything that affects them. Control includes

> All stages of a particular ... project—from conception to completion. [It] extends to the control of resources and review processes [associated with the project], the formulation of conceptual frameworks, data management, and so on. (First Nations Centre, 2007, p. 5)

Looked at another way, control "does not imply the right to exclusively conduct research, [instead] it is the right to be involved, to contribute, to approve and be aware of all aspects and impacts of the research as a project progresses" (Masching, Allard, & Prentice, 2006, p. 33).

Access. Access has two primary principles. The first reflects peoples' right to have direct access to information collected about them. "First Nations people must have access to information and data about themselves and their communities, regardless of where it is currently held" (First Nations Centre, 2007, p. 5).

The second is similar to the first but adds another dimension – others' access to information. This is described by Masching and her colleagues (2006) as follows, "[Access concerns the right] to decide who else will have access to this data" (p. 33).

Possession. Possession, literally, marks the importance of defining the processes for storage and control of information. According to Scharch (2004),

> While ownership identifies the relationship between a people and their data in principle, possession or stewardship is more literal ... possession [of data] is a mechanism by which ownership can be asserted and protected. When data owned by one party is in the possession of another, there is a risk of breech or misuse. (p. 81)

While physical possession of data is an important option, some communities may not have the infrastructure or personnel to "possess" their data directly. OCAP principles also allow for communities to designate a data steward that may manage and protect data on their behalf.

National forum guide to data ethics.   The United States' Department of Education convened a National Forum on Educational Statistics in 2010. The purpose of this forum was to "improve the quality of education data gathered for use by policymakers and program decisionmakers ... [of particular interest was] the ethical use and management of education data" (National Forum Guide to Data Ethics, 2010, p. iv).

The establishment and observance of data ethics are especially critical in the education sector—because:

> Each and every day, educators collect and use data about students, staff, and schools ... collecting, maintaining, reporting, and using data in an appropriate manner that is consistent throughout the organization ... will not happen unless ... data ethics ... [become] an important organizational priority ... by establishing standard procedures for collecting data, generating and reviewing reports, releasing publications, and communicating with the public, an education organization limits the opportunities for inappropriate behavior. (National Forum Guide to Data Ethics, 2010, pp. 1–3)

This guide includes nine canons that this *Cartography* uses as trail-markers. They describe the context within which all education sector data should be handled. The nine canons are organised according to three broad concepts: (a) integrity, (b) data quality, and (c) security. The canons are discussed in turn below.

Integrity. Data are used by schools and districts in a myriad of ways. For example, grade promotion, graduation status, attendance, staffing ratios, teacher qualifications—among many other school decisions—are informed by data. The individual(s) making these decisions must reflect on his or her understanding of appropriate data procedures as well as his or her personal and professional integrity to proceed properly. The five *Integrity* trail-markers are described in the sections that follow.

Demonstrate honesty, integrity and professionalism at all times. Data-driven decision making is a complex endeavour and nearly everyone throughout the education sector has access to various types of personal information about staff and students. "Regardless of an individual's job title [or responsibility], working in an education environment demands unwavering adherence to codes of appropriate conduct, operating expectations, and professional standards" (NFGES, 2010, p. 8).

Appreciate that, while data may represent attributes of real people, they do not describe the whole person. Data are indicators of individual and organizational behaviour—*not* definitive portrayals. Furthermore, while data may be either (a) narrative or numerical, and (b) individual or aggregate; they are attributable to individual people in real situations. This trail-marker reminds educationalists not to get lost in the numbers and remember to keep the focus on understanding the learning journeys of individuals even as we look at the "big" picture.

Be aware of (and follow) applicable statutes, regulations, practices, and ethical standards. Federal and provincial privacy legislation should be the foundations upon which ethical data cultures within schools and divisions are established. Everyone in the entire organization is bound by the legal requirements associated with personal information. "Ignorance of a legal requirement does not cancel the ethical obligation to meet it" (NFGES, 2010, p. 13). Additionally, data culture procedures and policies should delineate clearly the type of data to which persons at each level of the organization have access and ensure that information technology credentials delineate this differential access.

Report information accurately and without bias. With the rise of ED³M accountability structures, educational systems are looking more and more for data to support positions, decisions, and policies. Literature, both academic and non-academic, is rife with cautions to those who use statistics that they are to ensure accurate and appropriate representation of analyses. The pressure to provide evidence that particular interventions are "working" or that services are being delivered efficaciously might tempt individuals and/or districts to "fudge" statistics—especially when data reveal bad news. Furthermore, since statistics courses are not typically included in many educators' training programs—at either undergraduate or graduate levels—statistics may be misrepresented unknowingly. Nevertheless, it is incumbent upon education sector partners to ensure that results are reported accurately and responsibly.

Be accountable and hold others accountable for ethical practices. Even with the best of intentions, any policy cannot address absolutely every contingency. There are always "grey areas" and it is those areas that challenge us to be particularly careful. Organisations at every level of the education sector should be proactive in anticipating potential grey areas and ensure that unanticipated situations are incorporated into the fabric of policies and procedures as they arise and that changes in legislation are addressed as soon as possible.

Data quality. If decisions are to be informed by data, the data must be of the best quality possible. The following data quality trail-markers are associated with this theme.

Promote data quality by adhering to best practices and operating standards. Data, from individual student assessments and progress reports to provincial and district annual indicator reports, are generated, analysed, and reported at every level of the education sector. Multiple data systems both across the province and within school divisions present a challenge to data quality. Data that are similar in content or intent are also collected by various people using different information systems that reside on multiple technological infrastructures. Furthermore, while local and provincial expectations may require schools, divisions, and the province to report based upon the same information, albeit at different levels of aggregation, analysis procedures associated with the varying information systems may yield different results from the same data. This eventuality may lead to diminished confidence in both the results and the data themselves—resulting in skepticism about the education sector overall. According to the National Forum Guide, the following characteristics are essential to quality data:

- Utility – data should provide information that is both useful to the organization and essential to the decision-making process;
- Accuracy and validity – data must measure accurately and without bias what they purport to measure;
- Reliability – data should be consistent and reliable;
- Timeliness – if data are to be useful, they must be available when they are required for decision making, in addition, data must be entered and/or generated as soon as possible after they are created; and
- Cost-effectiveness – the benefits from collecting and maintaining the data should outweigh the burden of collecting the information in the first place.

Provide all relevant data, definitions, and documentation to promote comprehensive understanding and accurate analysis. At the core of this is the realization that no specific piece of data exists in a vacuum and is largely meaningless without context, both in terms of how it relates (or not) to other pieces of data and how it is to be interpreted in light of its origins.

> Education indicators are too often interpreted out of context … [consequently], data handlers are ethically obligated to provide sufficient information for data users [and, by extension, data interpreters] to reasonably interpret the meaning of data shared in reports and other publications. (NFGES, 2010, p. 23)

Consider the following example:

> Two schools—one with a graduation rate of 60% and another with a rate of 85%—report 5-year improvements of 20% and 5% respectively. At first glance, the audience would likely conclude that the first school (with the 20% improvement) was being more successful in graduating students overall as compared to the second school (with a 5% improvement). However, if the data are interpreted in context, we would see that the first school now has a graduation rate of 80%; whereas, the second school's graduation rate is 90%.

The challenge with this trail-marker is to provide enough information, in language appropriate for the audience, to allow efficacious analysis, interpretation, and understanding—without catching the reader in a blizzard of technical and operational minutiae. Furthermore, we must also consider progress over time—unless the data are from an entirely new initiative, they exist in both longitudinal and operational contexts. In other words, the core tenet of this trail-marker is that data must be placed in context and we must challenge our myriad of educational stakeholder audiences to interpret data in light of the contexts from which they are derived.

Security. Security has two trail-markers: (a) the potential value to the organisation of the data systems, and (b) the importance of keeping the data secure.

Data systems are valuable organisational assets. Currently and historically, a tremendous amount of resources—human, financial, and infrastructure—are expended generating, collecting, storing, and managing data throughout the education sector. For example, teachers administer, record, analyse, and interpret assessments; take attendance; and determine and record final grades. School districts monitor: (a) student-teacher ratios, (b) fixed and variable costs, (c) facility maintenance and repair progress, (d) transportation expenditures, and (e) facility usage rates. Considering the human and financial resources associated with these and other data activities, none of them would be taking place unless the education sector values the data themselves, as well as the resultant information that can be drawn from them.

Given this extensive outlay of resources, the entire education sector must provide everyone who has contact with data with training appropriate to the data they access and monitor. Furthermore, every effort must be made to ensure that data are accurate and used appropriately.

Safeguard sensitive data. In the broadest sense, all data are sensitive. They represent aspects of individuals' and groups' identities and can be misinterpreted and/or misused—especially when encountered out of context. However, we must make a distinction between data that are confidential and those which may be in the public domain or which may be general enough that they would do no harm if they were to be made public.

Personal information about students and employees, for example, fall into the confidential category and should receive the highest level safeguarding. Reports presented at open board meetings, on the other hand, live in the public domain—these data, while sensitive (especially if they report "bad news"), should be protected in the sense that context and meaning are ascribed to them in the report text but need not be subjected to high levels of security.

Data Sharing Agreement Considerations

Beyond the key guiding documents described above, ethical ED³M practices in the education sector can be informed by the results of others' journeys. Like rest stops along a highway, they are places we can pull over, examine progress to date, assess the adherence to the intended path, and make course corrections if required.

There is a profusion of examples of data sharing agreements as well as descriptions of the recommended steps to arrive at such agreements. Residing largely in the health care and corrections services sectors, these agreements usually govern both the processes for internal data sharing (e.g., records for individual patients residing on a central server in a large walk-in clinic that are accessed by the physicians within that clinic as they treat patients) and external data sharing (e.g., processes for external researchers to gain access to criminal records of those in the justice system).

In many ways, the education sector is analogous to the example of a large medical clinic—a hybrid made up of patients who (a) see the same physician over time, (b) see a "regular" physician but may occasionally see others for a variety of reasons, and (c) may not have a "regular" physician but who see whomever is available when and where it is necessary to do so. A great many students complete their entire pre K-12 education within a single school district (perhaps in a couple schools—an elementary school or two and a high school) or in a single pre K-12 school, especially in rural areas. However, there are also students who, for a myriad of reasons, migrate among schools—perhaps spread across numerous school divisions and First Nations education authorities. This phenomenon provides both an opportunity and a challenge to the education sector—schools, districts, and local education authorities have access to a great deal of valuable data that may be helpful in supporting student learning but may lack systems to make maximum use of those data.

Models for agreements. The literature in this field follows two primary threads: (a) recommended components for data sharing agreements (derived both from research and from governmental policy and/or legislation); and (b) examples of actual and/or model agreements. In broad terms, agreements of this type typically range from as few as five components to as many as twenty sections. Nevertheless, all models address data issues in similar ways. In general, there seem to be eight core components common to effective data sharing agreement models. These are listed below:

1. Definition of terms
2. Purpose of sharing data and of the agreement itself
3. Specific data to be shared
4. Procedures for data sharing
5. Accuracy of information—including procedures for requesting corrections
6. Security procedures and provisions
7. Retention and disposition of information
8. Consequences of improper use

These components are described in detail below.

Definition of terms. All stakeholders must have a common understanding of the main terms used in the agreement. Of particular importance to be made clear are the following:

- What do we mean by "data" (including "metadata")?
- What does it mean to "share data/information"?
- What is "personal information"—in particular, what are the differences between/ among information that is: (a) confidential, (b) personally identifiable, (c) private, (d) sensitive, and/or general information?
- Ownership, Control, Access, and Possession (OCAP terms)

Purpose of sharing data and of the agreement itself. The signatory organisations must be able to articulate clearly the purpose for sharing data. In other words, what objectives are not possible without disclosing data to others? Overall, the purpose statements provide important trail-markers for any data ethics map.

A useful guide for clarifying purpose lies in the findings from research of multi-agency data sharing processes in the UK—especially by reframing the benefits of data sharing into objectives for sharing local or provincial education sector data. For example, purposes may include:

- Improved engagement of sector partners,
- Earlier and more coherent interventions both for pupils who struggle and who require enrichment—leading to a reduction in the number of students who "fall through the cracks",
- Smoother transitions for students and their families,
- Enhanced profile of the role of data in the overall decision-making process, and
- Clearer foundation for tracking progress for continuous improvement (UK Home Office, 2013).

Further, as pointed out by the Treasury Board of Canada (2010), "organisation[s] requesting personal information should be able to clearly identify the purpose for which the information is needed" (sec. 6.1). Looked at another way, terms for external requests to data must also be defined clearly.

It is also best practice ... to clearly identify upfront all purposes for which the personal information may be used or disclosed, including secondary uses. Any prohibitions on secondary use(d) or further disclosure(s) of the information ... [should] be scrutinized and agreed upon by the parties to the agreement to avoid misunderstandings. (TBC, 2010, sec 6.5)

Specific data to be shared. Building on the definitions of "personal data", the agreement should set out the types of data that are eligible for sharing under the agreement – and which are not. One way to look at this section is to define the scope of the agreement. The Treasury Board of Canada cautions that *only those data that are required* should be shared. The education sector collects an immense variety of data. The Treasury Board of Canada (2010) cautioned

Organisations ... hold a lot of personal information on individuals but not all of this information ... [is] relevant to the purpose for which the ... information [is requested] ... disclosing too much information or collecting more personal information than is necessary to fulfill a particular purpose is contrary to the *Privacy Act* and also contradicts universally recognised privacy principles and standards. (sec. 6.5)

In any case, it is important for this map "to include a list of the personal data elements that will be exchanged along with the purpose [for collecting and disclosing] for each type of data" (TBC, 2010, sec. 6.5). Furthermore, the greater the specificity of data to be shared, the less likely that data will be shared improperly or that inappropriate data will be shared.

Procedures for data sharing. In large part, the principles of OCAP should frame the actual procedures for data sharing. It is important, though, to add specificity to the principles in context of the particular sector(s) for which the agreements is developed. In any education sector, OCAP must also be defined in terms of the macro- and micro- organisational levels. For example, OCAP structures may apply differently at the Ministry level as compared to the division or school levels. In addition, OCAP structures may apply differently to the provincial system as compared to First Nations local educational authorities.

Another facet of the procedural issue rests in the technological infrastructure via which data are shared and the precise nature of the data themselves. Standardised or common student information systems across school districts in a province or state are critical; otherwise, data will have to be manipulated or reformatted and transmitted from one setting to the next. Data security is addressed elsewhere in this chapter but it is important to keep this issue on the radar.

Accuracy of information—including procedures for requesting corrections. If data are to be shared, they must absolutely be accurate. Sharing inaccurate data could do a great deal of harm in many ways. Overall, the processes for data input, accuracy verification, cleansing, and, when necessary, correction must be clear and widely understood. There are many data access points in the system—from school-based personnel to Ministry staff. Research in the UK has found that the entire sector benefits from a common format for data input and management.

Security procedures and provisions. The importance of protecting both the process of sharing data and the data themselves cannot be overstated. There are three broad issues to consider:

- Administrative measures (e.g., policies and procedures, training, etc.)
- Technical measures (e.g., passwords, audit trails, firewalls, etc.)
- Physical measures (e.g., physical location of data, restricted access to physical offices and workstations, etc.)

All of these issues have implications at both the macro- and micro-levels. At the provincial level, core trail-markers can be developed in each area. All school divisions already have local policies, practices, and procedures. It is critical, however, that there is thorough alignment among the various levels not only to protect the individuals' privacy but also to protect the province, school divisions, local education authorities, and schools from litigation due to security breaches.

Retention and disposition of information. Certainly, it is important to retain certain personal information for the duration of students' pre K-12 education. However, a critical issue to consider is the length of time a student's Grade 2 reading score is relevant as he or she moves through the pre K-12 system. Research in this arena gives little guidance. Certainly from an academic perspective, retrograde analysis could be worthwhile to identify certain student characteristics or data points that may have been predictors of future academic or behavioural outcomes. From a pragmatic point of view, however, there is likely a point at which past data become irrelevant—or, at least, not terribly relevant—to present outcomes.

Consequences of improper use. Once the ethical data practices framework been finalised, there must be clarity regarding potential breaches in the protocols. These consequences may not be punitive *per se* but it will be important to draft procedures to mitigate potential harm associated with breaches as well as mechanisms to revise the map in light of unforeseen gaps in protocols that may have led to breaches in the system.

Further, multi-agency information sharing research in the UK (British Home Office, 2013) resulted in several findings that both extend the NFES canon and add additional facets of concern. Of particular importance for this project are (a) leadership and governance, and (b) communication.

Leadership and governance. The importance of strong leadership cannot be overstated in most situations. The findings from UK study till little new ground but do underscore the critical issues to be considered. Specifically,

- Engage relevant stakeholders as early as possible;
- Establish a governance committee to oversee the development of the agreement as well as its implementation;
- Overestimate the anticipated draw on organisational resources as the agreement is implemented;
- Consider the various levels of nested cultural norms across the organisation; and
- Anticipate infrastructure issues—especially technological complexities—and devise a plan to address them.

Communication. All stakeholders must have the opportunity to learn about the process for arriving at the data sharing agreement as well as the agreement itself; otherwise, "staff [may] try to circumnavigate the [new model] and revert back to old processes [due to a lack of understanding]" (NFGES, 2013, p. 9). Furthermore, effective communication reduces the likelihood of mistrust or lack of confidence in the process and/or product.

CONCLUSION: THE IMPORTANCE OF RELATIONSHIP

Reflecting upon the principles inherent in the TCPS, OCAP, and NFGES frameworks, all of them focus on the nature of the relationship among those who collect data, those from whom data are collected, the way in which the data will be used, and the data themselves. At the heart of these principles lies the fundamental foundation of mutual trust and respect.

OCAP has been described as "a political response to colonialism and the role of knowledge production in reproducing colonial relations" (Espey, as cited in Schnarch, 2000, p. 81). As pointed out by the Royal Commission on Aboriginal Peoples (1997), this political approach is entirely understandable because

> The gathering of information and its subsequent use are inherently political. In the past, Aboriginal people[s] have not been consulted about what information should be collected, who should gather this information, who should gather that information, who should maintain it, and who should have access to it. (p. 4)

Therefore, "much of the impetus for OCAP can be linked to the sorry history of research relations with Aboriginal Peoples in Canada" (Schnarch, 2004, p. 81).

Given the complexities of data-related processes and variable local capacity to conduct them, the question remains, how can the data ethics principles cited in this chapter be applied and implemented in an education sector that has several layers of assessment aggregation and loci of data collection. Schnarch (2004) stressed that "standardized, formal protocols" (p. 81) must be established to ensure that data are shared in a way that maximizes the distribution of data for the benefit of the individuals and communities involved while at the same time safeguards sensitive information. "The parties involved will have to judge: how to respect [ethical] principles and get [the work] done; what compromise is acceptable; whether to proceed with a project; and under what terms" (p. 90).

Finally, it is very important that an explicit *Cartography of Success* framework be developed and implemented honouring the ethical landmarks herein for the particular context as well as for the particular purpose(s) for which the information are collected and used. The spirit and intent of OCAP, TCPS, and NFGES with their focus on active and authentic local involvement, results in capacity building and leads to improvements in practice and service delivery—ideally at both the macro- and micro-levels—and leads to improvements. As Schnarch (2004) pointed out, "the most elegant … [process] in the world is only as valuable as the impact that it makes in people's lives" (p. 89).

In the education sector, there are a great number of complexities associated with enacting data ethics principles. For example, in contrast to the health sector, an individual student's information, even one from a First Nation, may be seen to be "owned" jointly by the student and his or her family, the school/teacher, the school division, and the student's First Nation (especially in situations with tuition agreements).

In summary, the following practices and training should be considered by the education sector to ensure data are handled with integrity and professionalism.

1. Create an ethical data culture that encourages honesty, integrity, and professionalism throughout the organization by adopting and enforcing the following:
   - Emphasize, through extensive staff training, that all employees are expected to handle data with integrity and in a professional manner—make sure that all those connected to the school division (such as vendors, volunteers, community partners, external funders, etc.) are aware of these expectations;
   - Explicitly include "honesty and integrity" in all job descriptions, contracts, policies, and staff supervisory documents;
   - Be intolerant of behaviour that contravenes the established data culture regardless of job type and level of authority.
2. Use data for the purpose they were intended and be cautious of any requests for secondary use of data.

3. Avoid release of any information that may result in physical, mental, or emotional harm to others and report publicly only aggregate data that protects individuals' personal information and identity.

4. Be transparent and inclusive as organizational data culture precepts are developed and provide extensive training as they are implemented.

5. Reinforce that there are limits to the extent to which data can describe people and be especially careful when making personal or professional observations about people based entirely on data.

6. Use data both to inform practice and challenge misconceptions.

7. Ensure that all data handlers understand the limits to the extent to which data can represent people and tailor training to job type.

REFERENCES

Black, P., & Wiliam, D. (2010). A pleasant surprise. *Phi Delta Kappan, 92*(1), 47–48, 81–90.

Canadian Institutes of Health Research, Natural Sciences and Engineering Research Council of Canada, and Social Sciences and Humanities Research Council of Canada. (2014). *Tri-council policy statement: Ethical conduct for research involving humans.* Retrieved from http://www.pre.ethics.gc.ca/eng/policy-politique/initiatives/tcps2-eptc2/Default/

Confrey, J. (2007). Teaching teachers to use data to inform issues of equity and instruction. *Philosophy of Mathematics Education Journal, 20*(1), n.p.

Crum, K. (2010). Building the foundation for data-based decision making: Creating consensus on language and concepts. *International Electronic Journal for Leadership in Learning, 13*(5), 1–23. Retrieved from http://files.eric.ed.gov/fulltext/EJ940626.pdf

Datnow, A., Park, V., & Wohlstetter, P. (2007). *Achieving with data: How high-performing school systems use data to improve instruction for elementary students.* Los Angeles, CA: University of Southern California, Center on Educational Governance.

First Nations Information Governance Centre. (n.d.). *First nations principles of OCAP.* Retrieved from http://fnigc.ca/ocap.html

Indian and Northern Affairs Canada. (1996). *Royal commission on aboriginal peoples.* Ottawa, ON: Government of Canada.

Kowalski, T., Lasley, T., & Mahoney, J. (2008). *Data-driven decisions and school leadership: Best practices for school improvement.* New York, NY: Pearson.

Mandinach, E., & Gummer, E. (2013). A systemic view of implementing data literacy in educator preparation. *Educational Researcher, 42*(30), 30–37. doi:10.3102/0013189X12459803

Mandinach, E., & Honey, M. (2008). Data-driven decision making: An introduction. In E. Mandinach & M. Honey (Eds.), *Data-driven school improvement: Linking data and learning* (pp. 1–9). New York, NY: Teachers College Press.

Masching, R., Allard, Y., & Prentice, T. (2006). Knowledge translation and Aboriginal HIV/AIDS research: Methods at the margins. *Canadian Journal of Aboriginal Community-based HIV/AIDS Research, 1*(1), 31–44.

National Forum on Educational Statistics, U.S. Department of Education. (2010). *Forum guide to data ethics* (NFES 2010-801). Washington, DC: National Center for Education Statistics.

Patterson, M., Jackson, R., & Edwards, N. (2006). Ethics in Aboriginal research: Comments on paradigms, process, and two worlds. *Canadian Journal of Aboriginal Community-based HIV/AIDS Research, 1*(1), 45–62.

Schnarch, B. (2004). Ownership, control, access, and possession (OCAP) or self-determination applied to research: A critical analysis of contemporary First Nations research and some options for First Nations communities. *Journal of Aboriginal Health, 1*(1), 80–95.

Treasury Board of Canada. (2010). *Guidance on preparing information sharing agreements involving personal information*. Retrieved from http://www.tbs-sct.gc.ca/atip-aiprp/isa-eer/isa-eer01-eng.asp

United Kingdom Home Office. (2013). *Multi-agency working and information sharing project: Early findings*. London, England: Government of the United Kingdom.

Wright, T. (1995). *Model data sharing agreement*. Toronto, ON: Information and Privacy Commission. Retrieved from http://www.ipc.on.ca/english/Resources/Best-Practices-and-Professional-Guidelines/Best-Practices-and-Professional-Guidelines-Summary/?id=301

PAMELA TIMANSON AND JOSÉ DA COSTA

7. LEARNING ORGANISATIONS AND THEIR RELATIONSHIP TO EDUCATIONAL IMPROVEMENT

A current trend in business and educational realms is the shift toward becoming learning organisations. In particular, Peter Senge's (1990) work initiated widespread interest in learning organisations through the publication of his book *The Fifth Discipline*, which encouraged companies to recognise the importance of becoming a learning organisation as a means to become more competitive in global markets. The learning organisation related literature that emerged subsequent to the publication of *The Fifth Discipline* is immense in terms of depth, breadth, and diversity.

Organisational learning and the learning organisation are intimately related concepts because the theoretical foundation for learning organisations originates in the organisational learning literature. If a distinction can be made, organisational learning literature focuses on the processes of learning in an organisation where the emphasis is on models and theories of how an organisation, as a collective, learns and evolves. The learning organisation literature tends to highlight characteristics of employee learning within an organisation; facilitating employee learning opportunities will allow the company to evolve sustaining its' competitiveness.

The literature on organisational learning extends back to the 1960s when interest in learning occurring at both the individual and organisational levels first appeared in the scholarly literature. Organisational learning is "the study of the learning processes of and within organizations [and researchers seek to] understand and critique what is taking place" (Easterby-Smith & Lyles, 2005, p. 2). It is "the deliberate use of individual, group, and system learning to embed new thinking and practices that continuously renew and transform the organization in ways that support shared aims" (Collinson & Cook, 2007, p. 8). Organisational learning is touted as being the vital component for an organisation's survival and its ability to adapt to the ever-changing dynamics of the work environment (Schechter & Feldman, 2010) because it provides an arena for innovation and transformation to occur within the organisation to sustain continuous improvement (Collinson, 2008).

A learning organisation, as defined by Easterby-Smith and Lyles (2005), is "an ideal type of organization, which has the capacity to learn effectively and hence to prosper" (p. 2). It is an organisation "where people continually expand their capacity to create the results they truly desire, where new and expansive patterns of thinking are nurtured, where collective aspiration is set free, and where people are continually

P. Newton & D. Burgess (Eds.), The Best Available Evidence, 99–112.

learning how to learn together" (Senge, 1990, p. 3). Having employees "who [can] think, work together, challenge each other, and innovate" (Forman, 2004, p. 2) resonates the importance of team learning in a competitive organisation (Rothwell, 2002). Companies who invest in human and knowledge capital encourage both the development of their enterprise and the development of their employees. They are a step ahead of their competitors, providing them with the potential to maximise their competitive advantage and maximise profit (Boud, 2003; Forman, 2004; Merriam, Caffarella, & Baumgartner, 2007; Rothwell, 2002).

HISTORICAL OVERVIEW

Organisational Learning

Four scholars have had a profound influence on the organisational learning literature, namely: John Dewey, Michel Polanyi, Edith Penrose, and Frederick Hayek. Learning organisation and organisational learning researchers have drawn upon Dewey's ideas of learning from experience and his description of the social construction of knowledge to explain the tools of the learning organisation and the individual learning that occurs within organisations. They have also drawn upon: (a) Polanyi's descriptions of tacit and explicit knowledge to describe the transfer of knowledge in organisational learning, (b) Penrose's argument on the importance of the human or internal resources of an organisation in explanations of human and knowledge capital, and (c) Hayek's economics perspective and his description of the importance of situated knowledge in descriptions of organisational learning (Easterby-Smith & Lyles, 2005).

Organisational learning originates in the work of Richard Cyert and James March (1963) who asserted that an organisation learns in ways that are independent of individual learning. As part of a decision-making model, they provided a general theory of organisational learning emphasising "the role of rules, procedures, and routines in response to external shocks and which are more or less likely to be adopted according to whether or not they lead to positive consequences for the organization" (Easterby-Smith & Lyles, 2005, p. 9). Their general theory pioneered the neorationalist tradition, the first tradition of organisational learning research. In 1965, Vincent Cangelosi and William Dill argued against the model proposed by Cyert and March declaring that the proposed model was only suitable for stable, established organisations. Their model of organisational learning focused instead on the series of interactions between the organisational and individual levels and the associated tensions or stresses in learning.

Just over ten years later, the work of Chris Argyris and Donald Schön (1978) contributed extensively to the organisational learning research field. They offered a critique of Cyert and March's rationalist model and deduced two models that described how an organisation inhibits (Model I) or enhances (Model II) learning. Argyris and Schön argued that human behaviour does not always follow the lines of economic rationality and that "both individuals and organizations seek to protect themselves from the unpleasant experience of learning by establishing defensive routines" (Easterby-Smith & Lyles, 2005, p. 10).

Much of the research following Argyris and Schön's initial contributions in the 1980s focused on providing definitions to terminology and to deepening understandings of organisational learning. In the 1990s, much of the research shifted back to focus on the neorationalist tradition, emphasising investigation into effective ways to use knowledge in organisations while balancing the realities of the various obstacles, such as human behaviour, prevalent in organisations (Easterby-Smith & Lyles, 2005). Some authors of note contributing to this era's research include: March (1991), Huber (1991), and Simon (1991). During this same time period, a parallel stream of research grounded in the social processes of organisational learning emerged. Authors such as Lave (1988), Lave and Wenger (1991), and Cook and Yanow (1993) made important contributions to this area of research. These streams are still prevalent in the organisational literature and continue to be distinctive, as research has progressed.

Learning Organisations

The organisational learning literature has focused on the processes of learning in organisation where the emphasis has been on models and theories of how an organisation learns and evolves. The concept of a learning organisation extends from the organisational learning literature and highlights the characteristics of employee learning within an organisation. It arose in the late 1980s in the UK from a few authors, the most notable being Arie de Geus (1988) who declared that in order for an organisation to be able to respond effectively to changes in the business environment, its members must focus on learning and in particular, institutional learning. A significant turning point in the learning organisation literature came from Peter Senge's (1990) research. Drawing upon technical and social systems theory from Jay Forrester, Chris Argyris, and Edgar Schein, Senge reconceptualised how organisations could renew and grow in order to increase their competition in global markets. Senge's (1990) work centred on five fundamental premises for the members of organisations:

1. systems thinking – a focus on the complexity of the world and how individuals are all connected to it, the whole represents a synergy of its parts which is greater than a simple sum of those parts;
2. personal mastery – recognition of the reciprocity between the individual and the organisation with commitment to ongoing learning through a constructivist lens that is focused on continuous improvement of the individual given his or her place in the larger organisation;
3. mental models – assumptions of how we understand the world are questioned and competing understandings are actively sought out to challenge that which is taken

101

for granted, a central goal is to learn from others and to be able to make one's reasoning explicit so others may understand and challenge;

4. building a shared vision – through intrinsic motivation people choose to excel and to learn, to do so requires individuals to come together through commitment to each other to imagine what a future might look like;

5. team learning – a process through which individuals, at least temporarily, suspend personal assumptions to engage in meaningful dialogue which respects and supports the individual members of the team.

His research inspired volumes of research and writing in this area, with most of the research being completed in Europe (Easterby-Smith & Lyles, 2005).

SCHOOLS AS LEARNING ORGANISATIONS

As with other organisations in the 1990s, schools were also strongly encouraged to become learning organisations. The emphasis in the schools as learning organisations literature and research has been predominantly on teacher collaboration to solve problems of teaching and learning. In these schools, learning networks were established to provide teachers with opportunities to talk, deliberate, and share ideas with each other (Schechter & Feldman, 2010). "[S]chools would develop innovative structures and processes that enable them to develop the professional capacity to learn in, and respond quickly and flexibly to, their unpredictable and changing environments" (Giles & Hargreaves, 2006, p. 126). Within the context of schools as learning organisations, teachers collaborated in ways that highlighted the connections between intra- and interpersonal learning and the importance of organisational learning at the school level. The end goal of these activities focused on enabling their schools to be able to change and succeed (Giles & Hargreaves, 2006). As in other organisations, schools were encouraged to shift away from traditional, individual, and isolated learning to learning that was collective and interdependent (Collinson, 2008). The most prevalent and popular way schools demonstrated their transition to becoming learning organisations was in the creation of communities of practice (CoPs) or professional learning communities (PLCs), emphasising the tradition of social processes of organisational learning.

Traditions of Organisational Learning in Schools

Social processes of learning. Many different types of community-oriented approaches have, and continue to be, used in education. These include: (a) Inquiry Communities, (b) Professional Learning Communities, (c) Teacher Professional Communities, (d) Communities of Learners, and (e) Communities of Practice (Levine, 2010). Each of these communities provides a space for teachers to participate in professional conversations and engage in ongoing collaboration to produce teacher learning (Levine, 2010; Levine & Marcus, 2007). However, they differ in what teachers create together, the mechanisms of learning, and in their limitations (Levine, 2010).

A CoP is characterised as staff members, from all levels of career development, learning together. It is "groups of people informally bound together by shared expertise and passion for a joint enterprise" (Wenger & Snyder, 2000, p. 1). Learning is brought about through a sense of belonging to the community, by developing individuals' professional identity, and constructing meaning out of experiences (Wenger, 1998). Individuals participate in the CoP, engaging in conversations examining practices, and generating ideas to solve problems. Participating in a CoP reflects the situated theory of learning where "knowing is intertwined with doing" within a sociocultural context (Merriam et al., 2007, p. 160). Language is "everything that has meaning" and for members of an organisation, this constitutes the main communication form through which they share and construct knowledge within their culture (Biesta & Burbules, 2003, p. 29).

A PLC is a variation of a CoP in which a group of teachers within a school work collaboratively to collectively improve pedagogy and student achievement (Levine, 2010). A PLC has a shared vision and "is seen as a powerful staff development approach and potent strategy for school change and improvement" (Cranston, 2009, p. 2). Giles and Hargreaves (2006) contended that PLCs in schools emphasise "collaborative work and discussion among the school's professionals, a strong and consistent focus on teaching and learning within that collaborative work, and the collection and use of assessment and other data to inquire into and evaluate progress over time" (p. 126). The potential benefits of PLCs include enabling schools to make sustainable improvements and "through teamwork and dispersed leadership, they build the professional capacity to solve problems and make decisions expeditiously" (Giles & Hargreaves, 2006, p. 126). The PLC concept is strongly ingrained within many school systems and jurisdictions, particularly in North America, where schools have been strongly encouraged to develop PLCs through various government or district-level policies and initiatives.

Neorationalist tradition. In order for organisations to maintain a competitive advantage, they have to be able to learn at both the individual and organisational level and be able to generate and manage knowledge. Quite often in the literature, the differences between learning and knowledge are confounded as these terms are used interchangeably. For the purposes of this chapter, learning is the process of acquiring an understanding or comprehension, and knowledge encompasses beliefs and casual understandings that are accumulated when different groups within organisations gain a new understanding or comprehension through reflection and abstraction (Chakravarthy, McEvily, Doz, & Rau, 2005).

An organisation maintains an advantage against its competitors when it possesses a deep knowledge base, particularly with respect to resource conversion and market positioning knowledge. Resource conversion knowledge refers to organisations' abilities to create unique products and services using the same generic resources that are available to all organisations. Market positioning knowledge is evident in organisations able to survey their work environment and perceive potential opportunities or avoid threats or obstacles (Chakravarthy et al., 2005). Other ways organisations can maintain competitive advantage include the ability to: (a) reflect periodically on their deep knowledge base; (b) effectively balance their resource conversion knowledge with their market positioning knowledge; (c) have more specific, complex, and tacit knowledge in their knowledge base; (d) be able to apply their deep knowledge base to new tasks or objectives in order to refine that knowledge and enrich and synthesise it with other knowledge resources; and (e) allow their employees opportunities for networking and frequent exchange between experts, thus enabling a diversity of knowledge bases to be shared and a variety of approaches to be discussed (Chakravarthy et al., 2005).

Schools are faced with the need to best serve their students in order to standard student learning, typically measured and reported through rudimentary achievement tests and high school completion rates. Interestingly, many teachers engage in these growth-oriented activities in hopes that their students will achieve at higher levels on various standardized measures than they have before or than students at other schools, focusing on the achievement measures as the end. This is not surprising given the trend over the past several decades toward simplistic rating systems drawing comparisons across schools within school jurisdictions, jurisdictions across provinces or states, and across countries internationally (e.g., PISA, TIMSS). Schechter and Feldman (2010) argued that in their efforts to maintain a competitive advantage, schools have tended to focus more on learning of subject content than on their knowledge management. They argued that schools place an "overemphasis on contents to be learned, instead of on the processes of knowledge acquisition, creation, dissemination, and integration" (p. 493). The learning opportunities provided to teachers, according to Schechter (2008), should "lead to new and diverse knowledge bases be[ing] developed" (p. 158). Teachers should be provided with opportunities to network and exchange information on a continual basis, shifting the focus to knowledge management, thus providing another alternative for achieving sustainable school improvement.

CONCEPTUALISING ORGANISATIONAL LEARNING

From Argyris and Schön's perspective that organisational learning occurs as individuals are learning within the organisation and Cyert and March's argument that organisations learn in the same fashion as individuals, there has been a wealth of research completed attempting to conceptualise organisational learning. One such area is a cultural perspective on organisational learning. Culture, as defined by Cook and Yanow (1993), is "a set of values, beliefs, and feelings, together with the artifacts of their expression and transmission, that are created, inherited, shared, and transmitted within one group of people and that, in part, distinguish that group from others" (p. 379). Culture is embodied in the language used by the individuals in the organisation, their artifacts or material objects, and in their routines. There is an inherent dialectic, as learning is an intrinsic part of culture and an awareness of culture is an essential component for facilitating learning (Weick & Westley, 1996).

The embedded knowledge of communities includes rituals, routines, practices, and past history of experiences of what worked and did not work. Weick and Westley (1996) argued that CoP are able to socially construct knowledge through "routines consisting of small continuous changes in the interest of frequent, adaptive updating rather than less frequent convulsing and crisis" (p. 443) in order to guide future practice and action. In this case, learning occurs as a result of individuals' active participation and interaction within their CoP and from their questioning, debate, and contemplation. Within this cultural perspective, organisations endeavor to create opportunities for individuals to continually interact and work with one another. Individuals do not learn in isolation nor away from their workplace, instead they are immersed in a sociocultural context where they learn with and through others.

Robinson (2002) conceptualised organisational learning as attempts to generate new solutions to organisational problems either through deliberative or non-deliberative learning processes. The deliberative learning process is a classical approach and represents learning that is strategically created, planned, and organised through meeting processes. The day-to-day work is interrupted in order for individuals to have the opportunity "to deliberate on symbolic representations of relevant tasks. New organisational routines and practices arise when task representations are manipulated through discussion, calculation and imagination, and the resulting symbolic products are implemented" (Robinson, 2002, p. 783). Motivation and communication are the primary concerns of this deliberative process. Learning is often decontextualised, since the knowledge required exists within the heads of the individuals participating in the deliberations (Robinson, 2002). The deliberative learning process is a common occurrence in schools, as teachers are routinely removed from their classrooms in order to attend conferences, meetings, or professional development days.

In the non-deliberative learning process, organisational learning occurs through feedback mechanisms embedded in tasks. It is unreflective and adaptive and occurs within the context in which it is to be applied (Robinson, 2002). Non-deliberative learning processes are context-based because knowledge is assumed to exist "in the heads of others with which [individuals] interact and in the tools and other cultural products that help them to do the work" (Robinson, 2002, p. 785). The historical artifacts of the organisation play a significant role in this learning process, as individuals use the tools and infrastructure of their organisation to complete their work tasks. The non-deliberative learning process is not used as often in schools because the emphasis is placed on new initiatives and improvements, as opposed to using educational tools and infrastructure from the past to refine teaching pedagogy.

Schechter (2008) conceptualised organisational learning as occurring through learning processes that are designed and implemented to promote learning. These processes can include activities, structures, and strategies that "focus on gathering and assimilating information from both internal (organizational) experiences and external (environment) changes that lead to better internal adaptations" (Schechter, 2008, p. 158). The learning processes are a part of the management science perspective and consist of five phases of an information processing or a learning cycle: (a) information acquisition (i.e., obtain knowledge), (b) information distribution (i.e., share information), (c) information interpretation (i.e., find meaning), (d) organisational memory (i.e., experiences are stored and coded), and (e) retrieving information from memory for organisational use (i.e., draw on encoded information) (Schechter, 2008; Schechter & Feldman, 2010). Individual learning in this cycle is perceived as being cyclical and interactive, as individuals work together to gather and process information. This cycle is an on-going process within the CoP, where individuals are active participants.

Schechter and Feldman (2010) asserted that organisations could support this cyclical learning process through structural and cultural perspectives. An example of this in schools is evident through the provision of time during the workday, by administration, for teachers to meet on an ongoing basis, thus allowing them the necessary time to share information and collectively construct understandings and knowledge. In this example, the administrators are implementing an integrated approach to organisational learning and supporting the cyclical learning process of their staff.

Organisational learning, according to Schechter (2008), is not simply the sum of the overall quantity of knowledge possessed by each individual; rather, it is more complicated and intricate. Just as individuals learn, organisations have a cognitive system that is distinct from individual cognition. The cognitive system of an organisation "enable[s] them to acquire, perceive, and interpret information in a way similar, although not identical, to the individual learning process" (Schechter, 2008, p. 159). An organisational cognitive system can be observed through organisational routines or in the procedures carried out by the individuals of the organisation. In a school, the organisational cognitive system can be found in the structure of classroom activities, the functioning of the school, the teaching strategies used, and in how the rules and/or policies are enacted.

In her conception of organisational learning, Collinson (2008) emphasised both the leaders and the followers of the organisation share the responsibility of establishing an environment conducive to organisational learning. The leaders and followers are responsible for influencing and sustaining the four environments affecting organisational learning: (a) intellectual (i.e., learning, inquiry and innovation); (b) ethical (i.e., explicit and tacit attitudes and values); (c) social (i.e., leveraging feedback, dissemination, and collective inquiry); and (d) political (i.e., members' ability to function as change agents). Collinson (2008) argued that there is great potential for organisational learning in schools and that more efforts need to be made to link the collaborative work of CoPs or PLCs to the establishment of the four environments. This conception of organisational learning in schools focuses on and encourages more in-depth learning experiences for both administrators and teachers, and would lead to enhanced school improvement initiatives.

IMPLICATIONS FOR SCHOOLS AND SCHOOL IMPROVEMENT

Evaluating Organisational Learning

As has been established through this chapter, the premise for school improvement initiatives are for schools to function as a learning organisation. School leaders are responsible for guiding their teachers through organisational learning processes, and indirectly influencing student learning and achievement (Kurland, Peretz, & Lazarowitz, 2010; Ylimaki & Jacobson, 2013). In their efforts, school leaders are confronted with various challenges; these include how "to create conditions that enable everyone in the school to have a sense of individual and collective vision and purpose while feeling a sense of ownership in the change processes in which they are involved and to engage their faculty in processes of learning and development at regular intervals" (Ylimaki & Jacobson, 2013, p. 13). Therefore, an evaluation of organisational learning processes can help a school leader determine their progress in establishing their school as a learning organisation and of the impact these processes are having on student learning (Levin-Rozalis & Rosenstein, 2005).

A primary concern for school leaders in the facilitation of teachers working together in PLCs and on various initiatives is the means of evaluating and supervising teachers. Traditionally school leaders have used an individual classroom approach (i.e., principal observes teachers in their classrooms) to instructional leadership in order to evaluate and improve instructional practices. However, teachers work together in PLCs and new means of evaluating and supervising teachers are needed in order to evaluate the quality and achievements of the teachers' collaborative efforts (Gajda & Koliba, 2008). Gajda and Koliba (2008) describe a teacher collaborative framework that can assist school leaders in improving the quality of teacher collaboration within their PLCs. This framework is based on the premise of having the principal be more transparent in his or her decision-making processes and expectations for, and examinations of, student learning. Principals should also be proactive in creating the necessary space, time, and learning opportunities for teacher collaboration. A framework such as this would provide a school leader the necessary means of evaluating the organisational learning processes within his or her school, ultimately continuing the progression of improved instructional practices and student learning.

Associated Issues with Schools as Learning Organisations

As schools have striven to become learning organisations, they have encountered issues. Schools are faced with the struggle of trying to facilitate social learning in conventional structures. Schools are challenged to create flexible learning spaces and the time necessary for learning. This has led to the criticism of teachers participating in contrived collaboration or "interactional congeniality" as opposed to delving into issues that may cause conflict between teachers (Giles & Hargreaves, 2006). Some school leaders and teachers have been able to successfully create the time and space within their schools to facilitate the social learning of their teachers and leaders. However, these schools often are not able to extend this social learning to other teacher communities. Thus, schools as learning organisations might be isolated to a small community of learners as opposed to extending outwards to the rest of their profession (Giles & Hargreaves, 2006).

This contrived collaboration and isolated teacher communities can lead to "groupthink". This manifests itself when "members insulate themselves from alternative ideas – turning shared visions into shared delusions" (Giles & Hargreaves, 2006, p. 127). Without having external influences and the opportunity for conflicting views to be expressed, teachers do not experience disruption to their norms, values, and exposure to alternative ideas. Further to this, the formal meeting of the PLC is encouraged and valued more so than the informal interactions that occurs amongst teachers outside of the PLC meetings. In this manner, school leaders promote the "formal cognitive processes of problem-solving, systems-thinking, and collective inquiry at the expense of the informal relationships and social networks that build a strong sense of professional community" (Giles & Hargreaves, 2006, p. 127). The interactions between teachers in and about their school are not considered as important as the ones occurring within the PLC environment.

Organisational Learning and School Improvement

The field of research on organisational learning that has emerged over the past decades is divergent in orientation, leading to confusion in the definition and feasibility of organisational learning (Schechter, 2008; Schechter & Feldman, 2010). Schools have been especially susceptible to this confusion and have sometimes been unable to move past the conceptual level of organisational learning. The literature focusing on schools becoming learning organisations seems to center around "coordinated group efforts, professional development programs, shared goals, active commitment to continuous improvement, horizontal networks of information flow, sufficient resources, open culture, and teacher leadership" (Schechter & Feldman, 2010, p. 493); it does not address in any substantive way how to translate these concepts into practical structures and processes in schools. Schools, instead, are floundering in their implementation of organisational learning because of a lack of structural guidance, leading to various conceptual interpretations, or perhaps misinterpretations, and a lack of notable change or improvement in schools. Ultimately, the term organisational learning "has come into wide usage without necessarily conveying clear meanings or reflecting a significant change in practice" (Schechter & Feldman, 2010, p. 493).

Evidence of how schools are floundering in their implementation of organisational learning is apparent in many school improvement initiatives. Schools are faced with many different problems as they strive to improve learning and increase student achievement. It is of upmost importance that teachers are able to differentiate between problems that are trivial and those that are crucial. If school staff members spend too much time focusing on trivial problems, then they will reduce the educational value that can be gained from organisational learning (Robinson, 2002). This is often evident in the various policies that have been implemented to encourage schools to reform and improve. These policies often emphasise the amount of learning experienced by teachers as opposed to focusing on the value of what the teachers are learning. Often, the focus of organisational learning in schools is more about superficial activities that can be easily quantified and give the appearance of change (Robinson, 2002).

It is possible, as Robinson (2002) argued, "that a great deal of organizational learning that goes on in educational settings is the learning of policies and procedures which are falsely assumed to have a positive impact on the learning of students" (p. 806). This is seen continuously in schools, with teachers and administrators being bombarded by new initiatives they are required to implement. It is believed that all of these initiatives will make significant improvements to school effectiveness and student achievement but very few of them last long enough or result in the improvements promised. The current state of organisational learning in schools is imbalanced and "perpetuates a limited capacity for noticing, developing and utilizing the cues and resources needed to tune organizational learning to matters of greater educational significance" (Robinson, 2002, p. 808). The emphasis for organisational learning in schools is placed on narrow conceptions of school improvement as a strategic process, rather than on improving student learning and the growth of teachers as professionals.

FINAL THOUGHTS

While the notions underlying the learning organisation and organisational learning hold much promise, and there do appear to be a few positive examples from which to draw, the true intent of the learning organisation does not seem to have been realised in the vast majority of schools over the past two decades. Any number of explanations can be provided for the failed promise of organisational learning. Perhaps the most compelling reason for this is the overemphasis on system-directed and administratively controlled learning imposed on teachers for the purposes of achieving external or governmental learning targets. This leaves little or no time for teachers to share and create meaningful knowledge and to implement change at the school level which can lead to improved learning for all children, learning that is not demonstrated merely through results on standardised tests, but demonstrated through student and professional engagement in authentic communities of practice.

Questions also remain about the roles teachers play in CoP or PLCs with regard to their fundamental abilities and willingness to engage each other as imagined by Senge (1990) in learning organisations. Some of these questions include:

1. Is there something about the inability of the individuals to suspend assumptions and to take a more complex systems view rather than a simple linear view of the world?
2. Is there something at a personal level that requires participants to trust and respect each other, both teaching colleagues and school administration, for a true learning organisation to materialise?
3. Is it possible that schools cannot be true learning organisations since visions of what it means to be an outstanding school are typically identified and provided in a top-down model (i.e., government defines the end goal of education systems and provides the measures by which this will be determined), school leaders and teachers simply *tinker* with minor deviations at the fringes of the vision to give the impression of engagement in vision development?

Furthermore, the very notion of publicly funded organisations may not lend themselves to conforming to the principles underlying learning organisations. Competition among school systems seems to exist only on a superficial level in which governments and *think-tanks* compare systems using easily obtainable and superficial measures. Measures commonly used such as PISA and TIMSS typically fail to measure how knowledge is created, shared, and managed. These measures also fail to take into account school level influences such as the socio-economic status of the learners and their families and the beliefs held by learners' families of the value of education.

This leaves us with a final question about schools as learning organisations: *How can stakeholders (i.e., leaders, teachers, students, families, community partners) in publicly funded organisations be motivated intrinsically to come together to learn from each other, to co-create a shared vision that is better than whatever the current circumstances might be?*

Many governments around the world have moved to commodify education by introducing systems that give, at least on some levels, decision-making autonomy about education to the local level. With this shift there has been devolution of resources to the local level (typically accompanied by school choice policies in which funding follows students), but at the cost of much higher accountability, often based on the very measures critiqued above, and highly centralised curricula. This Neo-liberal commodification of education is mostly in keeping with the principles underlying learning organisations. However, it does little to address issues of equity for those students and families who either live in communities where alternatives are simply not available or do not have the resources to move to the schools whose CoP or PLCs have resulted in competitive edges over other schools.

REFERENCES

Argyris, C., & Schön, D. A. (1978). *Organizational learning: A theory of action perspective.* Reading, MA: Addison-Wesley.

Biesta, G., & Burbules, N. (2003). From experience to knowledge. In G. Biesta & N. Burbules (Eds.), *Pragmatism and educational research* (pp. 25–54). Lanham, MD: Rowman & Littlefield.

Boud, D. (Ed.). (2003). *Current issues and new agendas in workplace learning.* Adelaide, Australia: National Centre for Vocational Education Research Ltd. Retrieved from www.ncver.edu.au

Cangelosi, V. E., & Dill, W. R. (1965). Organizational learning: Observations toward a theory. *Administrative Science Quarterly, 10*(2), 175–203.

Chakravarthy, B., McEvily, S., Doz, Y., & Rau, D. (2005). Knowledge management and competitive advantage. In M. Easterby-Smith & M. A. Lyles (Eds.), *Handbook of organizational learning and knowledge management* (pp. 305–323). Oxford, UK: Blackwell Publishing.

Collinson, V. (2008). Leading by learning: New directions in the twenty-first century. *Journal of Educational Administration, 46*(4), 443–460. doi:10.1108/09578230810881992

Collinson, V., & Cook, T. F. (2007). *Organizational learning: Improving learning, teaching, and leading in school systems.* Thousand Oaks, CA: Sage.

Cook, S. D. N., & Yanow, D. (1993). Culture and organizational learning. *Journal of Management Inquiry, 2*(4), 373–390.

Cranston, J. (2009). Holding the reins of the professional learning community: Eight themes from research on principals' perceptions of professional learning communities. *Canadian Journal of Educational Administration and Policy, 90*, 1–22.

Cyert, R. M., & March, J. G. (1963). *A behavioural theory of the firm.* Englewood Cliffs, NJ: Prentice-Hall.

De Geus, A. P. (1988). Planning as learning. *Harvard Business Review, 66*(2), 70–74.

Easterby-Smith, M., & Lyles, M. A. (Eds.). (2005). *Handbook of organizational learning and knowledge management.* Malden, MA: Blackwell Publishing.

Forman, D. C. (2004). Changing perspectives from individual to organizational learning. *International Society for Performance Improvement, 43*(7), 1–7.

Gajda, R., & Koliba, C. J. (2008). Evaluating and improving the quality of teacher collaboration: A field-tested framework for secondary school leaders. *NASSP Bulletin, 92*(2), 133–153. doi:10.1177/0192636508320990

Giles, C., & Hargreaves, A. (2006). The sustainability of innovative schools as learning organizations and professional learning communities during standardized reform. *Educational Administration Quarterly, 42*(1), 124–156. doi:10.1177/0013161X05278189

Huber, G. P. (1991). Organizational learning: The contributing processes and the literature. *Organization Science, 2*(1), 88–115.

Kurland, H., Peretz, H., & Hertz-Lazarowitz, R. (2010). Leadership style and organizational learning: The mediate effect of school vision. *Journal of Educational Administration, 48*(1), 7–30. doi:10.1108/09578231011015395

Lave, J. (1988). *Cognition in practice: Mind, mathematics and culture in everyday life.* Cambridge: Cambridge University Press.

Lave, J., & Wenger, E. (1991). *Situated learning: Legitimate peripheral participation.* New York, NY: Cambridge University Press.

Levin-Rozalis, M., & Rosenstein, B. (2005). The changing role of the evaluator in the process of organizational learning. *The Canadian Journal of Program Evaluation, 20*(1), 81–104.

Levine, T., & Marcus, A. (2007). Closing the achievement gap through teacher collaboration: Facilitating multiple trajectories of teacher learning. *Journal of Advanced Academics, 19*(1), 116–138.

Levine, T. H. (2010). Tools for the study and design of collaborative teacher learning: The affordances of different conceptions of teacher community and activity theory. *Teacher Education Quarterly, 37*(1), 109–130.

March, J. G. (1991). Exploration and exploitation in organizational learning. *Organization Science, 2*(1), 71–87.

Merriam, S. B., Caffarella, R. S., & Baumgartner, L. (2007). *Learning in adulthood: A comprehensive guide* (3rd ed.). San Francisco, CA: Jossey-Bass.

Robinson, V. M. J. (2002). Organizational learning, organizational problem solving and models of mind. In K. Leithwood & P. Hallinger (Eds.), *Second international handbook of educational leadership and administration* (pp. 775–812). Dordrecht, The Netherlands: Klewer.

Rothwell, W. J. (2002). *The workplace learner*. New York, NY: American Management Association.

Schechter, C. (2008). Organizational learning mechanisms: The meaning, measure, and implications for school improvement. *Educational Administration Quarterly, 44*(2), 155–186. doi:10.1177/0013161X07312189

Schechter, C., & Feldman, N. (2010). Exploring organizational learning mechanisms in special education. *Journal of Educational Administration, 48*(4), 490–516. doi:10.1108/09578231011054734

Senge, P. M. (1990). *The fifth discipline: The art and practice of the learning organization*. London: Century Business.

Simon, H. (1991). Bounded rationality and organizational learning. *Organization Science, 2*(1), 125–134.

Weick, K. E., & Westley, F. (1996). Organizational learning: Affirming an oxymoron. In S. R. Glegg, C. Handy, & W. R. Nord (Eds.), *Handbook of organization studies* (pp. 440–458). Thousand Oaks, CA: Sage.

Wenger, E. (1998). *Communities of practice: Learning, meaning, and identity*. New York, NY: Cambridge University Press.

Wenger, E., & Snyder, W. (2000). Communities of practice: The organizational frontier. *Harvard Business Review, 78*(1), 139–145.

Ylimaki, R., & Jacobson, S. (2013). School leadership practice and preparation: Comparative perspectives on organizational learning, instructional leadership, and culturally responsive practices. *Journal of Educational Administration, 51*(1), 6–23. doi:10.1108/09578231311291404

VICKI SQUIRES

8. THE ASSESSMENT IMPERATIVE

Evidence-Based Decision Making in Student Affairs

As discussed elsewhere in this volume, there is an increasing emphasis in post-secondary education on collecting and analyzing multiple forms and sources of data to support evidence-informed decision making (Black, 2010; Bresciani, 2006; Gotteil & Smith, 2011; Hollowell, Middaugh, & Sibolski, 2006; Laidler, 2005; Middaugh, 2010; Steele, 2010). This trend is evident throughout administrative units, such as student affairs, where previous assessment practices often consisted of metrics including enrolment numbers, and satisfaction surveys (Bresciani, Gardner, & Hickmott, 2009; Hardy Cox & Strange, 2010; Kuh, Kinzie, Schuh, & Whitt, 2010; Ouellete, 2010; Schuh, 2009). This chapter describes assessment practice as it is manifested currently in student affairs units in Canadian post-secondary institutions. Included in this description is a discussion of the emergent emphasis on accountability and institutional assessment. The chapter briefly outlines the role of student affairs in supporting the university's mission of teaching, learning, and research. Following this description is a summary of the changing expectations in student affairs concerning the role of data in informing practice. The chapter focuses on assessment project considerations, including types of assessment and forms of data, as well as analysis and communication of the results. In the final section, some examples of assessment projects are presented.

Assessment in Post-Secondary Education

The dialogue and action surrounding assessment in student affairs is situated within the larger context of the research, teaching and learning mission of the post-secondary institution, and the increasing emphasis on assessment. There is increasing scrutiny and emphasis on accountability from internal and external stakeholders, including governments, agencies, and the general public; the stakeholders expect evidence to demonstrate improved graduation and retention rates, enhanced student success including career transition (Bresciani, 2006; Hollowell et al., 2006; Schuh, 2009). Kuk, Banning, and Amey (2010) argued that this trend will continue. "As accountability and metrics assume a greater role in institutional decision making, emphasis on being able to measure and to justify the effectiveness of existing organizations, and their programs and services, will increase"

P. Newton & D. Burgess (Eds.), The Best Available Evidence, 113–128.
© 2016 Sense Publishers. All rights reserved.

(Kuk et al., 2010, p. 204). This is especially important in an environment of increasing competition for scarce resources (Kuk et al., 2010). Hollowell et al. (2006) contended that the "escalating emphasis on accountability is related, in part, to perceptions that colleges and universities do not plan carefully or assess their effectiveness" (p. 3). The purposeful use of data in post-secondary institutions to determine effectiveness and plan future directions will change that perception and enhance accountability and transparency.

Middaugh (2010) pointed out that this type of assessment is "different from scholarly research, more akin to action research. The primary objective of institutional assessment is to produce information that can be used in decision making and institutional improvement" (p. 124). Post-secondary institutions need to collect and analyze "robust evidence" (Fullan & Scott, 2009, p. 80), rather than relying on anecdotal evidence. In addition to measuring student performance, the data can be used to improve instructional practices, to gather feedback on program outcomes, and to enhance the student experience. Kuh et al. (2010) emphasized this point, and stated that "doing assessment right also contributes to a supportive campus climate" (p. 280). The process of assessment needs to incorporate all parts of the student lifecycle and all parts of the institution (Black, 2010). Interestingly, Laidler (2005) argued that "universities seem to respond to the desires of those who provide them with the resources they need to operate and if the importance of students in this respect is increasing, then they are likely to get more attention" (p. 44). As the importance of enrolment targets increases, so too will the emphasis on capturing and analyzing student outcomes and perceptions.

Not only must data about the current state of the institution be collected and analyzed, but it must be used to inform subsequent planning and action. Hollowell et al. (2006) asserted: "Quantitative and qualitative information about all facets of a college or university's operations—and how they relate to the institutional mission—is absolutely essential to good planning" (p. 69). According to Fullan and Scott (2009), a strong university-wide culture of assessment is demonstrated by a commitment to ongoing, systematic assessment and evaluation in order to generate information for two purposes. With a view of the present, the evidence can be used to determine what is working well and what needs modifying. With a view to the future, the evidence can be used to determine optimal directions and determine priorities that will promote sustainability for the university and position it well to respond to the changing environment (Fullan & Scott, 2009). Middaugh (2010) reiterated the point that the data needed to be used as the basis for strategic planning, decision making and resource allocation. The intentional gathering of data and the thorough analysis of the information are essential in informing future direction.

Student Affairs in Universities

Student affairs (also referred to as student services) in post-secondary education incorporates a variety of services that support students throughout their academic journey, encompassing the student lifecycle from the prospective student stage through graduation to alumnus (Black, 2010). The overall structure and array of services provided varies across post-secondary institutions. Ouelette (2010) posited that student services encapsulates a broad range of services, but noted that the range of services can be categorized as falling into three general groups: (a) recruitment, admissions and orientation services; (b) engagement and support services; and (c) graduating and career development services The movement towards viewing student issues holistically is critical, in Ouelette's opinion, because the issues that students encounter are not isolated problems; the individual issues and interrelated dynamics have an impact on overall student success.

This holistic approach to provision of services and programs can support the achievement of institutional and student goals. In their description of the work of student affairs administrators, Creamer, Winston, and Miller (2001) noted that these administrators perform essential roles that contribute to the organization's effectiveness and daily operations, and support student success. Through these actions, they contribute to the educational mission of the post-secondary institutions. Kuh, Siegel, and Thomas (2001) concurred, and noted that student affairs managers "are responsible for the stewardship of student and institutional resources and deploying those resources in ways that will have the maximum positive impact on student learning and personal development" (p. 60). Ouellete (2010) emphasized that explicit tying of the academic mission to student services and enhanced partnerships between academic and administrative units can result in better solutions and more effective supports for students. In Kuh et al.'s (2010) study of successful colleges and universities, those post-secondary institutions demonstrating exemplary student affairs practices had policies and services that were strongly "aligned with and complimented the institution's educational purposes and objectives" (Kuh et al., 2010, pp. 281–282). Part of the role of assessment in student affairs and throughout post-secondary institutions is the determination of whether articulated goals and objectives are being achieved.

Assessment in Student Affairs

The rationale for engaging in robust assessment practices in student affairs is similar to that of employing strong assessment practices throughout post-secondary institutions. Sullivan (2010) linked assessment in student affairs to priority setting, resource allocation, improved student success, and improved program outcomes. Because of the critical role that assessment played, it is essential that "Intentional and ongoing assessment of student learning and development and program outcomes should be part of each student services professional's mindset and of the institutional culture" (Sullivan, 2010, pp. 182–183). Kuk et al. (2010) pointed out that comprehensive assessment in student affairs can perform several functions. Assessment can provide information for determining strategic goals, for identifying progress in achieving prior goals, for demonstrating organizational effectiveness of

115

individual units or across all of the student services units, and for identifying gaps in service or areas for improvement. This view to the present and to the future was also emphasized by Palomba and Banta (1999): "Assessment can help service units with strategic planning, focusing on big issues and preparing for the future, and can also assist with immediate decisions such as how to improve services and reach appropriate audiences" (p. 290). Assessment should be an integral part of all of the activities in student affairs (Reynolds & Chris, 2008).

Strange and Hardy Cox (2010) articulated eight principles of best practice in student affairs; two of those principles, efficiency and effectiveness, are strongly tied to assessment. Strange and Hardy Cox (2010) stated that "ultimately, the effectiveness of a service is a measure of its contribution to the overall learning mission of the university" (p. 241). They averred that post-secondary institutions needed to be efficient and sustainable and that the institutions needed to focus on results-oriented effectiveness. Efficiency can be conceived as producing the best outcome with the least cost, and ensuring that the program can be sustainable (Strange & Hardy Cox, 2010). Collection of data helps to determine if efficiency is being realized. Additionally, the data can demonstrate effectiveness. Sullivan (2010) attested that "effective units oversee the resources, mobilize and maximize system capacity and then assess outcomes to determine impact, stimulate learning, and guide continuous improvement" (p. 182). Ongoing assessment is a key piece of continuous improvement.

Similarly, Bresciani et al. (2009) proposed that there were three main reasons to engage in outcomes-based assessment: (a) accountability, resources and funding; (b) policy, planning, and programming; and (c) creating a culture of continuous improvement. First, assessment results can demonstrate to internal and external stakeholders how student support services contribute to student learning and development. The results can also demonstrate the effective use of resources and show the value added by student services in supporting student well being. Second, the data generated through assessment can inform decisions around strategic planning, determine strengths and weaknesses in programming, and identify priorities moving forward. Finally, through intentional development of a culture of assessment in student affairs, all stakeholders become engaged in a continual improvement process that becomes "systematic, pervasive, and collaborative" (Bresciani et al., 2009, p. 28). The assessment culture needs to become embedded within the way that student affairs units operate.

Schuh and Upcraft (2001) articulated seven reasons to engage in assessment in student affairs. In addition to quality, affordability, policy development and decision making, accreditation, and strategic planning, they added survival and politics to the list. They believed that "in the era of declining resources and increased competition for what precious few resources there are, student affairs has come under the institutional financial microscope" (Schuh & Upcraft, 2001, p. 9). Assessment results can help demonstrate the value and worth of the student services supports and programs; survival of these services requires proof of value to student success and to the institution itself. Although national studies may point to the effectiveness and value of particular services, local assessment efforts can demonstrate positive outcomes within the environment of a particular post-secondary institution (Schuh & Upcraft, 2001). Schuh and Upcraft (2001) contended that "all assessment is political" (p. 12); staff and faculty engaging in assessment projects need to keep that viewpoint in mind in the design, implementation, and dissemination stages of assessment.

The Assessment Process

The cyclical process of assessment must include an intentional connection to the mission and goals of the unit and of the university. Palomba and Banta (1999) stated: "The assessment plan should include a clear purpose related to the mission, goals, program objectives, and learning outcomes of the institution as a whole, and of the student affairs office" (p. 17). It is also critical to engage the appropriate stakeholders in the planning (Palomba & Banta). This process requires the necessary support from institutional leaders as they need to commit resources, including financial and human resources, to assessment initiatives and projects. According to Palomba and Banta (1999), "academic leaders—including presidents, provosts, deans, department chairs, and leaders in student affairs—must be public advocates for assessment and provide appropriate leadership as well as support for the faculty and staff closest to the assessment process" (p. 11). Ongoing support includes professional development regarding effective assessment because, as Banta, Jones, and Black (2009) noted, this type of learning is important not only for faculty but also for student affairs leaders and staff. The use of data and assessment in crafting mission statements, strategic plans and foundational institutional documents is a strong indicator of an institutional culture of assessment (Bresciani et al., 2009).

The steps of the assessment cycle include identifying the problem or question, determining the participants, designing the assessment process or tool, collecting and analyzing data, disseminating the results, determining adjustments and implementing those changes; then the cycle begins again (see Kuk et al., 2010; Palomba & Banta, 1999; Schuh & Upcraft, 2001). An important consideration throughout the assessment process is assurance that the assessment project is conducted ethically. Schuh (2009) outlined a basic framework for conducting assessments ethically on campuses. Elements of ethical assessments that are required to ensure protection of the welfare of the participants include informed consent, respect for autonomy, data access procedures, and dissemination of results in an ethical manner. The protocol varies from institution to institution; consultation with the particular Research Ethics Board ensures that proper ethical procedures are being followed (Schuh, 2009). Often, assessment projects that are undertaken as quality assurance methods do not require separate ethics protocol submissions. Part of the decision process regarding application for ethics approval includes identifying how the results will be used. If the information will be used to make internal decisions on how to improve a program, ethics approval is probably not required. If the information will be included in reports and presentations, and perhaps published in a journal, ethics approval is required. However, it is essential that particular campus procedures are followed.

Ethical considerations play a part in ongoing assessments throughout the program (formative assessments) or in final assessments to determine the overall success at the end of a program or course (summative assessment). Palomba and Banta (1999) described formative assessment as the kinds of assessment conducted during a program in order to gather information that can be used to modify or improve a program while it is in progress, whereas summative assessment is conducted at the end of a program to evaluate it and make judgments about its efficacy. Both types of assessment are beneficial, depending on the purpose for the information gathered. The type of assessment chosen should align with the particular purposes for the data (Palomba & Banta, 1999).

Types of Assessment

In the context of student affairs assessment, it is important to differentiate among the terms *assessment, evaluation*, and *research*. Upcraft and Schuh (1996), who were among the first writers in the field of student affairs assessment, articulated the differences. They defined assessment as "any effort to gather, analyze and interpret evidence which describes institutional, divisional, or agency effectiveness" (Upcraft & Schuh, 1996, p. 18). Evaluation is linked to assessment; "evaluation is any effort to use assessment evidence to improve departmental, divisional, or institutional effectiveness" (p. 19). Evaluation includes the dissemination of results and the use of the evidence to implement improvements or changes, and to determine future directions. Similarly, assessment and research are related. Assessment is used to inform practice, whereas research is used to inform the development of theories and the testing of ideas. Additionally, assessment is institution-specific, while research has broader implications for student affairs practices across institutions (Upcraft & Schuh, 1996).

Shared definitions and a conceptual framework or philosophy of assessment must be constructed among the student affairs units, and ideally across the institution (Bresciani, 2006).

The development of an assessment framework or model is critical for laying the foundation of the entire process. Janice and Scott (2006) proposed a comprehensive model that integrated the multiple dimensions of service, development, and learning that are embedded within student-affairs services. They emphasized that "a strong assessment model should provide a step-by-step sequential process in order to ensure accuracy and success of implementation by practitioners. Finally, embedded in the systematic approach of the model, the assessment process should be iterative" (Janice & Scott, 2006, p. 212). According to Sullivan (2010), students need to be involved in the development of the assessment processes and framework; their participation can be accomplished by inviting them to comment on how best to gather feedback, including their opinions on the types of assessment, the timing, and the venue most appropriate for data gathering.

Bresciani et al. (2009) described five distinct types of assessment used in student affairs. Needs assessment is a process to determine if there any gaps in terms of supports or services that students require or would like. The other four types of assessment provide information based on student participation in particular programs or services. Utilization assessment generates information on the use of a service or program, including numbers of participants, and demographic data regarding the participants. Assessment of satisfaction determines levels of student satisfaction with a particular program or a service. Pre- and post-assessment determines student learning based on their participation. Lastly, outcomes-based assessment of student learning and development determines whether students met learning objectives as a result of their participation (Bresciani et al., 2009).

Banta et al. (2009) posited that the types of assessment utilized in student affairs have progressed from the collection of numbers of participants or event attendees, and the distribution of student satisfaction surveys, towards assessing student learning and development resulting from participation in a service or program. As Kuh et al. (2001) pointed out, there has been a change in perception regarding where learning takes place; learning used to be the domain of the formal learning environment but is now perceived as occurring everywhere. This change in perception regarding the notion of what constitutes learning implies that student affairs units need to consider learning outcomes in their assessment plans.

Keeling (2006) proposed that assessment in student affairs needs to be more intentionally focused on student learning and outcomes based assessment. This type of assessment can play a strong role in strategic planning. However, in order to carry out meaningful and effective assessment, campuses need to invest in training and professional development. According to Keeling (2006), there are two important steps in the process. First, professional development and training of faculty and staff helps build capacity by increasing "their ability to write learning outcomes, create assessment plans, use assessment methods and tools, and prepare reports that document the work" (Keeling, 2006, p. 55). Then, the campus needs to engage in "cultural adaptation that shapes the attitudes, perspectives, and working styles necessary for effective use of outcomes and assessment techniques" (Keeling, 2006, p. 56). Keeling added that developing the skills to write meaningful learning outcomes was an iterative process that required time and a cultural shift. Banta et al. (2009) also emphasized that "outcomes assessment can be sustained only if planning and implementation take place in an atmosphere of trust and within a culture that encourages the use of evidence in decision making" (p. 8). Effective and meaningful assessment will develop only in a supportive culture that understands and engages in intentional assessment processes.

The move towards learning outcomes assessment in student affairs is reflected in the work of The Council for the Advancement of Standards in Higher Education (CAS) to develop a set of standards. The standards are designed around six domains of student learning and development outcomes for student affairs programs and services. These domains include: knowledge acquisition, construction, integration and application; cognitive complexity; intrapersonal development; interpersonal competence; humanitarianism and civic engagement; and practical competence (Council for the Advancement of Standards in Higher Education, 2012). The eighth edition of the *CAS Professional Standards for Higher Education* (2012) includes descriptions of these domains, and associated learning outcome dimensions; in addition, the manual outlines standards and guidelines for 44 functional areas for student programs and services across campus, as well as examples of student experience outcomes across many campus settings. By using CAS standards, student affairs professionals can ensure that objectives and measurable outcomes are being intentionally and carefully constructed and assessed. The ninth edition of this popular manual—scheduled to be released in August of 2015—should be part of every student-affairs' assessment toolbox.

There are several manuals specifically written regarding assessment in student affairs (see, for example, Schuh & Upcraft, 2001); these manuals provide detailed information regarding the assessment process, the types of data that could inform practice, and the design of appropriate assessment tools. Choosing the correct assessment method or tool is contingent on the objectives for gathering the data. Simple metrics such as attendance numbers, or numbers of students within particular demographic groups, are useful snapshots of information for program purposes. However, when pulling data from information management systems, data teams need to recognize the inherent flaws within any student information system. "Every data system has hidden and unquestioned assumptions built into its design" (Birnbaum, 1988, p. 219). The data team must contend with those assumptions when designing the assessment project.

Statistics and statistical trends provide key data for decision making. However, to determine student perceptions or achievement of student learning outcomes, individual or small group assessments will be necessary. From a resource capacity perspective, student surveys are useful tools to gather information from many students quickly and cost-effectively. Large, institutional surveys include the Canadian University Survey Consortium (CUSC), the National Survey of Student Engagement (NSSE), and the National College Health Assessment (NCHA) (Sullivan, 2010). Sullivan (2010) noted that surveys such as the NCHA that gather data on specific student attitudes and behaviours are especially helpful in making decisions on how to align resources to best support students. "Such assessments are critical for conveying the purpose and effect of student services on campus and the role it plays in supporting students' success" (Sullivan, 2010, p. 242). These institutional surveys provide useful comparative information, as campuses are given not only their own data, but also aggregate data for comparator institutions. In addition to multi-institutional surveys, student surveys designed to elicit feedback on particular institution-specific programs and services are excellent sources of information for decision making and aligning resources.

Another common assessment process used in student affairs is the use of focus groups and occasionally, individual interviews. Focus group discussions can generate more detailed explanations and information regarding student experiences, expectations, and perceptions. Light's (2001) work is an example of this type of qualitative assessment. He designed a rigorous process of eliciting student feedback, including focus groups and individual interviews, to collect information from a wide spectrum of students on many facets of their academic and non-academic experiences at Harvard. With his colleagues, Light (2001) co-constructed a definition of assessment as "a process of evaluating and improving current programs, encouraging innovations, and then evaluating each innovation's effectiveness" (p. 224). Assessment should be a systematic process to gather data; the purpose of this data is sustained improvement, including enhanced student and faculty effectiveness and success (Light, 2001).

In addition to student assessment, information on the performance of individual units or the student affairs division as a whole can be expressed through benchmarking data and performance indicators. These types of data express performance of an individual unit or the whole division relative to past performance or performance compared to peers. Schuh (2009) described benchmarking as the comparison of one institution's performance to the performance of other institutions nationally and internationally, to industry standards or to its own performance along different dimensions over time. Hollowell et al. (2006) believed that institutions should engage in "as many benchmarking opportunities as possible to determine their relative position within the higher education marketplace" (p. 95). Understanding that position is imperative in determining optimal directions and in setting priorities.

Another type of comparison data is the performance indicator, which is occasionally referred to as a key performance indicator. Ewell and Jones (1996) defined a performance indicator as "a relevant, easily calculable statistic that reflects the overall condition of an enterprise" (p. 9). They articulated three types of performance indicators: indicators that compare relative performances of institutions or programs at a particular time; indicators that examine performance of a particular unit over time; and indicators that examine the impact of the implementation of a program or policy by comparing pre-implementation and post-implementation data (Ewell & Jones, 1996). These comparisons must communicate something useful; additionally, the comparisons must be made across similar settings (Ewell & Jones, 1996). Ewell (1999) outlined particular policy purposes that can be served using key performance indicators. First, for accountability purposes, these indicators provide publicly available information to demonstrate that public funds and resources are being used as intended. Second, for policy and decision-making purposes, performance indicators provide information on the current state of the institution and suggest future directions. Third, for improvement purposes, performance indicators can provide institutions with feedback on their progress regarding achievement of institutional goals or standards. Lastly, for recruitment purposes, performance indicators can provide information to potential consumers that can help them make informed choices about the institutions and programs that are the best fit for them (Ewell, 1999).

Key performance indicators are those indicators that are chosen as important barometers of overall performance along important institutional dimensions. For example, a key performance indicator in student affairs is enrolment and enrolment trends, including overall enrolment and enrolment of particular demographic groups over time. For example, the Ontario government's framework for reporting requires all post-secondary institutions to report performance on a number of key performance indicators such as graduation rates, employment rates, and Ontario loan default rates (Fallis, 2013).

A related assessment process, environmental scanning, is the process of gathering information on the current state of the institution and on the current national and international context. The information generated through environmental scanning can be used to analyze and formulate a description of the institution's position "quantitatively and qualitatively within the current higher education marketplace and describe changes in that marketplace that may affect that position. Within the context of that environmental data, the institution charts its direction; in other words, it plans" (Hollowell et al., 2006, p. 69). Environmental scanning uncovers relevant contextual information that can be instrumental for strategic planning purposes.

Analysis and Communication

Collection of data is not enough; careful analysis and then dissemination of the results are crucial steps in evidence-based decision making. These parts of the assessment process are not without contention, however. Birnbaum (1988) contended: "The collection, coding, and interpretation of data can never be done in the ambiguous world of organization and social interaction as carefully as they can be in the controlled environment of a laboratory" (p. 214). These dynamics have an impact right from the start of the process where the issue or assessment question is defined, through to the decisions on how to collect relevant data, how to interpret the results, and how to communicate the results to the appropriate stakeholders (Birnbaum, 1988). As Birnbaum (1988) stated, "What an institution measures, and how it is presented, can have a major effect on how the environment is sensed" (p. 218). All steps of the assessment process require careful consideration because of the possible impact of bias and political influences.

Presentation and sharing of the data are important considerations; the appropriate stakeholders should be engaged throughout the process but it is imperative that they are informed of the results (Banta et al., 2009; Bresecian et al., 2009; Palomba & Banta, 1999). As Breciani et al. (2009) pointed out, there should be a mechanism for public sharing of results from institutional assessment initiatives. How the information is shared may differ depending on the audience, but the key messages and information itself should be similar for all the stakeholder groups. Middaugh (2010) provided some tips for communication of results. He suggested that key messages should be conveyed in a simple fashion, using visuals such as charts or tables wherever possible. Another visual presentation tool is a dashboard that visually presents performance across a number of measures and can depict trends over time. As Middaugh noted: "Conveying assessment information entails getting the central points across quickly and comprehensively" (p. 191). Once the data has been disseminated, there should be opportunities for the various stakeholders to interact with the data and discuss possible implications (Birnbaum, 1988). "It is the application of data to interaction that permits information to inform preferences and possibilities and that leads to decisions grounded in reality" (Birnbaum, 1988, p. 220). The data should be instrumental in informing decisions, supporting strategic planning, and in determining next steps.

Strategic Enrolment Management

Student services can engage in a wide array of individual assessment projects as well as robust assessment projects that include many sources of data cutting across many of the services and programs. Perhaps one of the most illustrative uses of robust assessment processes to guide decision making is Strategic Enrolment Management (SEM). Gottheil and Smith (2011) identified that strategic enrolment management has become necessary for institutional success because of the changes to the Canadian post-secondary environment including the fiscal challenges and pressures from provincial governments, the changing demographics of the student population, and the upward and downward trends of enrolment across Canada. In an increasingly competitive environment, institutional leaders need to engage in data gathering and analysis with the goals of cost-effectiveness and revenue generation (Black, 2010).

Data play a crucial role in the SEM process. Indeed, Gottheil and Smith (2011) proposed that "data is what makes enrolment strategic" (p. 334). Black (2010) emphasized this point:

> For a SEM plan to be strategic, it must be guided by research and data that are sources of intelligence in decision making, in educating others, in targeting efforts, in planning, and in evaluating the effectiveness and return on investment of strategies introduced. (p. 81)

The data can be gathered from a number of sources including student information systems, academic programs information, future enrolment projections, student surveys, trend analysis, graduation and retention rates, student services data, national statistics, and market research (Christie et al., 2011). In order to determine what the institution's most productive enrolment and retention strategies are, institutional leaders need to "foster a culture of evidence" (Black, 2010, p. 19). The data needs to include important information about the students, including their demographics, their persistence patterns (graduation and retention rates), their goals, and the barriers to their learning (Black, 2010). In addition, the data should include information about the institution itself, as well as its competitors. The data collection and analysis must be ongoing so that the current needs of students are uncovered, and a corresponding action plan responding to those needs can be developed. As Black (2010) pointed out, "such an approach uses data to keep student services targeted and responsive to student needs" (p. 133). By providing the necessary and appropriate supports, student services can play an important role in student retention. The process for gathering and analyzing strategic intelligence must include the whole student life cycle so that a holistic array of initiatives and supports can be developed to recruit and retain students from the moment they show interest in the institution until after they become an alumnus (Black, 2010).

Large amounts of data represent a challenge. As Gottheil and Smith (2011) pointed out, the data analysis team needs to "turn large complex data sets into pieces of actionable insight" (p. 335). The data needs to be quality data that is accurate and reliable. Inconsistent definitions and self-identification of status (such as students self-reporting disabilities or landed immigrant status) can hamper accuracy and usefulness of data. Additionally, Gottheil and Smith (2011) pointed out that education being under provincial jurisdiction is a further complicating factor. "A key concern nationwide is that Canadians lack a common data set and a uniform approach to data collection" (Gottheil & Smith, 2011, p. 335). There have been some advances such as provincial centralized application centres and provincial student numbers that are assigned and stay with the student from their primary education through to their tertiary education experience. Gottheil and Smith (2011) proposed that a national mobility tracking system, rather than provincial systems, is needed for tracking students through their post-secondary experiences; the data would be especially beneficial for the SEM process.

Other Assessment Project Examples

Although SEM projects are increasingly common on campuses, there are many other types of assessment projects that can provide valuable feedback regarding student supports and services, recruitment and retention, resource allocation, and program design. The following are some examples of recent assessment projects undertaken by the University of Saskatchewan—the institution with which I am most familiar—as part of its strategic intelligence efforts.

Understanding our student parents. The university established a steering committee to address concerns regarding childcare for its student parents. The provincial government responded, as well, to the student union concerns and designated funds for building additional childcare spaces on campus. This allocation meant that the university could almost double its childcare spaces, as it already had two separate childcare centres on campus. These spaces were for children of undergraduate students, graduate students, staff, and faculty. In order to determine priorities for filling these additional spaces, the university engaged the Social Sciences Research Laboratory on campus to conduct a telephone survey of the undergraduate and graduate students so that the administration better understood the profile and needs of the university's student parents. The resulting data indicated that approximately 8% of the students were parents. They were interested in affordable, quality childcare that was either on campus or close to home. The information gathered will be used to construct principles and guidelines for distribution of the additional childcare spaces to address primarily the needs of the undergraduate and graduate students.

Successes of transfer-credit students. As part of discussions around enrolment strategies, several target enrolment groups, including transfer students, were identified. However, the success of students who transfer to the university was questioned. The answer would inform possible changes that could facilitate and encourage students to transfer credits and complete their degree at the University of Saskatchewan. Part of the initial issue was defining transfer credit students and determining the parameters of the study. The study required an examination of longitudinal data, a process that added to the complexity of the project. After interrogating the data, revising the parameters, and analyzing the data using several different lenses, the data team concluded that transfer credit students are generally as successful as, or more successful than, students who enter the program directly.

Understanding the employment and immigration goals of international students. In conjunction with the provincial government, the university wanted to determine what goals or aspirations international students held. The information would help inform how the university and the government could best support international students in achieving their goals, whether they intended to stay in the province or whether they intended to immediately return to their home country upon completion of their studies. In addition to gathering aggregate data from the student information system regarding programs of study, year in program, and countries of origin, student services constructed surveys to distribute electronically to all international students. The surveys generated valuable feedback on student perceptions regarding career goals, services and supports that they had accessed, types of services that were most necessary, and their sense of welcome and belonging at the university. Based on the data, student service units were able to construct recommendations and action plans to address the concerns and to build on the successes.

As these projects demonstrate, post-secondary institutions and their academic and administrative units can gather valuable strategic intelligence from multiple data sources. If institutional leaders intentionally construct a culture of evidence on their campuses, they can ensure that they are providing cost-effective and efficient services that maximize student success.

CONCLUSION

Transparency, accountability, and improved outcomes are especially important, given the context of increasing competition for resources and students, increased fiscal challenges, and the move by many institutions towards resource-based budgeting models where budgets are even more dependent on recruiting and retaining students. As Hardy Cox and Strange (2010) pointed out, student services in Canadian higher education are developing "a growing understanding of the complexities of the post-secondary experience, the need for greater responsiveness to students, demands for greater accountability in the service transaction, and the desire to achieve a higher standard of professional preparation and competence" (p. 15) in the delivery of those services. Assessment is a necessary and integral part of the process of designing, delivering and evaluating effectiveness of student services and programs; assessment is not an administrative task undertaken solely to satisfy reporting requirements. "Assessment should be seen as a natural responsibility to our students and each other" (Palomba & Banta, 1999, p. 346). When assessment becomes a core part of the way student affairs conducts its business, then evidence-based decision making will have become an integral piece of the culture. The outcome will be more cost-effective, targeted and efficient services that best support the mission of the university and promote student success.

REFERENCES

Banta, T. W., Jones, E. A., & Black, K. E. (2009). *Designing effective assessment: Principles and profiles of good practice*. San Francisco, CA: Jossey-Bass.

Birnbaum, R. (1988). *How colleges work: The cybernetics of academic organization and leadership*. San Francisco, CA: Jossey-Bass.

Black, J. (Ed.). (2010). *Strategic enrolment intelligence*. London: Academica Group.

Bresciani, M. J. (2006). *Outcomes-based academic and co-curricular program review: A compilation of institutional good practices*. Sterling, VA: Stylus Publishing.

Bresciani, M. J., Gardner, M. M., & Hickmott, J. (2009). *Demonstrating student success: A practical guide to outcomes-based assessment of learning and development in student affairs*. Sterling, VA: Stylus Publishing.

Christie, B., Metcalfe, J., & Fortowsky, K. (2011). Using data for strategic enrolment management. In S. Gottheil & C. Smith (Eds.), *SEM in Canada: Promoting student and institutional success in Canadian colleges and universities* (pp. 17–39). Washington, DC: American Association of Collegiate Registrars and Admissions Officers.

Council for the Advancement of Standards in Higher Education. (2012). CAS learning and development outcomes. In L. A. Dean (Ed.), *CAS professional standards for higher education* (8th ed.). Washington, DC: Author.

Creamer, D. G., Winston, R. B. Jr., & Miller, T. K. (2001). The professional student affairs administrator: Roles and functions. In R. B. Winston Jr., D. G. Creamer, & T. K. Miller (Eds.), *The professional student affairs administrator: Educator, leader and manager* (pp. 3–38). New York, NY: Brunner-Routledge.

Ewell, P. T. (1999). Linking performance to resource allocation: An unmapped terrain. *Quality in Higher Education, 5*(3), 191–209. doi:10.1080/1353832990050302

Ewell, P. T., & Jones, D. P. (1996). *Indicators of "good practice" in undergraduate education: A handbook for development and implementation*. Boulder, CO: National Center for Higher Education Management Systems.

Fallis, G. (2013). *Rethinking higher education: Participation, research and differentiation.* Kingston, ON: Queen's School of Policy Studies.

Fullan, M., & Scott, G. (2009). *Turnaround leadership for higher education.* San Francisco, CA: Jossey-Bass.

Gottheil, S., & Smith, C. (2011). *SEM in Canada: Promoting student and institutional success in Canadian colleges and universities.* Washington, DC: American Association of Collegiate Registrars and Admissions Officers.

Hardy Cox, D., & Strange, C. C. (2010). Foundations of student services in Canadian higher education. In D. Hardy Cox & C. C. Strange (Eds.), *Achieving student success: Effective student services in Canadian higher education* (pp. 5–17). Quebec City, QC: McGill-Queen's University Press.

Hollowell, D., Middaugh, M. F., & Sibolski, E. (2006). *Integrating higher education planning and assessment: A practical guide.* Ann Arbor, MI: Society for College and University Planning.

Janice, D. B., & Scott, J. H. (2006). Increasing accountability in student affairs through a new comprehensive assessment model. *College Student Affairs Journal, 25*(2), 209–219.

Keeling, R. P. (2006). Integrating learning reconsidered into strategic planning. In R. P. Keeling (Ed.), *Learning reconsidered 2: Implementing a campus-wide focus on the student experience* (pp. 53–58). Washington, DC: American College Personnel Association, Association of College and University Housing Officers International, Association of College Unions International, National Academic Advising Association, National Association for Campus Activities, National Association of Student Personnel Administrators, National Intramural-Recreational Sports Association.

Kuh, G. D, Siegel, M. J., & Thomas, A. D. (2001). Higher education: Values and cultures. In R. B. Winston Jr., D. G. Creamer, T. K. Miller and Associates (Eds.), *The professional student affairs administrator: Educator, leader and manager* (pp. 39–63). New York, NY: Brunner-Routledge.

Kuh, G. D., Kinzie, J., Schuh, J. H., Whitt, E. J., and Associates. (2010). *Student success in college: Creating conditions that matter.* San Francisco, CA: Jossey-Bass.

Kuk, L., Banning, J. H., & Amey, M. J. (2010). *Positioning student affairs for sustainable change: Achieving organizational effectiveness through multiple perspectives.* Sterling, VA: Stylus Publishing.

Laidler, D. (2005). Incentives facing Canadian universities: Some possible consequences. In C. M. Beach, R. W. Boadway, & R. M. McInnis (Eds.), *Higher education in Canada* (pp. 35–49). Kingston, ON: John Deutsch Institute for the Study of Economic Policy.

Light, R. J. (2001). *Making the most of college: Students speak their minds.* Cambridge, MA: Harvard University Press.

Middaugh, M. F. (2010). *Planning and assessment in higher education: Demonstrating institutional effectiveness.* San Francisco, CA: Jossey-Bass.

Ouellette, M. (2010). Student services in university. In C. Hardy Cox & C. C. Strange (Eds.), *Achieving student success: Effective student services in Canadian higher education* (pp. 208–220). Quebec City, QC: McGill-Queen's University Press.

Palomba, C. A., & Banta, T. W. (1999). *Assessment essentials: Planning, implementing, and improving assessment in higher education.* San Francisco, CA: Jossey-Bass.

Reynolds, A. L., & Chris, S. (2008). Improving practice through outcomes based planning and assessment: A counseling center case study. *Journal of College Student Development, 49*(4), 374–387.

Schuh, J. H., and Associates. (2009). *Assessment methods for student affairs.* San Francisco, CA: Jossey-Bass.

Schuh, J. H., Upcraft, M. L., and Associates. (2001). *Assessment practice in student affairs: An application manual.* San Francisco, CA: Jossey-Bass.

Steele, K. (2010). The changing Canadian PSE landscape. In J. Black (Ed.) *Strategic enrolment intelligence* (pp. 27–50). London, ON: Academica Group.

Strange, C. C., & Hardy Cox, D. (2010). Principles and strategies of good practice in student services. In C. Hardy Cox & C. C. Strange (Eds.), *Achieving student success: Effective student services in Canadian higher education* (pp. 237–245). Quebec City, QC: McGill-Queen's University Press.

Sullivan, B. (2010). Organizing, leading and managing student services. In C. Hardy Cox & C. C. Strange (Eds.), *Achieving student success: Effective student services in Canadian higher education* (pp. 165–191). Quebec City, QC: McGill-Queen's University Press.

V. SQUIRES

Upcraft, L. M., & Schuh, J. H. (1996). *Assessment in student affairs: A guide for practitioners.* San Francisco, CA: Jossey-Bass.
Winston, R. B., Creamer, D. G., Miller, T. K., and Associates. (2001). *The professional student affairs administrator: Educator, leader and manager.* New York, NY: Brunner-Routledge.

ROBIN MUELLER

9. CHANGE AND IMPROVEMENT IN
POST-SECONDARY EDUCATION

There is no shortage of criticism with respect to the current state of affairs in post-secondary education. It seems that most aspects of university policy, process, and function—in virtually every developed country worldwide—are being critiqued vociferously. Furthermore, the broad discourse about post-secondary education appears to be both contested and divisive, typically finding scholars from across disciplines firmly entrenched in one side or the other of a binary, neo-liberal/communitarian debate with respect to post-secondary issues. Regardless of which allegiance is felt most strongly by any particular scholar, however, it is evident that change to post-secondary systems and institutions is a desired outcome.

The call for change and improvement in post-secondary education is loud and clear (Christenson Hughes & Mighty, 2010; Côté & Allahar, 2007; Kirp, 2006; McInnes, 1995; Schafer, 2008; Stein, 2004; Wadsworth, 2006; Woodhouse, 2009). There are many types of change suggested as part of this discourse, including subtle and dramatic shifts to university structure, a re-examination of post-secondary priorities, a revival of "true" academic freedoms in the pursuit of knowledge, a shift in curricular emphases, and changes to university administration and governance, among many others. These suggestions are given based on varying levels of contextual understanding, meaning that the individuals who advocate change differ in their assessments of past and present politics, social dynamics, environmental issues, and cultural mores within university systems. An outward glance, then, suggests both alarm and disarray; the discourse pertaining to post-secondary change and improvement feels heated, unstable, and almost zealous in tone. This disarray is indicative of an absence within the higher education improvement movement: the absence of appropriate evidence in support of the change effort.

Much of the current debate about change in post-secondary education is rooted in reverie, or what often reads as a fond remembrance of what has been lost from the historical purpose and function of universities. My intent here is not to disparage the reverie, but to draw attention to un-asked questions: How do we know that the past conditions of higher education were better than current conditions? What mechanisms, visible and invisible, have contributed to current post-secondary environments? What is the purpose, or aim, of change and development in higher education? How should the change process be approached? Case studies, trend analyses, personal reflections, and theoretical analyses that highlight post-secondary

P. Newton & D. Burgess (Eds.), The Best Available Evidence, 129–146.

problems abound, but what has not been produced is any *compelling evidence* that suggests the need for, or the most effective direction of, change in post-secondary education. The use of evidence as a driver for improvement in post-secondary education is an idea that is, at best, underexplored. In this chapter, I suggest that considered use of sound evidence should be the driver of change and improvement in post-secondary education.

Before proceeding, I must offer a definition of what I mean by *post-secondary education*, because this term has been used variously in the literature over recent years. For the purposes of delimiting the discussion in this chapter, I will use the phrases post-secondary education and higher education in reference to universities only, meaning higher education institutions that typically confer four-year degrees. Although there are myriad institutions that are left out by this definition (vocational colleges, community colleges, theological colleges, and polytechnic institutions, for example), this delimitation serves the purpose of focusing the following discussion of the ways in which post-secondary change and improvement should be fuelled by evidence.

It should also be noted that my general discussion about universities and post-secondary change is intended to be exactly that: general. Post-secondary education is discussed in terms of trends noted within the university systems of developed countries. The scope of this chapter does not allow a nuanced discussion about post-secondary education in particular localities or contexts. However, trends in higher education have been remarkably similar among developed countries, and I have attempted to achieve a balance between the general and the specific by augmenting broad statements with contextual examples where appropriate.

In the remainder of this chapter, I endeavour to take the reader on a high-level journey through the past, present, and future of the university. I begin, as they say, at the beginning; I offer a history-in-brief of the university institution as a means to ground further exploration about how the move toward modularization in higher education influences current trends and the change movement. I provide an overview of the current trends in post-secondary education that are most pertinent to our discussion, concluding with a summary of the most prominent suggested frameworks for approaching university change efforts. I problematize the improvement movement in post-secondary education, and explore the current and potential roles of evidence in the change effort.

Context of Post-Secondary Education

When considering change in post-secondary education, it is useful to begin by elucidating the history of university education as a starting point. Much current dialogue about the state of post-secondary education is conducted without an adequate grasp of the ways in which the past continues to influence current trends. A brief historical inquiry, which is the "process of systematically searching for and organizing data to better understand past phenomena and their likely causes and consequences" (Gall, Gall, & Borg, 2010, p. 433), serves the purpose of establishing a descriptive baseline for understanding current situations.

History of post-secondary education. Historical accounts regarding the development of university organizational structures abound. The first universities were founded during the 12th century (Campayre, 2009; Cobban, 2009). A university in the 13th and 14th centuries was generally referred to as a *studium generale*, or an organized school with established infrastructure that attracted and served students from within and beyond the local region (Cobban, 2009). A studium generale was, in many ways, structured similarly to its modern cousins; the 13th century university was organized around such functions as coordinating student life, examinations, teaching methods, university-community relations, and licensure. Such schools had to be recognized by both papal and imperial authorities in order to be considered legally valid.

Universities have been referred to and described as institutions for hundreds of years. An *institution* is defined as a social structure that is shaped by rules, norms, beliefs, and material resources. Institutions are large-scale organizations, typically resistant to change, that characteristically endure across generations (Scott, 2008). Thus, universities are aptly described as institutions; in fact, Winchester (1986) identified several overarching characteristics of the university institution that have been constant since medieval times: (a) relative autonomy, (b) neutrality, (c) its role in creating and disseminating knowledge (research and teaching), (d) emphasis on linguistic or "bookish" knowledge, (e) emphasis on criticality, and (f) its role as a cultural center.

While widely considered institutions, universities bear some unique features that set them apart from other institutional organizations (Winchester, 1986). Of most interest in this case is the university's internal organization into *hierarchical silos,* which is paralleled by a largely modular system of educational delivery (Rothblatt, 2009; Winchester, 1986). Universities are led, managed, and regulated by over-arching governance bodies and associated administrative leaders, while the majority of academic or scholarly activity is focused in largely autonomous institutional silos, or *modules* (Rothblatt, 2009).

Rothblatt (2009) explored the emergence of modules in American higher education, and traced the growth of modular institutions back to 19th century educational developments. Prior to that time, European post-secondary educational processes had been adopted in North American systems, where students engaged in unified collegiate class systems. As part of *collegiate systems*, students entered a university in integrated cohorts and participated in pre-determined, common programs of study; examinations were comprehensive and administered to all students in the cohort at key points as they progressed toward degree completion. Around the 1820s, American institutions began to incorporate elective options, and influential academic leaders pushed to develop a post-secondary elective system that reflected the growing ideals of democracy, autonomy, and self-reliance. This trend was augmented by an emergent American affinity with consumerism and

131

an associated belief that the university system should offer wide choice among alternatives. Examinations were "uncoupled from the degree and instead attached to modules, where every kind of evaluation was possible" (Rothblatt, 2009, p. 394). As a result, the practice of continuous assessment within curricular modules became commonplace.

Emergence of curricular electives at American universities was paralleled by necessary shifts in university organizational structure (Rothblatt, 2009). First, widespread division of comprehensive curricula into discrete parts necessitated the development of accompanying regulatory policies and processes. The modular system of educational delivery required oversight of electives, development of regulations about 'credit units' and degree articulation, creation of instruments for continuous assessment, need for academic advising, and development of instruments for transfer credit, among other administrative needs. Consequently, large and complex non-academic organizational units developed at universities; this marked the inception of the field of university administration. Second, the modularization of university education led to the establishment of increasingly professionalized, curriculum-based organizational silos—colleges, departments, schools, units, and so forth. The nature of curricula in such a system requires highly specialized faculty, and leads to a preference for disciplinarity (Rothblatt, 2009; Swoboda, 1976). While universities have traditionally been separated into distinct colleges or schools of arts and science, modularity has emphasized and deepened the trend towards curriculum-based divisions, and universities are now typically composed of many relatively autonomous, differentiated, self-contained organizational units, or silos (Bess & Dee, 2012; Winchester, 1986).

The term *silo* is a metaphor; organizational silos are analogous to tall cylindrical containers used on grain farms to store a variety of commodities (Aaker, 2008). These commodities are all essential to the viability of a farm enterprise, but due to functional differences they are stored, processed, and used separately. The resemblance of farm silos to hierarchical structures in organizations is striking, as organizational silos in universities are similarly self-contained (Aaker, 2008). They each play a pivotal role in ensuring organizational success, but they tend to work in isolation from other units. Silos meet organizational needs for effective division of labour and need for highly specialized workers (Aaker, 2008; Schutz & Bloch, 2006). In universities, silos are established based on products (knowledge) and service (teaching) that are structurally organized according to disciplinary foci (Bess, 1988). Boundaries between such silos are further reinforced by a university-wide emphasis on research, where research units within academic silos focus on highly independent and discipline-specific contributions to academic discourse in their respective fields (Bess, 1988; Bess & Dee, 2012).

The movement toward modular education and institutional silos in post-secondary education, which began in the early 1800s, has yielded university environments that are prone to external influence. While universities have been subject to church and state controls since the inception of the institution (Cobban, 2009), most universities in developed countries enjoyed relative autonomy for a prolonged period of time. A recent shift, wherein universities have generally moved further toward modular education, has also left them more susceptible to political and corporate influence. As an example, governments prescribed a focus on particular, discipline-specific research during the 1940s in order to support North American efforts during World War II (Krismsky, 2008); this emphasis on differentiated, modularized research carried forward to today's campuses, and is evidenced in schools and research centers that are affiliated with universities but that remain outside of core university functioning. The adoption of a modular structure in post-secondary education thus created a context that has influenced and shaped current trends observed in universities world-wide.

Current Trends in Post-Secondary Education

There are dozens of current trends evident in post-secondary institutions, but a few of these are particularly noteworthy in context of our present discussion regarding higher education change and improvement. These trends are certainly linked to one another, and it is consequently difficult to discern causality with respect to their role in the higher education change movement. However, providing a brief description of these trends will allow us to explore the potential purposes of the improvement effort, as well as highlight the importance of evidence as part of this effort.

Funding to post-secondary institutions. Levels of public funding to post-secondary education have fluctuated significantly over the last century in developed countries (Fisher, Rubenson, Jones, & Shanahan, 2009). In the late 1980s and early 1990s, however, many universities experienced a "pull-back" of government subsidy; local and national governments responded to a world-wide economic recession by reducing funding to higher education (Shanahan & Jones, 2007). In Canada, for example, federal transfers allocated to provincial systems for higher education decreased over 40% between the early 1980s and the early 2000s (Fisher et al., 2009). Reduction in government money to fund post-secondary education has contributed to some pronounced changes with respect to the ways that universities secure operational funding. Although external stakeholders, including granting agencies, corporate sponsors, and individual donors, have long played a role on university landscapes due to their financial contributions to the university enterprise (Bok, 2004), they have become much more influential due to the pullback of government funding.

Recent years have seen an emphasis on the need for faculty members to generate revenue by way of grant proposals to external funders (Fisher et al., 2009); researchers who are able to secure substantial external funding are often considered the "superstars" of academia (Krimsky, 2008; Stein, 2004). In many countries, the importance of the individual researcher's ability to generate grant revenue for the university has been reiterated by the creation of government programs to supplement or match research dollars secured by faculty members. In Canada, for example,

133

fund-matching requirements are "imposed through the Canada Foundation for Innovation (CFI) and Canadian Research Chairs (CRC) programs," and tax incentives are offered as a reward for research and innovation activity (Fisher et al., 2009, p. 561). As a result, virtually all Canadian universities have aggressively positioned themselves to secure individual grants and increase research outputs (Shanahan & Jones, 2007).

In addition to a determined push toward securing research grants, universities have also been characterized as increasingly accepting of corporate sponsorship (Bok, 2004; Krimsky, 2008). Such sponsorship takes many forms; common sponsorship agreements include purchasing the naming rights for particular buildings, sponsoring high-profile athletic programs, creating venture capital companies affiliated with the university, and funding targeted research agendas (Bok, 2004). The levels of influence that funders maintain over the direction of and results generated by university research is debatable (Bok, 2004); however, the proliferation of scandal surrounding university research that has been compromised by inappropriate influence from private stakeholders suggests increasing corporate power over research processes (Schafer, 2008).

Emphasis on job/career preparation. Over the past two decades, shifting demographics and economic conditions have created burgeoning job markets. Consequently, provincial, state, and federal governments have indicated a desire to meet market demand with "human capital" in the form of well-trained professionals (Fisher et al., 2009; McInnes, 1995). This has fuelled the creation of myriad government policies, programs, and/or objectives, often geared toward producing a specific, targeted number of post-secondary graduates given the market needs of local communities (Armstrong, 1999; Fisher et al., 2009). The push for human capital has also prompted a post-secondary trend toward *vocationalism*, or the offering of university courses and programs that are designed to provide practical training for immediate use in the job market, usually in accordance with the "skills agendas" of local governments (Fisher et al., 2009). The "public" purpose of the university is thus emphasized, meaning that universities position themselves to highlight their contributions to local economies by providing training that gives graduates access to profitable employment opportunities (Grubb & Lazerson, 2005). Vocationalism in post-secondary education has been linked to a growing reliance by universities on market principles of governance and operation.

Introduction of market principles and market models of education. Dialogue about the commercialization of academia began in the early 1970s (Kirp, 2006), but has more recently become predominant among higher education scholars (Stein, 2004; Woodhouse, 2009). This discourse is centered on either critique or support of what has been labelled as the market model of education. According to critics, the *market model* is characterized by conditions where the "pursuit of knowledge, which is at the core of university research and teaching, is systematically devalued by the intrusion of market principles... into all the distinctive activities of these institutions" (Woodhouse, 2009, p. 10). Critique with respect to the market model of educational delivery is based on scholars' assessment of a current development wherein university students are perceived as consumers rather than learners, and professors as gatekeepers of quality and efficiency rather than facilitators of learning (Woodhouse, 2009). Accordingly, the critical assessment of market models yields an observation that higher education has become not only an institution, but an industry (Fisher et al., 2009).

Focus on standards and accountability. A by-product of the institutional shift toward market models of operation in higher education has been the widespread use of *managerialism* as a system of organizational control. Armstrong (1999) aptly described this shift:

> A key element of the... transformation of higher education was the need to guarantee value for money and provide public accountability. The concept of market forces was introduced to higher education in very much the same way as it was applied to many other areas of the public sector. It was clear the government wanted 'more for less'—the resources available for higher education had to grow at a slower rate than the participation rate and so higher education institutions therefore had to demonstrate the same efficiency gains as other public-sector institutions. The style of management of higher education institutions had to change as a result, 'managerialism' becoming the dominant motif. (p. 9)

Managerialism is a style of hierarchical organizational structure that aims to use centralized management as a mechanism to coordinate institutional efficiency, and to minimize institutional expenditures while maximizing output (Deem, 2008; Deem, Hillyard, & Reed, 2007). Accountability, of both individual employees and the organization as a whole, is a key focus within managerial cultures (Bergquist & Pawlak, 2008; Deem, 2008).

In concert with the establishment of managerialism in universities, systems of higher education experienced a gradual but marked shift toward regulation and accountability (Fisher et al., 2009). This is reflected in university policies and procedures that have emerged in the last two decades, including: (a) the introduction of minimum institutional and university graduate standards (Armstrong, 1999; Finnie & Usher, 2005; Harvey & Knight, 1996), (b) the use of benchmarking and other strategic approaches to quality assurance (Armstrong, 1999; Middaugh, 2010; Morley & Aynsley, 2007), (c) the establishment of quality assurance groups and policies (Clark, Moran, Skolnik, & Trick, 2009); (d) requirements for universities to make information about university performance available to the public (Clark et al., 2009); (e) the proliferation of university ranking systems (Dill & Soo, 2005; Finnie & Usher, 2005); and (f) the use of strategic planning as a means to frame institutional accountabilities (Finnie & Usher, 2005; Middaugh, 2010). The pronounced focus on accountability—and quality—in post-secondary education seems to drive current initiatives toward change and improvement.

Change and Improvement in Post-Secondary Education

The most predominant current trend in post-secondary education is the push toward change and improvement; several of the trends mentioned earlier are implicit in the change movement, and together they indicate that post-secondary education systems are on the brink of transformation. Scholars and higher education collectives from across the world have issued imperatives, stating that universities should:

- Engage "concerted action among all [higher education] stakeholders" (AACU, as cited in Kezar & Lester, 2009, p. 3);
- Recognize and act on the need for reform (Dickeson, 2010);
- Resist the unhealthy momentum created by current higher education trends (Woodhouse, 2009); and
- Restructure higher education to foster trust and collegiality in university environments (Deem et al., 2007).

Many scholars have posed theoretical solutions and suggestions for change frameworks in higher education. While this summary is certainly not exhaustive, for the purposes of this chapter the change strategies can be grouped into three general categories: (a) cultural approaches, (b) collaborative approaches, and (c) corporate approaches.

Cultural approaches to change and improvement in post-secondary education. Several scholars have proposed cultural approaches to change and innovation in post-secondary education. Accordingly, culture is considered to be ever-present in the organizational life of the university (Bergquist & Pawlak, 2008). *Culture* is the group ethos that distinguishes one organization from another (Hofestede, 1998); it includes a suite of attitudes, norms, values, processes, artefacts, and behaviours that help organizational members align with one another and with the organization as a whole (Schein, 1990, 1992). A dominant assumption implicit in the advocacy of cultural methods for improvement is that approaches to post-secondary change must be culturally sensitive (Kezar & Eckle, 2002); in other words, effective change strategies are those that align with the ethos created by existing organizational culture(s). Cultural models of organizational change have also been linked with the idea of collaborative approaches to improvement.

Collaborative approaches to change and improvement in post-secondary education. Collaborative approaches to change are founded on the premise that university systems are complex, and consequently, there is no one individual part of the university system that operates in isolation. Organizational silos notwithstanding, all aspects of the university institution are mutually influential. According to this view on university organizational life, advocates for post-secondary change often cite collaborative strategies as those with the most potential for gaining traction within the improvement movement. Such collaborative strategies are described variously, depending on the aspect of university life and/or function that is emphasized. Collaborative approaches are reflected in discourse on partnerships (Schroeder, 1999), organizational learning (Boyce, 2003; Kezar & Lester, 2009), and shared responsibility in post-secondary education (Kuh, Kinzie, Shuh, & Whit, 2005). The focus of collaborative strategies is typically on creating productive interpersonal and structural connections across the organizational silos that are evident in university environments. The purpose of creating such connections is to enhance the effectiveness of university processes and to facilitate organizational learning and collegiality (Kezar & Lester, 2009). Functional approaches to collaboration include collectively revising organizational purposes, forging stable social networks across the organization, and integrating organizational structures to support team-based functions (Kezar & Lester, 2009).

Corporate approaches to change and improvement in post-secondary education. Change resources from the corporate domain appear to be the most prevalent and influential in post-secondary improvement efforts. The language and processes adopted for the purposes of implementing change in higher education are reflective of those used in the corporate world, and it is frequently conceded that improvement strategies are borrowed from corporate domains and adapted to suit the purposes of post-secondary environments. Despite an acknowledgement that, for the most part, universities are not actually like businesses (Pattenaude, 2000)— neither in character nor in function—use of business models of improvement has become *status quo* in higher education when change is imminent.

Several corporate change trends have been implemented by universities over recent years. The first is the adoption of managerialism as a mechanism of organizational integration and control (Deem et al., 2007; Deem, 2008). Managerialism, as indicated earlier in this chapter, is a belief system grounded in the importance of free enterprise and a strategy of organization that is most concerned with ensuring financial viability or organizational economic advancement (Deem et al., 2007). While this type of organizational structure may seem an awkward fit given the traditional post-secondary emphasis on academic freedoms, serving public interests, and the value of discovery (Pattenaude, 2000), a world-wide government push toward transparency and efficiency in public institutions became an impetus for the adoption of managerialism in many universities. Managerial structures and processes have been used in universities, both implicitly and explicitly, to make progress with a change agenda that is focused on accountability and economic sustainability.

Universities, as part of a global change effort, have also endeavoured to mirror the corporate practice of creating a viable marketplace for their particular brand of activities (Duderstadt, 2004; Geiger, 2002; Kirp, 2006). Amid times of fiscal

137

restraint and reduction of government funding, universities responded with change efforts borrowed from the corporate world that would ensure their continued profitability. Such efforts included the practice of promoting university research as a commercially viable product (Duderstadt, 2004) and the creation of institutional competition in terms of recruiting the most (and the best) students (Geiger, 2002; Kirp, 2006). Research was rendered profitable through such mechanisms as technology transfer and the sale of patents (Duderstadt, 2004) and institutional competition for students, occasionally framed as "strengthening reputation" (Dickeson, 2010), was achieved by introducing both local and global university rating systems (Dill & Soo, 2005). This change effort has certainly demonstrated financial effectiveness at many universities, so much so that governments are subtly encouraging the commercialization of universities for the purpose of contributing to local economies and also issuing directives for universities to "keep pace" with the investments that commercial industries are making to post-secondary institutions (Duderstadt, 2004, p. 58).

Post-secondary institutions have also adopted corporate strategies for assessing and managing change. The *total quality management* (TQM) movement became popular in corporate domains in the 1980s. TQM is a method of ensuring continuous improvement in business that focuses on creating strategies to ensure stakeholder satisfaction and maximize the value of the corporate enterprise (Deming, 2000). The total quality approach was adopted by higher education as a change management strategy in the 1990s (Lewis & Smith, 1994), including the use of benchmarking as an assessment tool for monitoring change and progress (Appleby, 1999). *Benchmarking* is a corporate concept; organizations benchmark by creating metrics that are used to compare aspects of their economic performance against industry best practices (Appleby, 1999).

The total quality idea is still prevalent in post-secondary domains, but the most influential business practice adopted as a method for managing change in higher education has been *strategic planning*. Strategic planning is a systematic business process, wherein long-term strategy is formulated and articulated (Grünig & Kühn, 2011). In the arena of university administration, it is generally acknowledged that strategic planning is a process that was founded in the private sector, and that has now been adopted to facilitate higher education reform (Ellis, 2010). The activities of strategic planning may include: strategic success analyses (evaluating the strengths, weaknesses, opportunities, and threats within an organization); mission, vision, and values planning; systems analyses; network mapping; benchmarking; goal clarification; and development of specific strategies for implementation (Cook, 2010; Grünig & Kühn, 2011; Olsen, Olsen, & Olsen, 2004). Despite claims from some post-secondary scholars that strategic planning was a fleeting fad (Birnbaum, 2001), it has been embraced by higher education and has become a hallmark of university attempts to respond to both internal and external change forces. Universities invest substantially in coordinating institution-wide strategic planning cycles for the purpose of facilitating change and improving institutional functioning. Such planning is evidenced at universities by the persistent emergence of dedicated planning staff, working committees, and a profusion of publicly accessible university strategic planning documentation.

Results of the improvement movement in higher education. The drive to change is strong in post-secondary environments, and the intent to change is made clear by implicit and explicit university policies, practices, and investments. However, the results of this activity are unclear. While it is common for universities to engage in iterative strategic planning cycles, for example, there is little inquiry into or reporting about the substantive changes that occur as a result of such processes. There is a significant dialogue transpiring about the need for change and many ideas about how change might happen, but there is little to indicate whether or not improvement is actually taking place. This conspicuous lack of reflection with respect to the results of the change effort is but one problematic aspect of the current higher education improvement movement.

Problematizing the Change Movement in Higher Education

There are several problems pertaining to the various proposed strategies for implementing change in post-secondary education, but I will focus my examination on the matter by targeting what I believe to be the two most significant issues: (a) conceptions regarding the need for, purpose of, and meaning of change in post-secondary education are widely variant; and (b) this lack of focus regarding change parallels what appears to be institutional paralysis, or the inability of post-secondary systems to implement change in a responsive or comprehensive way. The criticisms offered and accompanying change imperatives advocated then achieve little purchase in the way of leading to meaningful higher education improvement.

Assessments regarding the need for post-secondary change and improvement vary substantially, and they are largely dependent on the person or group who is doing the assessing. Granted, there have been broad analyses of higher education trends that are frequently described by a specific lexicon, one that includes such words as *globalization, managerialism,* and *corporatization.* Many of these analyses have been rigorous and have included accompanying descriptive assessments of social, political, and cultural influences on post-secondary institutions. However, the rationale for change is not routinely nor concretely linked to these analyses; justifications for the improvement movement range from a nostalgic desire for a return to the academic freedoms of the past to a sweeping claim that higher education is not adequately meeting public need. Furthermore, the reasoning for change is based on variable understandings of both the long-term and local histories of higher education, and informed by views on current educational trends that appear to be limited at best, or biased at worst. There appears to be widespread agreement with respect to just two points: that there is a problem(s), and that change is warranted. However, there is a lack of clarity regarding the reasons for, and the purpose of, impending change efforts.

It is no surprise that, given the lack of focus regarding the purposes for higher education change and improvement, there is an absence of evidence-based, practical approaches to implementation within the change movement. The change strategies that are suggested most often tend to be broad and general and hold limited instructional value for those who are actually attempting to make change happen. Skeptics of this claim might argue that there are some change models that have been studied extensively in context of higher education—cultural change models, for example (Kezar & Eckel, 2002). However, the results of this inquiry have yielded general observations rather than specific, pragmatic suggestions, and the efficacy of such change models have yet to be demonstrated in any comprehensive way. In fact, when it comes to implementing change initiatives, it has been acknowledged that universities simply rely on "what seems to be an intuitively good idea" to the majority involved in the improvement effort (Kezar & Lester, 2009, p. 4). Moreover, it appears that intuitive ideas pertaining to post-secondary improvement are derived most often from corporate domains.

The widespread acceptance of corporate change models is, in my assessment, the most problematic aspect of the higher education improvement movement. Application of market models of higher education, including the use of corporate approaches to change, has occurred with little indication of critical thought and with scant acknowledgement of context or conditions. An issue exists in the startling absence of evidence pertaining to the use of corporate models in higher education decision making and change efforts. However, we can hardly blame the corporate world for the deficiencies inherent in their approaches to change when they are applied in the realm of post-secondary education. While the reliance on business models in higher education improvement is troublesome, in many ways what the corporate world has to offer is the "only show in town." Research and publication with respect to higher education administration and educational improvement in higher education is scant, leaving administrators to choose institutional change strategies from the suite of available options within corporate domains.

The Role of Evidence in Post-Secondary Change and Improvement

Evidence has played a central role in the historical purpose and function of post-secondary education; it is the hallmark of the kind of inquiry that we refer to as *research*. Research is an iterative process of disciplined questioning and collecting information in order to answer questions, and often to solve problems (Booth, Colomb, & Williams, 2008), and to do so in a way that provides us with meaningful and accurate insights that can be immediately put into practice. We can only answer questions and solve problems in a meaningful way if our inquiry has generated adequate evidence. *Evidence* is the information we collect—the grounds, or the proof—that helps us decide whether or not our ideas and beliefs are valid. We have to "search for evidence 'out there' in the 'hard' reality of the world, then make it available for everyone to see" (Booth et al., 2008, p. 111). Collecting evidence allows us to substantiate our claims, and to communicate to others about what we have learned.

The need to generate evidence in order to support our beliefs about histories, phenomena, events, processes, interactions, structures, and systems is universal in post-secondary education. In every discipline and tradition of inquiry, implicit in every paradigm and research method, the generation of evidence is what allows scholars to make a case for significance, or meaning, with respect to the research that is conducted. Evidence is what provides scholars with concrete links between theory and application, so that what is learned in academia might be best utilized in the real world. Evidence fuels the recommendations that are made and the associated action that occurs as a result of research.

Applying the ethos of research to change and improvement in post-secondary systems. Universities can be considered localized meccas of research activity; in recent years many universities have even created complex infrastructures to support research activity across institutional silos (Fisher et al., 2009). Universities are driven by research, yet, curiously, the inquiry conducted with respect to the theory and practice of higher education change and development is virtually non-existent within scholarly discourse. Although we are in the midst of unprecedented change in higher education, such change appears to be initiated in a largely unconscious manner, without supportive evidence pertaining to the descriptive history of post-secondary education, the dynamics of the current landscape, or the change mechanisms that might be most effective.

It is crucial to consider well-rounded and comprehensive evidence as a driver for change and improvement in post-secondary education for a number of reasons. First, our glance at the history of higher education indicates that the trends we have identified as being problematic in universities have actually been in motion for decades or even centuries. This points to a level of complexity in post-secondary systems that would not be well-addressed by the application of change strategies borrowed from a completely different and possibly incompatible system. Second, there are pragmatic concerns to consider: In a post-secondary landscape pre-occupied with financial viability, we simply cannot afford to invest in change efforts that do not work or that produce unintended results. Finally, university systems meet instrumental needs for many people; this is indicated by the variety implicit in current critiques of post-secondary education. Generating evidence will help to ensure that change is conducted in a way that is meaningful for a critical mass of those who are connected to post-secondary systems.

A focus on the consideration of evidence that is generated from sound inquiry will not only ground post-secondary change in a meaningful way, but will also have the potential to mediate a highly fractured discourse. When the members of a university community center their attentions on evidence, it forces a collective move away from dichotomized entrenchment in either neo-liberal or traditional stances regarding the nature of improvement; the prospect of inquiry encourages us to acknowledge that change in higher education is viewed and occurs from multiple perspectives and paradigms. Attention shifts from the advocacy of "best" answers to the asking of unanswered questions. How has the university institution come to be? What is the university right now? What characterizes current activity in post-secondary systems? What does post-secondary education mean to a wide variety of people and how do they experience it? The inquiry that is structured to collect evidence in answer to these types of questions will help scholars and practitioners uncover the mechanisms that make post-secondary change both meaningful and effective.

CONCLUSION

Over the past 200 years, universities have exhibited a relatively slow evolution that has been both structural and interpretive in nature. They have moved from the use of a collegiate style of education and its consequent infrastructure to the use of modular systems, structures, and processes in educational delivery. This evolution was not accidental and its impetus has been traced back to parallel public desires for individually tailored programs and greater consumer choice in higher education. In some respects, then, the current critique of higher education and accompanying call for post-secondary change is somewhat puzzling. It would appear that the university institution—which, as an institution, is inherently difficult to change—*has* changed. Outward appearances might suggest that this evolution occurred appropriately in the effort to meet public need. Nevertheless, the ongoing critique of current higher education trends, including market models of educational delivery, a shift toward managerialism, and an emphasis on accountability, suggests a deep-seated dissatisfaction with the state of post-secondary education worldwide.

Post-secondary change, or even transformation, is imminent; some would argue that change in higher education is already well underway. Numerous change strategies have been articulated and many of them have been attempted in various post-secondary contexts. However, the purposes of, meanings associated with, and results of higher education change are unclear. Figuratively speaking, the waters are muddy; it is difficult to identify any widely held perception of a comprehensive, evidence-based rationale for change or the intended direction or effect of improvement efforts. How, then, does the post-secondary institution begin to navigate such muddy waters?

I argue that the most reasonable and valuable place to begin is with evidence. Evidence is a hallmark of post-secondary life, and most people at universities— regardless of disciplinary focus—speak the "language" of evidence. Using evidence as a rationale for change and as a tool to leverage improvement is an inherently pragmatic approach because research, conducted for the purpose of generating evidence, is one of the most common and revered practices in post-secondary education.

Use of evidence as a driver of change is one of the only ways we will come to an understanding of the generalities we can apply to university systems and simultaneous hypotheses about the kinds of specific strategies that are most appropriate given the particular needs and environments in individual institutions. Gathering evidence allows us to gradually uncover the post-secondary phenomena in which we are interested. Consideration of evidence allows us to understand what is really "going on" in universities—how institutions are structured as systems, the kinds of activities that characterize university systems, and the mechanisms operating within university systems that bring about particular results. Furthermore, the search for evidence allows us to acknowledge that there is not one definitive truth but multiple and overlapping understandings of university life that influence perceptions of change and improvement. Finally, the use of evidence when crafting change strategies allows practitioners the opportunity to apply suites of well-considered solutions that acknowledge the multiplicity inherent in the reality of university life.

Some will read this chapter and argue that what I have offered is yet another theoretical take on a problem of practice that has already become bogged down in theory. I contend that the value in what I have suggested rests not necessarily in the idea but in the potential importance of the idea with respect to bridging theory and application. Reliance on evidence is a simple strategy for post-secondary change that is currently under-used in the very environment where it might be most successfully applied. The snapshot of the current landscape offered here, then, becomes a foundation for inquiry, where the next step is to engage in the design of specific research efforts that generate the evidence needed to begin a change movement in a manner that ensures meaning and significance in application.

<h2 style="text-align:center">REFERENCES</h2>

Aaker, D. A. (2008). *Spanning silos: The new CMO imperative*. Boston, MA: Harvard Business School Press.

Appleby, A. (1999). Benchmarking theory: A framework for the business world as a context for its application in higher education. In H. Smith, M. Armstrong, & S. Brown (Eds.), *Benchmarking and threshold standards in higher education* (pp. 53–69). London: Kogan Page.

Armstrong, M. (1999). Historical and contextual perspectives on benchmarking in higher education. In H. Smith, M. Armstrong, & S. Brown (Eds.), *Benchmarking and threshold standards in higher education* (pp. 7–34). London: Kogan Page.

Bergquist, W. H., & Pawlak, K. (2008). *Engaging the six cultures of the academy*. San Francisco, CA: Jossey Bass.

Bess, J. L. (1988). *Collegiality and bureaucracy in the modern university*. New York, NY: Teachers College Press.

Bess, J. L., & Dee, J. R. (2012). *Understanding college and university organization* (Vol. 1). Sterling, VA: Stylus.

Birnbaum, R. (2001). *Management fads in higher education*. San Francisco, CA: Jossey Bass.

Bok, D. (2004). The benefits and costs of commercialization in the academy. In D. G. Stein (Ed.), *Buying in or selling out?* (pp. 32–47). Piscataway, NJ: Rutgers University Press.

Booth, W. C., Colomb, G. G., & Williams, J. M. (2008). *The craft of research* (3rd ed). Chicago, IL: The University of Chicago Press.

Boyce, M. E. (2003). Organizational learning is essential to achieving and sustaining change in higher education. *Innovative Higher Education, 28*(2), 119–136. doi:10.1023/B:IHIE.0000006287.69207.00

Campayre, G. (2009). The rise of the universities. In R. Lowe (Ed.), *The history of higher education* (Vol. 1, pp. 67–80). London: Routledge.

Christensen Hughes, J., & Mighty, J. (Eds.). (2010). *Taking stock: Research in teaching and learning in higher education*. Montreal, QC, Canada: Queen's Policy Studies Series, McGill-Queen's University Press.

Clark, I. D., Moran, G., Skolnik, M. L., & Trick, D. (2009). *Academic transformation: The forces reshaping higher education in Ontario*. Kingston, ON: Queen's School of Policy Studies.

Cobban, A. B. (2009). Concept of a university. In R. Lowe (Ed.), *The history of higher education* (Vol. 2, pp. 4–17). London: Routledge.

Cook, L. P. (2010). Values drive the plan. *New Directions for Student Services, 132*, 27–38. doi:10.1002/ss.373

Côté, J. E., & Allahar, A. L. (2007). *Ivory tower blues: A university system in crisis*. Toronto, ON: University of Toronto Press.

Deem, R. (2008). Uravelling the fabric of academe: The managerialist university and its implications for the integrity of academic work. In J. L. Turk (Ed.), *Universities at risk: How politics, special interests and corporatization threaten academic integrity* (pp. 256–281). Toronto, ON: James Lorimer & Co.

Deem, R., Hillyard, S., & Reed, M. (2007). *Knowledge, higher education, and the new managerialism: The changing management of UK universities*. doi:10.1093/acprof:oso/9780199265909.001.0001

Deming, W. E. (2000). *Out of the crisis*. Cambridge, MA: MIT Press.

Dickeson, R. C. (2010). *Prioritizing academic programs and services: Reallocating resources to achieve strategic balance*. San Francisco, CA: Jossey Bass.

Dill, D. D., & Soo, M. (2005). Academic quality, league tables, and public policy: A cross-national analysis of university ranking systems. *Higher Education, 49*(4), 495–533. doi:10.1007/s10734-004-1746-8

Duderstadt, J. J. (2004). Delicate balance: Market forces versus the public interest. In D. G. Stein (Ed.), *Buying in or selling out?* (pp. 56–74). Piscataway, NJ: Rutgers University Press.

Ellis, S. E. (2010). Introduction to strategic planning in student affairs: A model for process and elements of a plan. *New Directions for Student Services, 132*, 5–16. doi:10.1002/ss.371

Finnie, R., & Usher, A. (2005). *Measuring the quality of post-secondary education: Concepts, current practices and a strategic plan*. Ottawa, ON: Canadian Policy Research Networks. Retrieved from http://immagic.com/eLibrary/ARCHIVES/GENERAL/CPRN_CA/C050407F.pdf

Fisher, D., Rubenson, K., Jones, G., & Shanahan, T. (2009). The political economy of post-secondary education: A comparison of British Columbia, Ontario and Quebec. *Higher Education, 57*(5), 549–566. doi:10.1007/s10734-008-9160-2

Gall, M. D., Gall, J. P., & Borg, W. R. (2010). *Applying educational research* (6th ed.). Boston, MA: Pearson.

Geiger, R. L. (2002). The competition for high-ability students: Universities in a key marketplace. In S. Brint (Ed.), *The future of the city of intellect: The changing American university* (pp. 82–106). Stanford, CA: Stanford University Press.

Grub, W. N., & Lazerson, M. (2005). Vocationalism in higher education: The triumph of the education gospel. *The Journal of Higher Education, 76*(1), 1–25. doi:10.1353/jhe.2005.0007

Grünig, R., & Kühn, R. (2011). *Process based strategic planning*. Heidelberg, Germany: Springer. Retrieved from http://www.springerlink.com.cyber.usask.ca/content/978-3-642-16714-0/#section=813091&page=4&locus=45

Harvey, L., & Knight, P. T. (1996). *Transforming higher education*. Buckingham, UK: Society for Research into Higher Education.

144

Henkel, M. (2005). Academic identity and autonomy in a changing policy environment. *Higher Education, 49*(1/2), 155–176. Retrieved from http://link.springer.com.cyber.usask.ca/journal/10734/49/1/page/1

Hofstede, G. H. (1998). Attitudes, values and organizational culture: Disentangling the concepts. *Organization Studies, 19*(3), 477–492. doi:10.1177/017084069801900305

Kezar, A., & Eckel, P. D. (2002). The effect of institutional culture on change strategies in higher education: Universal principles or culturally responsive concepts? *The Journal of Higher Education, 73*(4), 435–460. Retrieved from http://www.jstor.org/stable/1558422

Kezar, A., & Lester, J. (2009). *Organizing higher education for collaboration*. San Francisco, CA: Jossey Bass.

Kirp, D. L. (2006). This little student went to market. In R. H. Hersh & J. Merrow (Eds.), *Declining by degrees: Higher education at risk* (pp. 113–129). New York, NY: Palgrave Macmillan.

Krimsky, S. (2008). When sponsored research fails the admissions test: A normative framework. In J. L. Turk (Ed.), *Universities at risk: How politics, special interests and corporatization threaten academic integrity* (pp. 70–95). Toronto, ON: James Lorimer & Co.

Kuh, G. D., Kinzie, J., Schuh, J. H., & Whitt, E. J. (2005). *Student success in college: Creating conditions that matter*. San Francisco, CA: Jossey Bass.

Lewis, R. G., & Smith, D. H. (1994). *Total quality in higher education*. Delray Beach, FL: St. Lucie Press.

McInnes, C. (1995). Less control and more vocationalism: The Australian and New Zealand experience. In T. Schuller (Ed.), *The changing university?* (pp. 38–51). London: Society for Research into Higher Education. Retrieved from http://files.eric.ed.gov/fulltext/ED415725.pdf

Middaugh, M. F. (2010). *Planning and assessment in higher education*. San Francisco, CA: Jossey Bass.

Morley, L., & Aynsley, S. (2007). Employers, quality and standards in higher education: Shared values and vocabularies or elitism and inequalities? *Higher Education Quarterly, 61*(3), 229–249. doi:10.1111/j.1468-2273.2007.00353.x

Olsen, N. D., Olsen, E. J., & Olsen, H. W. (2004). *Strategic planning made easy*. Retrieved from http://library.books24x7.com.cyber.usask.ca/toc.aspx?site=D7375&bookid=9741

Pattenaude, R. L. (2000). Administering the modern university. In J. Losco & B. L. Fife (Eds.), *Higher education in transition: The challenges of the new millennium* (pp. 159–175). Westport, CT: Bergin & Garvey.

Rashdall, H. (2009). What is a university? In R. Lowe (Ed.), *The history of higher education* (Vol. 2, pp. 18–35). London: Routledge.

Rothblatt, S. (2009). The American modular system. In R. Lowe (Ed.), *The history of higher education* (Vol. 4, pp. 391–404). London: Routledge.

Schafer, A. (2008). The university as corporate handmaiden: Who're ya gonna trust? In J. L. Turk (Ed.), *Universities at risk: How politics, special interests and corporatization threaten academic integrity* (pp. 43–69). Toronto, ON: James Lorimer & Co.

Schein, E. H. (1990). Organizational culture. *American Psychologist, 45*(2), 109–199.

Schein, E. H. (1992). *Organizational culture and leadership* (2nd ed.). San Francisco, CA: Jossey Bass.

Schroeder, C. C. (1999). Partnerships: An imperative for enhancing student learning and institutional effectiveness. *New Directions for Student Services, 87*, 5–18. doi:10.1002/ss.8701

Schutz, P., & Bloch, B. (2006). The "silo-virus": Diagnosing and curing departmental groupthink. *Team Performance Management, 12*, 31–43. Retrieved from www.emeraldinsight.com/1352-7592.htm

Scott, W. R. (2008). *Institutions and organizations* (3rd ed). Thousand Oaks, CA: Sage.

Shanahan, T., & Jones, G. A. (2007). Shifting roles and approaches: Government coordination of post-secondary education in Canada, 1995–2006. *Higher Education Research & Development, 26*(1), 31–43. doi:10.1080/07294360601166794

Stein, D. G. (2004). A personal perspective on the selling of academia. In D. G. Stein (Ed.), *Buying in or selling out?* (pp. 1–16). Piscataway, NJ: Rutgers University Press.

Swoboda, W. (1979). Disciplines and interdisciplinarity: A historical perspective. In J. Kockelmans (Ed.), *Interdisciplinarity and higher education* (pp. 49–92). University Park, PA: Pennsylvania State University Press.

Wadsworth, D. (2006). Ready or not? Where the public stands on higher education reform. In R. H. Hersh & J. Merrow (Eds.), *Declining by degrees: Higher education at risk* (pp. 23–38). New York, NY: Palgrave Macmillan.

Winchester, I. (1986). The future of a mediaeval institution: The university in the twenty-first century. In W. A. W. Neilson & C. Gaffield (Eds.), *Universities in crisis: A mediaeval institution in the twenty-first century* (pp. 269–290). Montreal, QC: The Institute for Research on Public Policy.

Woodhouse, H. (2009). *Selling out: Academic freedom and the corporate market*. Montreal, QC: McGill-Queen's University Press.

ERIKA E. SMITH AND RICHARD HAYMAN

10. DECISION MAKING AND PROBLEMS OF EVIDENCE FOR EMERGING EDUCATIONAL TECHNOLOGIES

To support what is commonly referred to as twenty-first century learning, those in decision-making roles are often urged to quickly adopt and integrate the newest educational technologies and abandon older processes—or risk becoming obsolete. This impetus to quickly adapt can be witnessed in the discourse surrounding the impact of technologies in today's educational landscapes. The past decade has been witness to considerable discussion regarding the purpose and value of educational technologies, especially regarding the potential of e-learning to "transform" learning in the twenty-first century. Those in favour of these innovations, such as Garrison and Anderson (2003), believe that "E-learning will inevitably transform all forms of education and learning in the twenty-first century... E-learning cannot be ignored by those who are seriously committed to enhancing teaching and learning" (p. 2). As such, many technology advocates see the choice as no longer concerning *if* technologies should be used, but rather *what* and *how* technologies will be implemented in the learning environment. As some argue, "Universities no longer have a choice about whether to implement e-learning: they must in order to remain competitive in the market place ... E-learning is now at the heart of a university's core business of learning and teaching" (Kregor, Breslin, & Fountain, 2012, p. 1382).

Related to this discussion of educational transformation via technologies around the turn of the twenty-first century, various depictions of the *Net generation* or Millennials as "digital natives" (Prensky, 2001a, 2001b; Tapscott, 1998, 2008) emerged. Digital natives are purported to: (a) be native speakers of the language of technology; (b) learn differently from preceding generations of students; and (c) demand a new way of teaching and learning involving technology (Thomas, 2011, p. 4). Digital native proponents have been criticized for presenting a problematic utopian vision of technology that is tied to an exoticized picture of liberated young people (Buckingham, 2011), with critics arguing that such popular claims regarding the Net generation as digital natives are largely unsupported by substantive research evidence. Such critics contend that, rather than being theoretically or empirically informed, such kinds of discourse about educational and technological transformation and, relatedly, the debates regarding the needs of digital native students, equate to a form of "moral panic" that restricts critical and rational consideration

P. Newton & D. Burgess (Eds.), The Best Available Evidence, 147–166.
© 2016 Sense Publishers. All rights reserved.

(Bennett, Maton, & Kervin, 2008; Smith, 2012, 2013). Indeed, similar tropes defining a crisis in education, as we will see in the following paragraphs, can be witnessed in the paradigms informing debates on evidence-based education as well (Pirrie, 2001). As a result, there is a need to revisit and perhaps redevelop approaches that enable research-informed decision making regarding emerging technologies in our educational settings.

With the ever-expanding range of emerging educational technologies that could be introduced to learning environments, making evidence-informed decisions about whether and how to effectively use e-learning tools for pedagogical purposes is a critical yet challenging task. How can educators, learners, and administrators make informed decisions about the use of particular emerging technologies to achieve desired pedagogical transformation when, due to their relative newness, there is often a perceived lack of available and "up-to-the-minute" research on the latest technological trends that may impede evidence-based educational practice? This is a key problem of evidence for technology use in higher education.

This chapter discusses several exigent problems of evidence for decision making regarding emerging technologies, particularly for higher education, beginning with a brief overview of evidence-based practice (EBP) and twenty-first century learning. We reflect upon strategies that educational practitioners may employ when facing a perceived lack of up-to-date evidence to support their decision-making processes. By discussing strategies for identifying affordances and employing environmental scanning, we describe approaches for mitigating potential research gaps when considering use of emerging technologies within academic learning contexts.

EMERGING EDUCATIONAL TECHNOLOGIES
IN THE TWENTY-FIRST CENTURY

Notions of teaching and learning in the twenty-first century involve many diverging views on and visions of the future of education. However, within this range of views, a key recurring theme is the need to integrate technology and education effectively and beneficially in the new century (Brown, 2006; Brown & Adler, 2008; Garrison & Anderson, 2003). Illustrative of such discussions, Wan and Gut (2008) asserted the following:

> In many ways, new media and information are already changing the way that we learn and teach in the new century. The field of education is faced with the challenge of redefining teaching and learning to adapt to a rapidly changing world and what it means to be a teacher and a student. (p. 175)

In this environment, technology proponents assert that such tools change learning and should be woven into an interactive and responsive learning space, such that the virtual classroom is just as important as the physical one. Together, these inform an institutional context where constant *connectedness* has become so commonplace that it is often seen as being inseparable from the twenty-first century learning environment itself (although here we prefer the term connectedness, for alternative discussions of *connectivism*, see Siemens, 2005). Today, educators and learners experience education not just through the face-to-face classroom, but also via hardware and networking infrastructures, learning management systems, social media, mobile devices, and Internet ubiquity.

Emerging Technologies

Coupled with this focus on transforming learning via an information revolution happening in the twenty-first century, a core conundrum of the term *emerging technologies* is that it is often misunderstood and remains ill-defined despite its frequent use. Broadly, emerging educational technologies can perhaps be understood as "tools, concepts, innovations, and advancements utilized in diverse educational settings...evolving organisms that experience hype cycles...not yet fully understood, and not yet fully researched" (Veletsianos, 2010, pp. 3–4). Even though they are still in a developmental stage of design and production, emerging technologies are often seen as inherently strategic, in that they are tied to aspirations, investment, planning, and thinking about the future (Einsiedel, 2009).

With this future-looking lens, and reflecting views similar to the e-learning thinkers already mentioned, emerging technologies experts typically focus on tools that will be "revolutionary" or that alter traditional relationships and cause social disruption. For example, technologies that will have broad impacts on day-to-day life, just as historically the automobile, and more recently the Internet and World Wide Web, dramatically reshaped the known world (Einsiedel, 2009, pp. 3–4). Given this future-looking and aspirational focus of those concerned with emergence, a key challenge surrounding research and policies for such technologies in education, then, is contextualizing and applying relevant knowledge that can be used today and in the future, and which will not become quickly out-dated.

Convergence

Amidst all of these discussions of technological emergence, to make sense of the problems facing those in decision-making roles today, there is great potential in the notion of the *converging technologies* as understanding the evolving qualities, integrations, and merger of such tools. According to McLuhan (2002), changes in pattern or interaction are of utmost importance: "the 'message' of any medium or technology is the change of scale or pace or pattern that it introduces into human affairs" (p. 8). The idea of emerging technologies as related to convergence underscores the fact that many technologies we use have evolved and been synergized in a unifying way (Kaldis, 2010), building upon and integrating the qualities of previous technologies. From another standpoint, media convergence may be understood as "the flow of content across multiple media platforms, the cooperation of multiple media companies, and the migratory behaviour of media audiences" (Jenkins, 2006, p. 2). As such, these technological or media patterns and scale changes can be seen as the message.

An example of the convergence of emerging technologies is Google Apps (increasingly used in educational settings), which now combines the traditionally separate features of email with amalgamated features of calendars, documents, and talk (voice over IP and chat), and further enhanced by online storage and cloud software (e.g., for document creation and sharing), to name a few. Another example can be seen in social microblogs such as Twitter, which has combined previously discrete forms of short message service (SMS), really simple syndication (RSS) feeds, direct messages (DM), and weblogs (or blogs), all within a micro 140 character setup. Finally, convergence may be seen in the increasing prominence of a platform across other technologies; for instance, the increasingly common option to use one's Facebook, Google+, or Twitter account to login and connect to other third-party social networking applications, such as Pinterest or Academia.edu. This synergy, unification, or merging of technologies can be a critical point of consideration when searching for evidence, particularly for those who use technology in their educational practice, and one to which we will return in our case study.

Emerging web technologies are increasingly used in academic learning environments, and include a host of social media tools, such as blogs, wikis, instant messengers (IM), social bookmarks, podcasts, and vodcasts (Saeed, Yun, & Sinnappan, 2009). Willcockson and Phelps (2010) provided a useful overview of emerging technologies, in which they list many social media and web-based technologies, but also include serious games and virtual worlds. Recent editions of the New Media Consortium's annual *Horizon Report* (Johnson et al., 2013; Johnson, Adams Becker, Estrada, & Freeman, 2014, 2015) have outlined key emerging technologies that they assert will impact higher education in the next five years, including ubiquitous social media, massively open online courses (MOOCs), tablet computing, games and gamification, learning analytics, 3D printing, makerspaces, and wearable technology. In addition to these sources, and within higher education specifically, information on trending emerging technologies is easily discoverable via the *ECAR Study of Undergraduate Students and Information Technology* (see EDUCAUSE reports, e.g., Dahlstrom, Walker, & Dziuban, 2013; Dahlstrom & Bichsel, 2014), not to mention various conferences, journals, magazines, and blogs all interested in detailing new developments in educational technologies. Notably for higher education, current discussion about transformation and disruption has centred to a large extent on MOOCs, a topic with widespread media coverage that is debated as either a revolutionary game-changer (Leckart, 2012) or as an over-hyped and problematic venture (Schuman, 2013).

EVIDENCE-BASED PRACTICE IN EDUCATION

As the diversity of chapters included in this publication illustrates, ways of using the best available evidence in education are much discussed, and there are many perspectives on the process and constitution of evidence-based practice (EBP) and decision making for educational contexts. We can see that relating research evidence and practice is, unsurprisingly, an important focus for many professional areas. Evidence-based practice has fully emerged in disciplines such as education, health care (as illustrated by journals such as *Evidence-Based Medicine*), and library and information sciences (for further discussion of evidence-based decision making in professional library contexts, see Hayman & Smith, 2015). These fields have influenced one another in their definitions of evidence-based practice, and so while EBP is intended to have specific disciplinary and professional application, EBP should be understood broadly as an overwhelmingly interdisciplinary and interprofessional concept. Furthermore, the overlap between evidence and practice within these disciplines reflects the relationship between research and education as concomitant endeavours involving the discovery and application of new forms of knowledge for societal and individual betterment. Clearly, this relationship is especially relevant to universities whose mandates reflect research-teaching relationships through educational programs at the undergraduate and graduate level, and who are increasingly involved in lifelong learning and continuous professional development programs.

Within discussions of evidence-based education, proponents argue for transformation through increased incorporation of evidence in education to better inform policy and practice. For instance, Slavin (2002) saw great promise in an EBP "scientific revolution" that will change education with a "focus on rigorous experiments evaluating replicable programs and practices" (p. 15). Similarly, Davies (1999) argued for an increase in evidence-based approaches that involve utilizing and establishing high-quality research (systematic reviews and meta-analyses, often relying on scientific means and criteria), to inform a set of principles and practices that enhance and support professional judgment in the field. Davies (1999) explicitly noted crossover between these characteristics of evidence-based education and those in evidence-based healthcare, and likewise Slavin (2002) drew direct connection to medical interventions and experiments. Such approaches to evidence-based education have been taken up with goal of improving policy and practice; for example, through initiatives such as the Best Evidence Encyclopedia (http://www.bestevidence.org/) created by the Johns Hopkins University Center for Data-Driven Reform in Education.

Several criticisms have been levelled against such approaches to EBP in education, including the strong relationship to scientific and quantitative strategies at the exclusion of other approaches. For example, in response to arguments from thinkers like Slavin (2002) who advocate for a prescriptive or replicable "what works" approach to education, Olson (2004) proposed that we must examine critically the underpinning "beliefs, goals, and intentions of those supposedly affected by the treatments" (p. 24) offered. Other critics, such as Pirrie (2001), point out that these arguments reflect a form of "moral panic" that precipitates an inflated "crisis of legitimation" (p. 124) underscoring the rationale for transformation, a stance similar

151

to that presented by Bennett, Maton, and Kervin (2008) in response to problems of evidence within the digital native debate. What these critics present is a concern about the limited range of methodologies and toolkits (i.e., those solely reflecting scientific or instrumental paradigms) accepted as a part of evidence-based education. Such points underscore the need for critical acknowledgement that research and education should not and cannot take a context-free, one-size-fits-all-approach.

It is our view that, by being reflexive about these issues, educators conducting research-informed EBP can intentionally take into account a wider range of paradigms, methodologies, and strategies in ways that avoid unnecessary prescription. One way that we may do so is by leveraging emerging frameworks that articulate relational aspects of practice. Such flexible frameworks, as we outline in more detail below, can also include approaches to environmental scanning and identifying aims and affordances that may widen the available sources of useful evidence. In recognizing both the benefits and limitations of an evidence-based approach, we can balance the value of evidence-informed decision making with the need for contextualized practice.

PROBLEMS OF EVIDENCE FOR EMERGING TECHNOLOGIES IN EDUCATION

As the preceding discussion suggests, discovering information on the features of new technologies themselves is relatively easy given the variety of sources describing and forecasting technology trends. However, when little is known about these technologies in practice, such as how tools in production interface with existing technological infrastructures, policies, and processes, there still exists a significant challenge: how do we make informed decisions regarding if, where, and when new technologies should be incorporated into our teaching and learning environments? This is the crux of the evidence problem at hand: when it comes to any given emerging technology, where there is a perceived lack of substantive up-to-date research regarding its educational use, value, and impact on pedagogy, how can we address potential barriers and support evidence-based decision-making models?

Wicked Problems

Facing the challenges outlined above, decision makers may see the development of theoretical and empirical evidence that informs use of emerging technologies in practice as unavailable, or perhaps as too slow or unrealistic, given the ever-changing and evolving nature of such innovations. As the nature of these issues are seen to be complex and constantly changing, it can be helpful to understand decision making and planning related to emerging educational technologies as an *unstructured* or *wicked* problem.

Particularly relevant to planning and policy development, *wicked problems* were first defined by Rittel and Webber (1973) as those societal issues that differ from problems of math and science precisely because they do not have clear true-false answers. In other words, finding "one-best answer" is impossible with wicked problems, as they do not have a definitive formulation or solution. As a result, rather than searching for value-free or "true" answers, with wicked problems the (social) context must inform meaningful and iterative judgment of information to resolve, rather than solve, the items at hand (Rittel & Webber, 1973). Furthermore, there is no opportunity for trial-and-error testing of the proposed solutions to wicked problems, for all implementations and decisions (or, attempted reversal of decisions) will have real-world impacts and consequences that cannot be undone. As Rittel and Webber argued with an example from education, the "effects of an experimental curriculum will follow the pupils into their adult lives" (p. 163). Along these same lines, *unstructured decisions* are seen as those "decision processes that have not been encountered in quite the same form and for which no predetermined and explicit set of ordered responses exists in the organization" (Mintzberg, Raisinghani, & Théorêt, 1976, p. 246). As we have seen, the characteristics of wicked problems and unstructured decisions can be witnessed in discussions regarding the conundrum of emerging technologies and their educational impact.

It is useful to understand the issues surrounding decision-making for emerging educational technologies through the lenses of unstructured or wicked problems and EBP in education, since there is often an articulated concern about quickly adapting to technological innovations that have not been encountered in the same form and for which there is no pre-set response. Rather than searching for the "one-best answer" or looking for "the best evidence" or even "best" solutions or practices to follow as we encounter wicked technological and educational problems, it is instead more useful to consider approaches to the meaningful and iterative judgment of high-quality information within our social and educational contexts.

Identifying Problems of Evidence

While several problems of evidence exist regarding emerging educational technologies, in this chapter we focus on what we have come to understand as a perceived lack of new "up-to-the-minute" research on evolving technological innovations. Through our own professional practice working in technology-enhanced education settings, this is a concern we face regularly in our own educational roles, and one that we regularly see in our consultations with other academics and educators. In seeking to effectively adopt emerging technologies, this perceived lack of evidence leads to a potentially dichotomous position. Must we: (a) quickly adopt emerging technologies without applying the evidence, therefore falling short of a true research-informed decision-making process, or else (b) delay the adoption cycle until evidence exists, in the form of educational research, but risk missing opportunities for innovation and being seen as out-dated due to the delay in time-to-adoption? If the problem is presented to us in this manner, as is so frequently the case, then there is no ready solution and no clear answer.

However, we argue that several approaches can be used to identify and mitigate such problems of evidence, approaches that do not limit us to these dichotomous options. Even though new and emerging technologies can (and do) shape practice, a lack of formal research around a particular new technology does not mean there is no useful evidence base of information to be found. The following discussion outlines the complementary approaches of identifying aims and affordances, along with environmental scanning, and we argue that these methods can be used to recognize and address the perceived lack of traditional evidence available for effectively incorporating new technologies into practice.

APPROACHES TO INFORMED DECISION MAKING
REGARDING EMERGING TECHNOLOGIES

When implementing emerging technologies, there are a variety of possible methods one can use to address the problem of evidence. In this section we highlight two tried-and-tested methods: identifying aims and affordances, and the information seeking environmental scan. We then use a case study to highlight how these two methods can be applied in an academic environment for practical results. And while it makes sense to identify affordances before the conducting the environmental scan, we are not suggesting that this is a rigid, step-by-step process. Ultimately, we propose that these are complementary methods that are relational in nature and should be used in tandem, so that each iteratively informs the other.

Identify Aims and Affordances

When facing a lack of up-to-date evidence on a specific new technology, it is often helpful for practitioners to (re)focus on the aims and affordances related to the questions and problems at hand. Willcockson and Phelps (2010) called this focus "keeping learning central," and make sound recommendations for examining the learning theories, learner characteristics, and instructional goals when determining whether or not to use an emerging technology. This may include determining items of theoretical or philosophical importance. As Kanuka (2008) aptly demonstrated, we can best understand technologies in practice by first understanding our philosophies in practice, to avoid simply following the latest trends by taking time to ask *why* what we are doing is important. There is a range of helpful literature and empirical experiences to draw upon regarding pedagogical strategies and philosophical underpinnings that can support and align to the educational goals in mind and inform use of a particular technology.

When implementing emerging technologies for education, Willcockson and Phelps (2010) recommended finding the connection between the *affordances* of the technology being considered for implementation and the learning problem, objective, or goal it is hoped the technology will address. They defined an affordance as "the way a technology or software can be used and what it allows the user to do or not to do" (para. 9). In other words, an affordance is the characteristic that allows (or disallows) one to carry out an action within an environment or via an object. In our physical environment, an example of an affordance is a knob that can be twisted, or an elevator button that can be pressed. In the virtual world an example of an affordance is an on-screen button that the user can click or touch when using a mouse or trackpad or touchscreen, i.e., the button affords clicking. Willcockson and Phelps provided multiple examples of affordance-learning goal matching, such as using a wiki to meet the outcome of providing students an online mechanism to collaborate on content creation, or establishing student blogs to create opportunities for reflective learning via journaling (para. 10).

The idea of affordances has influenced a number of fields, including industrial design, human-computer interaction, and instructional design. In designing learning interactions for the physical or virtual environment, we can leverage the notion of affordances to make informed choices that can enhance optimal aspects or reduce sub-optimal ones. For example, certain affordances of educational media or e-learning technologies may be designed to enable optimal presentation, engagement, or interaction with material (e.g., via graphics, text, sound, etc.), and when used according to design principles can aid in comprehension (see, e.g., Clark & Mayer, 2011; Mayer, 2005). By considering affordances or the properties of learning environments and objects, educators can use instructional design to meet goals, and to make informed choices about the selection and use educational technologies. They can intentionally design learning objects that use media features, for instance, to promote learning, to reduce cognitive load, and ultimately to help learners achieve the intended learning goals (Rabinowitz & Shaw, 2005, p. 51). Perhaps most importantly, educators and decision makers can endeavour not to simply forecast technological trends, but to observe and forecast changes and patterns of interaction between learners, their environment, and the content.

Speaking generally, to connect pedagogical goals with affordances, we suggest conducting a literature review or evidence search that seeks other implementations of comparable pedagogical outcomes achieved with similar technologies (or similar affordances), to understand the pedagogical and technological impact in situations akin to the one at hand. During this evidence search the guiding questions may change, for instance, from "How can I use this emerging technology in my teaching?" to "How can I design learning, given the affordances available, to meet this pedagogical goal?" However, it is important to remember that the affordances discovered within technologies, whether emergent or long-standing, do not necessarily inherently lead or connect to learning outcomes. As Day and Lloyd (2007) argued, it is important to recognize that affordances should be understood as "products of a whole learning context, of which online [and other] technologies are an integral part, rather than being inherent properties of the technologies in isolation from the context in which they are used" (p. 20). When we recommend identifying affordances to inform decision making when facing a problem of evidence, it is this more broad perspective we envision, a perspective that accounts for one's proposed learning outcomes, learning environment, and learner characteristics.

The importance of discussing affordances with regard to decision making for emerging educational technologies here comes back to our earlier point that an evidence base must be contextualized to the learning goals and outcomes intended. After identifying learning goals and affordances within our educational setting, objects, and materials, we can then create an evidence base by searching for and utilizing existing research literature and empirical observations on similar goals and affordances. Thus, rather than simply focusing on a current technological trend or on a newly launched innovation in isolation, there can be a focus on learning from research on, and experiences with, pedagogical goals and affordances that have existed and perhaps evolved or converged over time. When we critically examine whether these characteristics or features can enhance or subvert our intended educational purpose, we can make informed decisions about how best to work within the constraints of our circumstances to achieve the desired educational results. If we adhere to the argument that there exists no one-size-fits-all approach to making evidence-based decisions that will work for every circumstance, then looking at goals and aligning the intended outcomes with appropriate affordances becomes a powerful way to find and refine useful information from similar areas that will hold relevance.

Although emerging technologies are often perceived to be so revolutionary and new that no formal research around their use exists, it is important to emphasize that often these technologies build upon and incorporate lessons learned and information from publications and empirical observation of established features, functionalities, and affordances. There is a well-established body of literature on educational strategies, instructional design, and e-learning that can be leveraged when one has identifiable pedagogical outcomes and affordances in mind, regardless of whether a particular trend or theme is at play. Thus, we recommend that practitioners seeking an evidence base should look for recent implementation of similar affordances or features that may have converged across similar, related technologies, rather than focus on the one specific technology under consideration. For example, someone who is considering whether to implement Google Talk for synchronous chat- and text-based communication in a distance education setting may consult existing research on chat and talk tools within learning management systems, or within older or established technologies like Skype and MSN Messenger. Consulting existing research on converging technologies with similar characteristics that reflect the particular learning goals to be met through implementation is one recommended method for addressing the problem of evidence.

Environmental Scanning

When faced with an important decision around adoption of a new technology, particularly in situations where technology integration is deemed to be required, but where formal, specific evidence is perceived to be lacking, the use of *environmental scanning* is a tried and tested method of information gathering. Many post-secondary institutions and other organizations do this as part of a strategic and often future-looking planning process (Gibbs, 1996; Grummon, 2012). In many respects, the aforementioned *ECAR Study* and the *Horizon Report* both use environmental scanning as the foundation for their reporting.

Environmental scanning takes many forms depending on the discipline or focus of the scan, and there are various definitions and types depending on the need and anticipated outcome. From an information-gathering standpoint, the activity of scanning the environment can perhaps best be understood as the "acquisition and use of information about events, trends, and relationships in an organization's external environment, the knowledge of which would assist management in planning the organization's future course of action" (Choo, 2001, para. 1). Further to this definition, Chrusciel (2011) defined an environmental scan as a crucial part of the strategic planning process for organizations, particularly for identifying quality of service, customer expectations, and anticipating future needs. However it is worth noting that an environmental scan itself must be more than just an exercise in information gathering, and that the resources must be assessed for applicability to one's situation and context. As Zhang, Majid, and Foo (2010) concluded, the environmental scan requires important information literacy skills that involve the evaluation and use of the information discovered, and connecting that use to the intended outcomes.

Though discussions of environmental scanning are often framed within a managerial or organizational planning lens, we believe that an understanding of these activities should be expanded to include educational practitioners across all levels of the institution. The ES can be conducted by undertaking information-gathering, observation, and experimentation with technologies. In this way, environmental scanning and information gathering activities can help in constructing shared knowledge-bases via networks, within communities of practice (Wenger, 1998) and communities of inquiry (Garrison, Anderson, & Archer, 2000, 2010), both inside and beyond an individual's own institutional systems.

To put it simply, when it comes to decisions around new technologies, creating an evidence base may be realized by establishing an *empirical foundation* using a range of strategies that incorporate the experiences, observations, and experimentation done by others. This is not to devalue the literature review process, which is an essential undertaking, but rather underscores the importance of going beyond the extant research literature during the information gathering process, especially when faced with an initial dearth of recorded evidence. As Alderman, Towers, and Bannah (2012) described in their study on student feedback mechanisms, "although the main emphasis is on sources demonstrating evidence-based research supported by sound theoretical underpinnings, other relevant resources such as observational studies, reports and conference papers are also taken into account" (p. 262) to inform their research.

When engaging in decision making with respect to putting new or unfamiliar technologies into practice, we recommend information seeking via Internet searching, one of the most common forms of environmental scanning. The ES may incorporate readily accessible (public) websites and news sources, along with sometimes hard to discover reports, white papers, and other informally published resources traditionally classified as grey literature. The kinds of resources discovered for the ES may depend on the type of technology and pedagogical setting that is the subject of the scan, and naturally there are limits to this type of scanning. For instance, Internet scanning success can be hit-or-miss depending on whether one's selected search terms match against indexed metadata recognized by the search engine being used. Moreover, typically this type of scan will not successfully discover material in the Deep Web, such as material behind a password-protected portal (e.g., an institution's employee-only intranet or LMS), potentially missing key resources that would be helpful for constructing a more fulsome evidence base. Nevertheless, to address the problem of evidence this type of scanning is still useful.

Increasingly, social media applications and online social networks can further aid in environmental scanning. For instance, Academia.edu provides not only availability of some online resources, but also provides connections to a community of researchers and practitioners with whom one may discuss issues of interest. Tools for community building, such as online forums and online news sources, may also prove useful for connecting with a community of academics, practitioners, or other user groups also in the midst of exploring similar questions and issues. Of course, ethical and privacy issues may limit the availability or effectiveness of information shared in online contexts, however it is not within the scope of this chapter to discuss those items in detail. Ultimately, the scanner must then account for the credibility and utility of these resources through applying information-literacy skills, and then determine how these examples can be applied and contextualized within their own scenario.

In regards to both strategies of identifying aims and affordances and conducting an environmental scan, clearly each approach should inform the other as decision makers refine their own understandings and make sense of the available evidence related to pedagogical aims and outcomes, as well as technological features and affordances. As a wicked problem, the challenge of finding evidence for emerging educational technologies may be mitigated by refocusing on the purpose and characteristics of the pedagogical and technological items at hand.

CASE STUDY: IPADS IN AN ACADEMIC LIBRARY

At this juncture, an example of early adoption of an emerging technology in a practice-based pedagogical setting is useful. Our case study involves the 2010 launch of the Apple iPad, which generated immediate educational interest at the time of release while also maintaining ongoing relevance for today's educators. It is worth noting that there are multiple other emerging technology examples we could have selected to make this case, but at nearly 94% of the market share for tablet products for education as of late 2013 (AppleInsider, 2013; Cheng, 2013), the dominance of iPads in education make it a highly relevant example even today. The case study is built from one author's direct experience implementing iPads in an educational setting shortly after the device appeared on the market, and therefore provides first-hand insights into ES strategies and implementation issues faced with this particular emerging technology.

Case Study Background

While upon release the iPads received a lot of attention from academic communities, it should come as no surprise that at that time there was no available academic research on successful implementation of this specific iPad technology in an educational setting. The problem of a lack of evidence in this case is a striking example of how the impetus to quickly adopt a new and emerging technology poses immediate challenges. With no iPad-specific evidence to consult to assess what kind of pedagogical impact would emerge when students began taking the devices into their classrooms, let alone how to address the logistical challenges of ensuring access, keeping the devices secure, and providing a support mechanism for users, those seeking to implement iPads in their learning environments required alternative evidence gathering opportunities.

In 2010, a medium-sized undergraduate university in Alberta, Canada looked to implement an iPad-lending program through the library. The iPads were made available to all members of the university community via a sign-out process within the library, with a focus on availability first and foremost to students. The project team identified a number of goals for the project, such as meeting the library's commitment to introduce new and innovative technologies into the students' learning experiences, along with a determination to provide users with an option for mobile computing that went beyond traditional desktop or laptop computers. The selection of iPads was also influenced by a number of external factors outside the original scope of the project, including the fact that some faculty members and instructors were expressing an interest in tablets and ereader technologies, and that the university bookstore was independently exploring options for etextbooks. The timely release of the iPad commercially, and its potential for both general and educational use, presented an excellent opportunity to take this emerging technology into an academic setting.

Aims and Affordances

The methods discussed above for addressing the lack of evidence were useful in identifying how best to proceed, first by identifying outcomes and recognizing affordances, and then via a web-based environmental scan. Regarding affordances, the project team recognized that some characteristics of iPad technology could be easily matched to the expressed project outcomes, as illustrated in Table 1.

Table 1. Connecting affordance to outcome for iPads available via the library

Desired outcome	Technological use or characteristic
Provide mobile computing options for users to incorporate into their learning	Tablet computer with wireless Internet connection; mobility provides anytime, anywhere access
Improve access to ebooks and electronic scholarly resources and articles	Can be used as an ebook and PDF reader through web browser or downloadable applications
Make available to as many users as possible	Can be easily erased and restored through centralized account management, does not need to be attached to a single user

For instance, one driving factor of the project was the desire to improve access to the ebook and electronic article content available to users via the library's online resource collection. Since an iPad can be used as an ereader via the built-in web browser, via its ability to open common document formats including PDFs, and through the downloadable iBooks application, this technology provided multiple options for users seeking mobile access to ebooks and electronic articles.

Upon deeper examination of the technology under consideration, it became clear that the original iPads contained features that were similar to those found within existing ereader technologies. Recognizing this convergence, and identifying ereader affordances as important, led the project manager to consult existing literature about how various ereaders had been implemented in university and classroom settings. Ereaders had been commercially available in North America since as early as 2004, while popular devices including the Sony Reader, Amazon's Kindle, and Barnes & Noble's Nook ensured the adoption of ereader technology, and as such the project team had little trouble identifying various examples of how ereaders had been successfully implemented in classrooms and other academic settings. Now more informed about how those ereader devices had impacted pedagogically on learners and educators, particularly within the context of higher education settings and academic libraries, the project team then looked for other convergences. For example, the team recognized that some education institutions were using other Apple mobile devices, such as the iPhone and iPod Touch, in their classroom settings. Examining the formal and informal evidence base from those implementations provided additional insights regarding what we might expect from the iPad project.

Environmental Scanning

The other recommended method for addressing the lack of research evidence, conducting an environmental scan, proved invaluable for the success of the iPad project. Despite the novelty of iPads, web-based environmental scanning was helpful in identifying other institutions that had implemented, or were in the process of implementing, projects also using iPads in their academic settings. As an information gathering process, this environmental scan relied upon general Internet searching using keyword searches in a search engine (e.g., targeted to find institutional materials, etc.), and returned an astounding number of hits that were not always specific to the project. Sifting through and assessing the results of this Internet search required patience on the part of those conducting the scan, a potential shortcoming of this type of information seeking behaviour mentioned above. However, by revealing where and how similar institutions were using iPads, especially those in academic library and university settings, the environmental scan itself was a worthwhile endeavour.

The compiled results of an environmental scan will look different for each project, but generally speaking should seek to document and categorize each scan result itself (and its source) for later reference, along with comments on the source's utility or application to the project at hand. As shown in Table 2, for the iPad project scan, results were categorized into two main types: primary sources (e.g., a website about an existing project) and secondary sources (e.g., a news site which mentioned a project), accompanied by a note on general information included in the result, and comments on the source's overall usefulness for the project at hand.

Table 2. Example – Documenting results of the iPad project environment scan

Scan source	Category	Information revealed	Useful for local project?
Project website	Primary	Existing and current iPad project at an academic institution; identifies aims and outcomes; logistical details outlined.	Yes, very. Logistical items and aims are of relevance to this project.
News story	Secondary	Mentions specific iPad project; gives details of student reception.	Yes. Details of student engagement especially helpful.
News story	Secondary	Convergent technology; broad discussion of ereaders in schools.	No. Not specific enough to project context or learning audience.
Academic article	Secondary	Convergent technology; discusses learning outcomes met by using ereaders.	Yes. Educational outcomes met by ereaders apply to iPads.

Note: Table data has been adapted for the purposes of this chapter (e.g., sources anonymized, etc.)

Sources categorized as "primary" are those which yielded the best results related to the iPad project, in that they typically identified existing and current iPad projects in a similar university setting. While information contained in the secondary sources was less impactful to local implementation than primary sources, it was important to document and consult secondary sources that identified similar projects using the same technology or else a convergent technology, no matter whether those projects were in progress or under development. As discussed below, both primary and secondary sources may bear additional fruit. Information garnered from the iPad project environmental scan results included general details (such as over-arching project goals and desired outcomes), as well as project-specific details about other institutional iPad lending programs (such as logistical solutions that had yet to be resolved by the project team). These ES results proved to uncover unique and useful insights for the local project. Generating this informal evidence base about other, similar projects, also aided the team in developing successful implementation criteria at the host institution.

Though not specifically discussed above, we suggest that an important part of the environmental scan is to follow the most relevant sources as far as possible to their root. In the case of the iPad project, this meant contacting those responsible for the projects at similar institutions to informally discuss any methods and evaluation techniques not explicitly revealed by the environment scan results. The project lead contacted a number of institutions involved in similar iPad projects in an attempt to learn more about how those projects were implemented, how they were received by users, and what impact, if any, their respective projects had on the teaching and learning process, on service levels, and how those impacts were evaluated or assessed. Attempting contact in this manner had mixed results, as some respondents were more than happy to share their experiences, while others declined to share for various reasons. However, this measure is still worthwhile, since uncovering additional information from the respondents who did share insights with the project team in this case proved invaluable.

Overall, the small effort spent reaching out to other institutions paid large dividends when the project team was able to rely on this connection for sharing and discussing additional evidence. This extension of the environmental scan certainly bore additional fruit: in one instance an external contact not only provided information about their local project, but served as a secondary source, by pointing toward yet another institution which had not been discovered during the online search. Arguably, then, despite the ease of electronic environmental scanning via the Internet, human connections and contexts are still an important component of the environmental scan, and not to be ignored.

Case Study Summary

As this case study shows, the methods of *identifying goals and affordances* and *environmental scanning* have great potential for building and applying a useful informal evidence base, especially when also accounting for *convergence*. With regard to the iPad project, when applied in tandem, the information gathered during planning and early implementation more than accounted for the lack of formal research evidence, assisting the project team in launching a successful project, as ultimately revealed by the measures used to evaluate the project. We recognize that the case study used to support the strategies was based on a specific project with a readily identifiable technology that would no longer be considered emergent (iPads are now mainstream technology). Nevertheless, we propose that the case study serves as a recent, practice-based example of how the methods discussed can be effective techniques for evidence gathering when considering how best to implement a new, emerging technology initiative in one's own educational setting.

CONCLUSION

Making decisions regarding the introduction of emerging educational technologies in learning environments is not always an easy task. However, the challenges presented with a perceived lack of up-to-date evidence regarding emerging technologies in educational practice may be mitigated through a reframing of these issues as wicked problems. There is value to be gained in widening the paradigmatic approaches to issues of evidence-based decision making beyond traditional positivistic lenses, to include alternative frameworks and viewpoints that are relational, iterative, and flexible, and take into account a range of viewpoints, contextually. We offer one example of an information gathering framework via the iPad case study, demonstrating a proposed approach that: (a) identifies aims and affordances, and (b) employs information seeking via environmental scanning to widen the available range of useful evidence and support informed decisions regarding emerging technologies.

As the case study illustrates, environmental scanning can take various forms depending on the goals, approaches, and disciplinary foci. For the purposes of integrating emerging technologies into pedagogical practice in the face of problems of evidence, the environmental scan is a carefully planned search to discover other instances where the new technology under consideration has been applied in a similar scenario, or failing that, instances where non-identical but similar technological affordances have been adopted in a pedagogical setting similar to that under consideration. Moreover, the environmental scan should be meaningful, taking into account the educator's original purpose for integrating the technology into practice. Finding an ideal or exact match is itself a challenge given the large amount of information available via multiple channels, such as the Internet. This is why it is of utmost importance to go beyond the extant formal research (or lack thereof), to carefully plan a wider analysis and engagement of additional empirical sources and observations, including sharing of information between institutions and educators.

As we look forward to the wicked problems posed by the educational and technological opportunities and issues of the future, a deeper discussion of the nature of technological or media convergence may broadly help to further build responsive and flexible approaches to such problems of evidence. Greater discussion of whether there is, in fact, convergence apparent in the technologies at hand also works to widen our understanding of a long lineage of scholarship in instructional design and e-learning that can be leveraged today and in the future, including the rigorous and established research on similar affordances and patterns of interaction that are so often reflected in those technologies viewed as new or emerging.

REFERENCES

Alderman, L., Towers, S., & Bannah, S. (2012). Student feedback systems in higher education: A focused literature review and environmental scan. *Quality in Higher Education, 18*(3), 261–280. Retrieved from http://dx.doi.org/10.1080/13538322.2012.730714

AppleInsider. (2013, October 28). Apple's education sales breached $1B for first time ever in Q3, iPad share at 94%. *AppleInsider.* Retrieved from http://appleinsider.com/articles/13/10/28/apples-education-sales-breached-1b-for-first-time-ever-in-q3-ipad-share-at-94

Baker, B., & Welner, K. G. (2012). Evidence and rigor: Scrutinizing the rhetorical embrace of evidence-based decision making. *Educational Researcher, 41*(3), 98–101. Retrieved from http://dx.doi.org/10.3102/0013189X12440306

Bennett, S., Maton, K., & Kervin, L. (2008). The 'digital natives' debate: A critical review of the evidence. *British Journal of Educational Technology, 39*(5), 775–786. Retrieved from http://dx.doi.org/110.1111/j.1467-8535.2007.00793.x

Brown, J. (2006). New learning environments for the 21st century: Exploring the edge. *Change: The Magazine of Higher Learning, 38*(5), 18–24.

Brown, J. S., & Adler, R. P. (2008). Minds on fire: Open education, the long tail, and learning 2.0. *EDUCAUSE Review, 43*(1), 16–32. Retrieved from http://www.educause.edu/ero

Buckingham, D. (2011). Foreword. In M. Thomas (Ed.), *Deconstructing digital natives: Young people, technology and the new literacies* (pp. iv–xi). New York, NY: Routledge.

Cheng, R. (2013, October 28). Apple CEO: We've locked up 94% of education tablet market. *CNET News.* Retrieved from http://news.cnet.com/8301-13579_3-57609699-37/apple-ceo-weve-locked-up-94-of-education-tablet-market/

Choo, C. W. (2001). Environmental scanning as information seeking and organizational learning. *Information Research, 7*(1). Retrieved from http://www.informationr.net/ir/

Chrusciel, D. (2011). Environmental scan: Influence on strategic direction. *Journal of Facilities Management, 9*(1), 7–15. Retrieved from http://dx.doi.org/10.1108/14725961111105691

Clark, R. C., & Mayer, R. E. (2011). *E-learning and the science of instruction: Proven guidelines for consumers and designers of multimedia learning* (3rd ed.). San Francisco, CA: Pfeiffer.

Dahlstrom, E., & Bichsel, J. (2014). *ECAR study of undergraduate students and information technology.* Retrieved from http://www.educause.edu/library/resources/study-students-and-information-technology-2014

Dahlstrom, E., Walker, J. D., & Dziuban, C. (2013). *ECAR study of undergraduate students and information technology.* Louisvile, CO: EDUCAUSE Center for Analysis and Research. Retrieved from http://www.educause.edu/ecar

Davies, P. (1999). What is evidence-based education? *British Journal of Educational Studies, 47*(2), 108–121. Retrieved from http://dx.doi.org/10.1111/1467-8527.00106

Day, D., & Lloyd, M. (2007). Affordances of online technologies: More than the properties of the technology. *Australian Educational Computing, 22*(2), 17–21. Retrieved from http://acce.edu.au/journal/

Einsiedel, E. F. (2009). Introduction: Making sense of emerging technologies. In E. F. Einsiedel (Ed.), *Emerging technologies: From hindsight to foresight* (pp. 3–9). Vancouver, BC: UBC Press.

Garrison, D. R., & Anderson, T. (2003). *E-learning in the 21st century: A framework for research and practice.* New York, NY: RoutledgeFalmer.

Garrison, D. R., Anderson, T., & Archer, W. (2000). Critical inquiry in a text-based environment: Computer conferencing in higher education. *Internet and Higher Education, 2*(2/3), 87–105. Retrieved from http://dx.doi.org/10.1016/S1096-7516(00)00016-6

Garrison, D. R., Anderson, T., & Archer, W. (2010). The first decade of the community of inquiry framework: A retrospective. *Internet and Higher Education, 13*(1/2), 5–9. Retrieved from http://dx.doi.org/10.1016/j.iheduc.2009.10.003

Gibbs, A. (1996). The role of environmental scanning in effective fundraising. *New Directions for Higher Education, 94*, 57–67. Retrieved from http://dx.doi.org/ 10.1002/he.36919969408

Grummon, P. H. (2012). A primer on environmental scanning in higher education. *Planning For Higher Education, 41*(1), 69–74.

Hayman, R., & Smith E. E. (2015). Sustainable decision making for emerging educational technologies in libraries. *Reference Services Review, 43*(1), 7–18. Retrieved from http://dx.doi.org/10.1108/RSR-08-2014-0037

Jenkins, H. (2006). *Convergence culture: Where old and new media collide.* New York, NY: New York University Press.

Johns Hopkins University Center for Data-Driven Reform in Education. (n.d.). *Best evidence encyclopedia.* Retrieved from http://www.bestevidence.org/

Johnson, L., Adams Becker, S., Cummins, M., Estrada, V., Freeman, A., & Ludgate, H. (2013). *NMC horizon report: 2013 higher education edition.* Austin, TX: The New Media Consortium. Retrieved from http://www.nmc.org/pdf/2013-horizon-report-HE.pdf

Johnson, L., Adams Becker, S., Estrada, V., & Freeman, A. (2014). *NMC horizon report: 2014 Higher education edition.* Austin, TX: The New Media Consortium. Retrieved from http://www.nmc.org/publication/nmc-horizon-report-2014-higher-education-edition/

Johnson, L., Adams Becker, S., Estrada, V., & Freeman, A. (2015). *NMC horizon report: 2015 higher education edition.* Austin, TX: The New Media Consortium. Retrieved from http://www.nmc.org/publication/nmc-horizon-report-2015-higher-education-edition/

Kaldis, B. (2010). Converging technologies. In D. Guston (Ed.), *Encyclopedia of nanoscience and society* (pp. 126–131). Thousand Oaks, CA: Sage. Retrieved from http://dx.doi.org/10.4135/9781412972093.n71

Kanuka, H. (2008). Understanding e-learning technologies-in-practice through philosophies-in- practice. In T. Anderson (Ed.), *The theory and practice of online learning* (2nd ed., pp. 91–118). Edmonton: AU Press. Retrieved from http://www.aupress.ca/index.php/books/120146

Kregor, G., Breslin, M., & Fountain, W. (2012). Experience and beliefs of technology users at an Australian university: Keys to maximising e-learning potential. *Australiasian Journal of Educational Technology, 28*(8), 1382–1404. Retrieved from http://ascilite.org.au/ajet/

Leckart, S. (2012, March 20). The Stanford education experiment could change higher learning forever. *Wired.* Retrieved from http://www.wired.com/wiredscience/2012/03/ff_aiclass/3/

Mayer, R. E. (2005). *The Cambridge handbook of multimedia learning.* Cambridge, UK: University of Cambridge.

McLuhan, M. (2002). *Understanding media: The extensions of man.* Cambridge, MA: MIT Press.

Mintzberg, H., Raisinghani, D., & Théorêt, A. (1976). The structure of "unstructured" decision processes. *Administrative Science Quarterly, 21*(2), 246–275.

Olson, D. R. (2004). The triumph of hope over experience in the search for "what works": A response to Slavin. *Educational Researcher, 33*(1), 24–26. Retrieved from http://dx.doi.org/10.3102/0013189X033001024

Pirrie, A. (2001). Evidence-based practice in education: The best medicine? *British Journal of Educational Studies, 49*(2), 124–136. Retrieved from http://dx.doi.org/10.1111/1467-8527.t01-1-00167

Prensky, M. (2001a). Digital natives, digital immigrants part 1. *On the Horizon, 9*(5), 1–6. Retrieved from http://dx.doi.org/10.1108/10748120110424816

Prensky, M. (2001b). Digital natives, digital immigrants part 2: Do they really think differently? *On the Horizon, 9*(6), 1–6. Retrieved from http://dx.doi.org/10.1108/10748120110424843

Rabinowitz, M., & Shaw, E. J. (2005). Psychology, instructional design, and the use of technology: Behavioral, cognitive, and affordances perspectives. *Educational Technology, 45*, 49–53.

Rittel, H. W. J., & Webber, M. M. (1973). Dilemmas in a general theory of planning. *Policy Sciences, 4*(2), 155–169.

Saeed, N., Yun, Y., & Sinnappan, S. (2009). Emerging web technologies in higher education: A case of incorporating blogs, podcasts and social bookmarks in a web programming course based on students' learning styles and technology preferences. *Journal of Educational Technology & Society, 12*(4), 98–109.

Schuman, R. (2013, November 19). The king of MOOCs abdicates the throne: Sebastian Thrun and Udacity's "pivot" toward corporate training. *Slate*. Retrieved from http://www.slate.com/articles/life/education/2013/11/sebastian_thrun_and_udacity_distance_learning_is_unsuccessful_for_most_students.html

Siemens, G. (2005). Connectivism: A learning theory for the digital age. *International Journal of Instructional Technology & Distance Learning, 2*(1). Retrieved from http://www.itdl.org/index.htm

Slavin, R. E. (2002). Evidence-based education policies: Transforming educational practice and research. *Educational Researcher, 31*(7), 15–21. http://dx.doi.org/10.3102/0013189X031007015

Slavin, R. E. (2008). Perspectives on evidence-based research in education—What works? Issues in synthesizing educational program evaluations. *Educational Researcher, 37*(1), 5–14. Retrieved from http://dx.doi.org/10.3102/0013189X08314117

Smith, E. E. (2012). The digital native debate in higher education: A comparative analysis of recent literature. *Canadian Journal of Learning and Technology, 38*(3). Retrieved from http://cjlt.csj.ualberta.ca/index.php/cjlt/index

Smith, E. E. (2013). Are adult educators and learners 'digital immigrants'? Examining the evidence and impacts for continuing education. *Canadian Journal of University Continuing Education, 39*(1). Retrieved from http://ejournals.library.ualberta.ca/index.php/cjuce-rcepu/index

Tapscott, D. (1998). *Growing up digital: The rise of the net generation*. New York, NY: McGraw-Hill.

Tapscott, D. (2008). *Grown up digital: How the net generation is changing your world*. New York, NY: McGraw-Hill.

Thomas, M. (2011). Technology, education, and the discourse of the digital native: Between evangelists and dissenters. In M. Thomas (Ed.), *Deconstructing digital natives: Young people, technology and the new literacies* (pp. 1–11). New York, NY: Routledge.

Veletsianos, G. (2010). A definition of emerging technologies for education. In G. Veletsianos (Ed.), *Emerging technologies in distance education* (pp. 3–22). Edmonton: Athabasca University Press. Retrieved from http://www.aupress.ca/index.php/books/120177

Wan, G., & Gut, D. M. (2008). This issue. *Theory into Practice, 47*(3), 175–177. Retrieved from http://dx.doi.org/10.1080/00405840802153700

Wenger, E. (1998). *Communities of practice: Learning, meaning, and identity*. Cambridge, UK: Cambridge University Press.

Willcockson, I. U., & Phelps, C. L. (2010). Keeping learning central: A model for implementing emerging technologies. *Medical Education Online, 15*. Retrieved from http://dx.doi.org/10.3402/meo.v15i0.4275

Zhang, X., Majid, S., & Foo, S. (2010). Environmental scanning: An application of information literacy skills at the workplace. *Journal of Information Science, 36*(6), 719–732. Retrieved from http://dx.doi.org/10.1177/0165551510385644

PAUL NEWTON AND DAVID BURGESS

EPILOGUE[1]

Evidence and the Research-Practice Gap in Education

Although the subject of a research-practice divide in education has been much discussed, much of the criticism centers on the relevance of academic research and knowledge diffusion practices of the academic research community. In fact, we would argue that practitioners and policy makers share responsibility for the paucity of educational research utilisation with those from the academe. The contributors in this volume have highlighted several issues with respect to evidence in educational research. To this, we add a few other observations related to political and epistemological challenges to research utilization.

In 1998, Hillage, Pearson, Anderson, and Tamkin reported on a study that implicated the research community in the failure of research to realise gains in school improvement. They argued that flaws in the research process, flaws in research dissemination, a lack of research quality, and issues with research funding were the primary causes of the failure of research to have an impact on educational practice and policy making. Further, Abbott, Greenwood, Tapia, and Walton (1999) argued that the failure of research to make inroads into educational practice has resulted from "the traditional, top-down educational research model, with the researcher targeting the problems and planning the solutions and the teacher implementing with fidelity" (p. 339).

While these may be valid criticisms, it is also clear that practitioners and policy makers have not adequately addressed their role in the research-practice divide. The politicization of research by policy makers, a lack of capacity to appropriately utilise research in school systems, and systemic processes that inhibit change are significant elements of the problem. Further, an epistemological divide between the field and the research community (in particular, notions of what constitutes "good" evidence) has, as yet, not been satisfactorily addressed. This chapter concludes with suggestions for improving the research dialogue among the researchers, practitioners, and policy makers.

Those in the research community have often grappled with the question of why educational research has failed to realise desired results in educational improvement. Frequently, researchers have self-deprecatingly accepted the bulk of the responsibility for the failure of educational research to achieve educational impact. It is clear, however, that this is a complex problem with constraining factors on both sides of

P. Newton & D. Burgess (Eds.), Issues in Materials Development, 167–174.

the divide. Our purposes for this chapter are to explore the issues on both sides and to put forward a few suggestions for narrowing the gap.

Research Impact

Wilson (2004) stated, "over the years, educational research has taken some serious stick from practitioners. Its findings have been widely viewed as cloudy, complex, contradictory and irrelevant to classroom practice. This reputation has deterred teachers from using research to inform their practice" (p. 1). Educational research is experiencing a significant public relations problem. Critics of educational research include those in government agencies, teachers, policy makers, and (to some extent) the general public. In general, the criticism centres on the ability of educational research to realise measurable and tangible positive effects in the academic, behavioural, and social achievement of students. A daunting task, but nonetheless, we think it is fair to say that the various publics have an expectation that research should be able to provide clear answers about how teachers ought to teach and how educational policies ought to be constituted.

Educational research (and social research in general) rarely provides conclusive research outputs. There is evidence from a number of jurisdictions (e.g., Canada, the United States, Australia, and the United Kingdom) that educational research is experiencing a crisis of credibility.

> Social research in general, and especially education research, has been criticized for failing to provide a coherent, cumulative knowledge base. Much of this problem can be traced... to failures to link the research to relevant theory and failures in connecting research findings to that theory. (Hood, 2003, p. 34)

The complexity of social research and the difficulty in developing a coherent theory base (due in large part to the influence of values, ideologies, and differing epistemologies in education) make it unlikely that educational research will provide unequivocal answers to educational problems.

Kanefsky (2001) defined research impact as:

> comprehending the whole research agenda and process, but with special emphasis on transforming research knowledge into worthwhile and new approaches and useful products—artefacts, teaching materials, improved policies, improved practice, new research approaches and techniques. It also means ensuring that as many of the potential beneficiaries as possible in all our audience groups are aware of these products and apply them to their circumstances as they judge appropriate. (p. 4)

Kanefsky's characterisation of research impact highlights a trend in the literature in this area, that of academic authors accepting the majority of the responsibility for the lack of research impact. This is not surprising, as even the writing on the research-practice gap fails to engage people on both sides of the gap in a meaningful dialogue. Academic writers have sought the perspectives of policy makers and practitioners; however, this process has generally been unidirectional (e.g., Cordingley, 2000; Fielding et al., 2005; Helmsley-Brown & Sharp, 2003; Hillage et al., 1998; Kanefsky, 2001; Wilson, 2004). In Kanefsky's previous statement, the definition of research impact suggests that researchers need to improve at generating practitioner awareness and in designing *worthwhile* and *useful* research. The onus for improving research impact is clearly the research community's.

Criticisms of the Research Community

One of the areas in which there seems to be general agreement with respect to the research community's role in the research-practice gap is in the area of dissemination of research to practitioner and policy maker audiences. The primary criticisms centre around: (a) the inaccessibility of academic research journals to practitioners and policy makers, (b) the inaccessibility of the *language* of research for practitioner and policy makers, and (c) the lack of motivation for those in the research community to develop research materials for a practitioner or policy-maker audience (Hillage et al., 1998).

Hillage et al. (1998) referred to the process of dissemination of educational research as a "rampant *ad hocery*" (p. x). They claimed that there appears to be no comprehensive, coherent strategy for ensuring that research is disseminated to practitioner and policy-maker communities. The dissemination strategy for research that is intended for a researcher audience is not the subject of this chapter; however, dissemination to audiences outside of the academe is an issue that requires further investigation. We will discuss the dissemination to practitioner audiences later in this chapter; however, it may be that this type of dissemination is best coordinated and resourced through the practitioner and policy-maker communities (There are some excellent examples of where this works well).

Wilson (2004) argued that "teacher-to-teacher dissemination was more effective than researcher-to-teacher (i.e. top-down dissemination) because it was seen as more reliable and relevant" (p. 5). This sentiment can undoubtedly be traced back to a general criticism of the role of university research communities by the practitioner community. This will be discussed later in this chapter; however, Kanefsky (2001) suggested that "the perception that research is mainly a top-down activity of little relevance to practice is still prevalent among practitioners" (p. 2). Whatever the reason for this perception, practitioners appear to believe that research is an activity directed from "above" with little connection to their lived experiences in the school. Furthermore, it has been suggested that school administrators also share a dim view of the value of university-led research initiatives.

University faculties of education were viewed among important sources [of new developments in education] by both postgraduate students and professional associations, but not by school principals... At the present time only a minority (around 25 per cent) felt that universities were important sources of recent new developments in their school. (Holbrook et al., 2000, pp. 28–30)

Another major critique concerns the quality of educational research. Hillage et al. (1998) argued that "there was widespread concern about the quality of much educational research, especially, but by no means exclusively, from those involved in policy formation, although we found no single objective definition of what actually constitutes 'good quality' research" (p. x). This critique may have more to do with practitioners' and policy makers' perceptions about the purposes of research. Those who believe that educational research ought to be predictive or explanatory in nature will undoubtedly be disappointed by much of the educational research currently being produced. In spite of these critiques, the approaches currently being used in educational research are "diverse and... methods such as interpretive and participatory research are now much more frequently used" (Holbrook et al., 2000, p. 27). This may, in part, be at the root of the critique of the quality of educational research. It has taken the academe many years to come to terms with new innovative research approaches, and it may take more time yet for the field to come terms with these approaches.

Criticisms of Practitioner and Policy Maker Communities

In many education policy areas we simply do not really know enough to support a clear decision. However, decisions must be made. If the concept of using evidence as a basis for policy and practice is to prevail, then we need to avoid making exaggerated claims based on limited knowledge. (Hood, 2003, p. 29)

There are considerable potential issues with the use of research in the policy-making environment. Policy decisions are often supported *a posteriori* through the presentation of research findings. This is not a new criticism, but bears repeating—educational decisions are rarely objective, and most issues in education are emotionally charged and value-laden. Additionally, policy making is a political process, and research findings are often used to build or reinforce consensus in policy-making groups. "The use of research depends on the degree of consensus on the policy goal. It is used if it supports the consensus and is used selectively if there is a lack of consensus" (Black, as cited in Hood, 2003, p. 31). It is therefore not surprising that research data have been retrospectively applied to justify decisions that are either ideologically or politically motivated.

In a study by Holbrook et al. (2000) they stated, "most of the examples of influential research that were cited [by policy makers] had been specifically commissioned, or had at least been sought out in some form or other such as through a commissioned review or a special policy forum" (p. 31). They summarised the response of a policy maker and stated, "one senior official commented that 'schools will only accept policy changes that are strongly evidence based' and that 'the research has helped to de-politicise educational reform" (p. 31). In this case, we hypothesize that such a use of educational research, while de-politicising educational reform, has the consequence of inappropriately politicising educational research.

What is the effect of the politicisation of research? Once again, anecdotally, we can assert that those in the practitioner community may feel that their views and their practitioner knowledge have been marginalised by the research. In this case, research can have the result of subjugating the voice of teachers in the policy-making process. Researchers understand that research is rarely conclusive and that a dialogue among researchers exists in which support for research findings and critiques of research findings exist simultaneously. Educational personnel often do not have these understandings and can be led to believe that the research has *trumped* their professional knowledge. That is, although they may disagree with the policy position, they may feel that the use of research findings to substantiate a policy decision leaves them (and their professional knowledge) little political leverage for dissent.

The Epistemological Divide: The Privileging of Practitioner Knowledge

> The concept of "evidence" is problematic. Evidence is not value-free. Try to get a roomful of teachers, politicians or researchers to agree on the meaning of even something as apparently simple as "effective practice." Opponents of the "evidence-based" approach cite the value-laden nature of all "evidence." There are no universal solutions or quick fixes. Education is so complex that subtle differences in contexts can make large differences in the effects or outcomes of changes in policy or practice. This contextual effect makes it unlikely that simple, universal strategies will produce the improvements intended everywhere. A more useful kind of evidence that is required is detailed information that would identify exactly which features of the context are important in affecting various desired outcomes. (Hood, 2003, p. 28)

In studies of research utilization in K-12 schools, teachers appear to accept research findings more readily if there appears to be "field credibility" attached to the individuals brokering the research. Fielding et al. (2005) stated that transfer of best practice was more likely to occur when teachers believed that those presenting the practices to them had "hands on understanding of being a teacher" (p. 3).

Comments such as "this doesn't work in the real world" or "that may work in school X, but this school is very different", point to an epistemological gap between the academe and the field. What is at issue is how practitioners engage the evidence. That is, practitioner epistemology ranks first-hand practitioner knowledge higher than all other forms of knowledge—followed by second-hand practitioner knowledge and other knowledge sources that are directly transferable to classroom practices. Helmsley-Brown and Sharp (2003) stated "teachers judged a study's merits on the basis of whether the findings could be translated into procedures that worked in their classrooms" (p. 3). This is not an indictment, it makes perfect sense—practitioners want practical solutions to real-life practical problems. They also stated that teachers believed that research "sometimes had ambiguous results or untrustworthy findings; was often full of jargon and statistics they did not understand; and was too theoretical and unhelpful or irrelevant to their teaching" (p. 4).

Cordingly (2000) also stated that teachers preferred research that was reported in the form of case studies. This may be because case studies replicate the conditions in which teachers believe evidentiary claims are justified. That is, they replicate first-hand, experiential, practitioner knowledge. Arguably, practitioners hold first-hand experience (their own or other practitioners') in higher esteem than research data, which researchers hold in the highest esteem.

Suggestions for Improving the Research Dialogue

In the K-12 context, it is crucial that teachers and policy makers become research-literate, and develop capacities to become interpreters of research. Redefining teachers as builders of knowledge and interpreters of research promises to move research responses from "this won't work here" to "how can we make this work here?" or "this won't work here for these reasons, but we owe it to our students and to our profession to keep looking for what will work here"? To that end, it seems to make apparent good sense that pre-service education programs consider delivering seminars on how to understand educational research. In addition, there is great potential for postgraduate students to "provide a direct link between the fields of knowledge generation and knowledge utilisation" (Holbrook et al., 2000, p. 29). Postgraduate education students are positioned at the nexus of educational research and educational practice. School districts that promote advanced study for their staff members (e.g. generous educational leave and bursary policies or agreements) are much more likely to realise research-based improvements in their schools.

Further, Kanefsky (2001) proposed *change agents* to facilitate and expedite the implementation of research findings. He also recommends that researchers become "customer focused" (p. 8) and develop research products that are designed for practitioner audiences. Some educational institutions employ research consultants to, among other duties, sift through research reports and journals and develop research briefs targeted to the practitioner audience. There are also examples of educational organisations that produce research briefs or summaries for practitioner or policy-making audiences. Again, this would appear to make good sense for professional and other educational organisations to consider similar initiatives.

This discussion would not be complete without, at least, a cursory discussion of the purpose of educational research—is it to advance understanding of the field of education, or to justify existing and promising educational practices? Arguably, educational research seeks truth about the value of educational practices, structures, processes, and so on. Aristotle (1976) spoke of five modes of thought "by which truth is reached" (p. 206): *episteme, techne, phronesis, nous,* and *sophia.* In the words of Aristotle, *episteme* (or scientific knowledge—also *sophia,* or wisdom, is associated with scientific knowledge—in particular, universal scientific laws) requires an understanding of the underlying principles of knowledge.

A person has scientific knowledge when his belief is conditioned in a certain way, and the first principles are known to him; because if they are not better known to him than the conclusion drawn from them he will only have knowledge incidentally. (p. 207)

Phronesis (or practical wisdom) is concerned with reflecting and thinking on establishing ends and determine methods to achieve ends. Aristotle does not privilege *episteme,* or any of the other modes of thought. Aristotle's prescription for finding truth has some utility in this discussion. "The challenge for applied research, development, and service agencies will be to provide assistance in developing and interpreting research evidence in ways that promote effective integration with professional wisdom" (Hood, 2003, p. 36). It seems apparent that a balance between practitioner wisdom and research evidence is essential if we are to realise gains in school improvement.

NOTE

[1] Adapted from: Newton, P. M. (2009). The research-practice gap in education: A view from both sides. In K. Anderson (Ed.), *The leadership compendium: Emerging scholars of Canadian educational leadership* (pp. 56–68). Fredericton, NB: The Atlantic Centre for Educational Administration and Leadership (ACEAL).

REFERENCES

Abbott, M., Walton. C., Tapia, Y., & Greenwood. C. R. (1999). Research to practice: A "blueprint" for closing the gap in local schools. *Exceptional Children, 83*(3), 339–362.

Aristotle. (1976). *Ethics.* London: Penguin Books.

Cordingley, P. (2000, September 7–9). *Teacher perspectives on the accessibility and usability of research outputs.* Paper presented at the BERA Annual Conference. University of Cardiff, Cardiff, Wales. Retrieved October 1, 2006, from http://www.ncsl.org.uk/mediastore/image2/randd-engaged-cordingley-perspectives.pdf

Fielding, M., Bragg, S., Craig, J., Cunningham, I., Eraut, M., Gillinson, S., ...Thorp, J. (2005). *Factors influencing the transfer of good practice.* London: DfES (DfES RR615) [Online]. Retrieved September 10, 2006, from http://www.dfes.gov.uk/research/programmeofresearch/index.cfm?type=0&keywordl ist1=0&keywordlist2=0&keywordlist3=0&andor=or&keyword=RR615&x=70&y=14

Helmsley-Brown, J., & Sharp, C. (2003, December). How do teachers use research findings to improve their professional practice? *Oxford Review of Education, 29*(4).

Hillage, J., Pearson, R., Anderson, A., & Tamkin, P. (1998). *Excellence in research on schools* (Research Report #74). Brighton, UK: The Institute for Employment Studies. Retrieved October 14, 2006, from http://www.dfes.gov.uk/research/data/uploadfiles/RR74.doc

Holbrook A., Ainley J., Bourke S., Owen J., McKenzie P., Misson S., & Johnson T. (2000). Mapping educational research and its impact on Australian schools. In *The impact of educational research* (pp. 15–278). Canberra: DETYA Higher Education Division.

Hood, P. (2003). *Scientific research and evidence-based practice.* San Francisco, CA: WestEd.

Kanefsky, J. (2001, September). *Research impact and the ESRC teaching and learning research programme*. Paper presented at the BERA Annual Conference, University of Leeds, Leeds. Retrieved September 15, 2006, from http://www.tlrp.org/acadpub/Kanefsky2001.pdf

Wilson, R. (2004). Taking control: How teachers use research, *TOPIC*, 31, [Item 2]. Retrieved September 15, 2006, from http://www.topiconline.org.uk/31_f.pdf

ABOUT THE CONTRIBUTORS

David Burgess is Department Head and Associate Professor in the Department of Educational Administration at the University of Saskatchewan in Saskatoon, Canada. His research interests include philosophy of organization, organizational theory, organization modeling, educational law, and methods in legal instruction and research. Burgess holds university teaching concentrations in history of organizational theory, philosophy of organization, and educational law.

Sabre Cherkowski is an assistant professor in the Faculty of Education at the University of British Columbia, Okanagan. She teaches and researches in the areas of leadership in learning communities; professional development and collaboration; organizational development; mentoring and coaching; and diversity and education. She brings her experiences as a teacher, coach and parent to her current research on organizational well-being, focusing on what it means for teachers and other school leaders to flourish at work in schools.

José (Joe) da Costa is a Professor of Educational Administration and Leadership (Department of Educational Policy Studies, Faculty of Education, University of Alberta) where he teaches courses in educational administration and leadership, generally, and supervision of instruction, specifically. He has also taught a variety of introductory and advanced research methods courses (drawing on rationalist and naturalist paradigms). Joe's research focuses on how educational programming and administrative structures impact student success in school; particularly for students who are academically disadvantaged due to socio-cultural backgrounds and experiences, or economic circumstances. His research program has included work on pre-kindergarten, full-day kindergarten, small class-size at the grade one level, in-school mentoring, school choice, and teacher and administrator professional development.

Richard Hayman is Assistant Professor and Digital Initiatives Librarian at Mount Royal University in Calgary, Alberta, Canada. His professional practice includes library instruction, subject area outreach and liaison work, as well as project management and administration of the library website, e-journal publishing system, and institutional repository. He is regularly involved in and promotes scholarly communication issues to the university community, with a focus on sustainability and open access initiatives. His research interests include evidence-based practice, open movements, and the meaningful implementation of educational technologies.

Robin Mueller is an Educational Development Consultant and faculty member at the Taylor Institute for Teaching and Learning, University of Calgary. In this role, Mueller engages the scholarship of teaching and learning (SoTL) across the University of Calgary campus, consults with campus partners to help strengthen their teaching and learning initiatives, and supports the teaching development of individual instructors. Her areas of teaching interest include leadership development, faculty development, research methods, organizational theory, and self-regulated learning. Robin also maintains an active research agenda, and is currently involved in inquiry projects that investigate the evolving field of educational development, strategic planning in higher education, and higher education history and structure.

Paul Newton is an Associate Professor and Graduate Chair in the Department of Educational Administration at the University of Saskatchewan. His research interests are school improvement, the principalship, staff development, and the role of theory in educational administration.

Erika Smith is Assistant Professor and Faculty Development Consultant in the Academic Development Centre at Mount Royal University in Calgary, Alberta, Canada. She is completing her PhD with a specialization in Adult, Community, and Higher Education in the Department of Educational Policy Studies in the Faculty of Education, University of Alberta. Erika's research focuses on building evidence-informed understandings of undergraduate student learning, particularly regarding undergraduate student perceptions and uses of technology (e.g., social media) in their learning, with the goal of improving both policy and practice. With over ten years of experience, her professional practice focuses on educational development, instructional design, and educational technology within higher education settings.

Vicki Squires is an Assistant Professor in the Department of Educational Administration at the University of Saskatchewan. Prior to becoming a faculty member, Squires served as a special education teacher, classroom teacher, and vice principal in Saskatchewan Rivers School Division and Saskatoon Public Schools. After completing her doctoral studies, she worked in Student and Enrolment Services Division (SESD) at the University of Saskatchewan, working with senior leadership, managers and staff of SESD to facilitate the development of an integrated strategic plan, and to design assessment methods to determine their progress in implementing those strategies. Squires' research interests include leadership, organizational theory including organizational change and development, strategic planning, and assessment and evaluation.

Bonnie Stelmach is an Associate Professor in the Department of Educational Policy Studies at the University of Alberta in Edmonton, Canada. Her research focuses on the role of parents in school improvement. She has designed and instructed courses on qualitative research methodologies and methods.

Derek Stovin is a PhD Candidate in the Department of Educational Policy Studies at the University of Alberta. His specialization is Educational Administration and Leadership with a particular focus on higher education. Stovin has B.A. (Economics) and M.Sc. (Agricultural Economics) degrees from the University of Saskatchewan as well as B.Ed. and M.Ed. (Post-Secondary Studies) degrees from the University of Windsor and Memorial University respectively. He is currently a Research and Policy Analyst living in Saskatoon, Saskatchewan. He has been a university-based institutional analyst, research faculty member, and professional administrator. Stovin also taught in the pre K-12 public education system in Saskatchewan. His previous research as an Economist, an Institutional Analyst, and a consultant often relied heavily on quantitative methods. For his doctoral research, however, he is currently enjoying using a narrative approach to study academic administration in Canadian universities.

Pamela Timanson is a PhD candidate in the Educational Administration and Leadership stream of the Department of Educational Policy Studies at the University of Alberta. Her educational background includes a Bachelor of Education and a Master's of Education (Workplace and Adult Learning) both from the University of Calgary. She has taught courses at the secondary and post-secondary levels and received recognition for her teaching. Her research interests include professional learning and knowledge practices and management, and she is completing her doctoral research on how teachers are learning informally within a knowledge culture.

Scott Tunison is the Coordinator for Research and Measurement at the Saskatoon Public School Division as well as an Adjunct Professor in the Department of Educational Administration at the University of Saskatchewan. His research and teaching interests focus on the intersection between education sector strategic planning and evidence-informed decision making as well as the application of research ethics principles to education sector data-handling practices.

Keith Walker enjoys a joint appointment in the Department of Educational Administration and the Johnson-Shoyama Graduate School of Public Policy at the University of Saskatchewan. His recognized areas of work include educational governance and policy-making, leadership philosophies and practices, community and interpersonal relations, organizational development and capacity-building, and applied and professional ethics. He brings over 35 years of experience as a manager, teacher, minister, leader, scholar and educational administrator in public and social sectors. His formal education has been in the disciplines of physical education, sports administration, theology, education, educational administration and philosophy.

INDEX

Lightning Source UK Ltd.
Milton Keynes UK
UKOW04f1132250816

281418UK00001BA/2/P

9 789463 004367